Science and Religion
in the Twenty-First Century

Science and Religion in the Twenty-First Century

THE BOYLE LECTURES

Edited by

Russell Re Manning and Michael Byrne

scm press

© The Editors and Contributors

Published in 2013 by SCM Press
Editorial office
3rd Floor
Invicta House
108–114 Golden Lane,
London
EC1Y OTG

SCM Press is an imprint of Hymns Ancient & Modern Ltd
(a registered charity)
13A Hellesdon Park Road
Norwich NR6 5DR, UK

www.scmpress.co.uk

British Library Cataloguing in Publication data

A catalogue record for this book is available
from the British Library

978-0-334-04594-6

Kindle edition 978-0-334-04595-3

Typeset by Regent Typesetting, London
Printed and bound by
CPI Group (UK) Ltd, Croydon

This book is dedicated to
Edmund Robert Re Manning
and to the memory of
the late Niall Byrne

Contents

Acknowledgements

The editors would like to express their sincere thanks to all the Lecturers and Trustees who have made the first ten years of the revived series of Boyle Lectures such a success.

The Lecturers delivered stimulating and engaging public lectures that are models of academic rigour and public accessibility. They also generously agreed to revise their works for publication in this volume. All ten Lecturers have been a pleasure to work with and we have learnt much from their careful exploration of issues in the relationship between science and religion, in these lectures and elsewhere.

The Trustees have generously given their time to steward the revived series through to its ten-year milestone. As Michael Byrne's Foreword shows, this is a distinguished group of contemporary Trustees who follow in the footsteps of an equally distinguished original group.

The lectures collected here were followed by substantial Responses when they were first given. For reasons of space – and with much regret – we have been unable to include those Responses in this volume. We are grateful to all the Respondents – The Rt Revd and Rt Hon. Dr Richard Chartres, Professor Niels Gregersen, Professor Lord Rees of Ludlow (Martin Rees), the Revd Dr Fraser Watts, Professor Geoffrey Cantor, the Revd Professor Alan Torrance and Professor Fount LeRon Shults.

We have been privileged to hold all but two of the lectures at St Mary-le-Bow in the City of London, a beautiful Wren church and one of the venues for the original series of Boyle Lectures held in the late seventeenth and early eighteenth centuries. We are grateful to the Rector the Revd George R. Bush, the Verger Nick

Cressey and the Parish Secretary Matthew Power, for their kind welcome and impeccable administrative assistance.

The lecture series has received generous financial support from The Worshipful Company of Grocers, Gresham College, The Worshipful Company of Mercers, the Bishop of London, Lord Cork and Orrery and the parish of St Mary-le-Bow. We are grateful to these sponsors for their kind encouragement and assistance over the past decade.

We acknowledge permission to reprint revised versions of the following lectures:

John F. Haught, 'Darwin, Design and the Promise of Nature', *Science and Christian Belief* 17.1 (2005), pp. 5–20.

Simon Conway Morris, 'Darwin's Compass: How Evolution Discovers the Song of Creation', *Science and Christian Belief* 18.1 (2006), pp. 5–22.

Philip Clayton, 'The Emergence of Spirit: From Complexity to Anthropology to Theology?', *Theology and Science* 4.3 (2006), pp. 291–307.

Malcolm Jeeves, 'Psychologising and Neurologising about Religion: Facts, Fallacies and the Future', *Science and Christian Belief* 21.1 (2009), pp. 25–54.

Jürgen Moltmann, 'Is the World Unfinished? On Interactions Between Science and Theology in the Concepts of Nature, Time, and the Future', *Theology* 114.6 (2011), pp. 403–13.

Celia Deane-Drummond, 'Christ and Evolution: A Drama of Wisdom?', *Zygon* 47–3 (2012), pp. 524–41.

Contributors

John D. Barrow is Research Professor of Mathematical Sciences at the University of Cambridge. His publications include *The Book of Universes* (2011), *New Theories of Everything: The Quest for Ultimate Explanation* (2008) and *The Constants of Nature* (2003).

Jonathan Boyle is 15th Earl of Cork and Orrery and Chairman of the Boyle Lecture Trustees.

John Hedley Brooke is the Emeritus Andreas Idreos Professor of Science and Religion at the University of Oxford and a past President of the International Society for Science and Religion. His published works include *Reconstructing Nature: The Engagement of Science and Religion* (with Geoffrey Cantor, 2000), *Thinking About Matter: Studies in the History of Chemical Philosophy* (1995) and *Science and Religion: Some Historical Perspectives* (1991).

Michael Byrne is founder and co-convenor of the revived series of Boyle Lectures and co-editor (with George R. Bush) of *St Mary-le-Bow: A History* (2007). He holds postgraduate degrees in history, theology and history of science and is a Fellow of Birkbeck College London.

John F. Haught is Senior Research Fellow at the Woodstock Theological Centre and was formerly Landegger Distinguished Professor of Theology at Georgetown University in Washington DC. His published works include *Is Nature Enough? Meaning and Truth in the Age of Science* (2006), *Deeper Than Darwin:*

The Prospect for Religion in an Age of Evolution (2003) and *God After Darwin: A Theology of Evolution* (2000).

Philip Clayton is Dean of Faculty at Claremont School of Theology and Provost of Claremont Lincoln University. His published works include *Adventures in the Spirit: God, World, Divine Action* (2008), *The Oxford Handbook of Religion and Science* (with Zachary Simpson, 2006) and *Mind and Emergence: From Quantum to Consciousness* (2004).

Simon Conway Morris is Professor of Evolutionary Palaeobiology at the University of Cambridge. His publications include *The Deep Structure of Biology* (2008), *Life's Solution: Inevitable Humans in a Lonely Universe* (2003) and *The Crucible of Creation: The Burgess Shale and the Rise of the Animals* (1998).

Celia Deane-Drummond is Professor in Theology at the University of Notre Dame. Her publications include *Religion and Ecology in the Public Sphere* (with Heinrich Bedford-Strohm, 2011), *Christ and Evolution: Wonder and Wisdom* (2009) and *Ecotheology* (2008).

Malcolm Jeeves is Emeritus Professor of Psychology at the University of St Andrews. His published works include *Neuroscience, Psychology, and Religion: Illusions, Delusions, and Realities about Human Nature* (with Warren Brown, 2009), *Psychology Through the Eyes of Faith* (revised with D. Myers, 2002) and *Science, Life, and Christian Belief* (with R. Berry, 1998).

Jürgen Moltmann is Emeritus Professor of Systematic Theology at the University of Tübingen. His publications include *Science and Wisdom* (English translation in 2003), *The Crucified God* (English translation in 1973) and *Theology of Hope* (English translation in 1967).

John Polkinghorne is former President of Queens' College, Cambridge. Among his publications are *The Polkinghorne Reader: Science, Faith, and the Search for Meaning* (edited by Thomas Jay Oord, 2010), *Quantum Physics and Theology: An Unex-*

pected Kinship (2007) and *Reason and Reality: The Relationship between Science and Theology* (1991).

Russell Re Manning is the Lord Gifford Fellow in Natural Theology at the University of Aberdeen and co-convenor of the Boyle Lectures. His publications include *The Oxford Handbook of Natural Theology* (2013), *New Varieties of Natural Theology* (2013) and *The Cambridge Companion to Paul Tillich* (2009).

Keith Ward is Emeritus Regius Professor of Divinity at the University of Oxford and a former Professor of Divinity at Gresham College, London. Among his publications are *Why There is Almost Certainly a God: Doubting Dawkins* (2008), *The Big Questions in Science and Religion* (2008) and *Religion and Human Nature* (1998).

Preface

JONATHAN BOYLE,
Earl of Cork and Orrery
Chairman of the Boyle Lecture Trustees

On behalf of the trustees of the Boyle Lectures, I am delighted to introduce this collection of essays by ten distinguished scholars working in the field of science-and-theology. The range of contributions to that growing discipline represented here is truly impressive, and we are grateful to each of the authors for the enthusiasm that they brought to delivering their lectures over the last ten years and to revising them for publication in this collection. This book represents a significant showcase of leading commentaries in science-and-theology, and we are grateful to all our lecturers for their distinguished contributions.

The original Boyle Lectures were held in London over the 40-year period from 1692 to 1731, and were resuscitated for various shorter periods in the years since then. The new series was founded in 2004, so we are as yet a mere quarter of the way to meeting the target set by the first series, but we will get there! The original lectures were endowed by the Hon. Robert Boyle, fourteenth child and seventh son of Richard Boyle, my forebear as 1st Earl of Cork. Robert Boyle's contribution to developing what we now call science, but what was known in those days as natural philosophy, is widely appreciated. Less well known is Boyle's deep Christian devotion and his clear sense that science could undoubtedly serve to deepen the Christian faith. Today, over 300 years later, both science and Christian theology have developed in significant ways since Boyle's time, but the original hopes of the founder remain as relevant today as they were in the seventeenth century. I am confident that in reviving his original lecture series we are continuing to honour the memory of its remarkable founder.

Robert Boyle was born at Lismore Castle, County Waterford, in Ireland. It seems fitting that another Waterford man, Dr Michael Byrne, should have had the idea of reviving the lectures in 2004, and his enthusiasm for the venture has paid off handsomely. The Revd George Bush, the Rector of St Mary-le-Bow, was instrumental in seeing that the lectures found a home at one of the two churches that hosted the original series. I should also pay tribute here to the distinguished group of trustees who have supported the venture since its foundation: Dr Richard Chartres, Lord Bishop of London; David Vermont, a past Master of the Mercers' Company; Julian Tregoning, a past Master of the Grocers' Company; the Revd Dr John Polkinghorne KBE, a Past President of Queens' College, Cambridge; Dr Russell Re Manning of the University of Aberdeen; and not least my own brother, the Hon. Robert Boyle. I would also record our thanks to two former trustees, the Earl of Selborne and Sir Brian Jenkins, who contributed their share of energy to developing the series.

Russell Re Manning and Michael Byrne are to be commended for gathering the first ten Boyle Lectures of the new series into this handsome volume, and I hope that those who read these essays will feel inspired and welcome to join us in person for further lectures at St Mary-le-Bow in years to come.

Jonathan Cork and Orrery

Foreword

The Boyle Lectureship and its Trustees – Then and Now

MICHAEL BYRNE

On the 7th of March 1692, at the fashionable Westminster church of St Martin-in-the-Fields, the Revd Richard Bentley delivered the first sermon in a new lectureship endowed by Robert Boyle, the distinguished natural philosopher who had died the previous year. The audience that evening included many leading members of London society who had come to hear Bentley preach on *A Confutation of Atheism*. Also present were the four Trustees nominated by Boyle to manage his lectureship: Thomas Tenison, newly appointed Bishop of Lincoln and a future Archbishop of Canterbury; John Evelyn, the noted horticulturalist and diarist; Sir John Rotherham, a lawyer and former judge; and Sir Henry Ashurst, a leading figure in the City's Levant trade. One month later, Bentley delivered the second of the eight sermons scheduled for that year, this time at St Mary-le-Bow in the City. Rebuilt by Sir Christopher Wren only 12 years previously, St Mary's had been the London seat of the Archbishops of Canterbury in the Middle Ages and was one of the City's most celebrated churches.

St Mary-le-Bow was also the venue when Professor John Haught from Georgetown University, Washington DC, delivered the first in a new set of Boyle Lectures 312 years later. The original series had run without a break from 1692 until 1731, and occasional sermons bearing Robert Boyle's name had been preached since then, but the lectures had effectively died out during the eighteenth century. John Haught's audience in January 2004 was in some ways very similar to that which Bentley had faced three centuries earlier. It included seven Trustees who had been invited (or were soon to be invited) to oversee the new lecture series. Jonathan Boyle, 15th Earl of Cork and Orrery, who held his title in descent from Richard Boyle (1566–1643), 1st Earl of Cork and father of the original Robert Boyle, was to become Chairman of the new group of Trustees. Also present were the Bishop of London, Dr Richard Chartres, who spoke in response to Professor Haught's lecture; a former Lord Mayor of the City of London (Sir Brian Jenkins); former Masters of the Mercers' Company (David Vermont) and the Grocers' Company (Julian Tregoning); a Fellow of the Royal Society and former Professor of Mathematical Physics at Cambridge (the Revd John Polkinghorne) and the Rector of St Mary-le-Bow, the Revd George R. Bush.

Quite what Boyle would have made of his lectureship being revived at the hands of an Irish Catholic convenor (the present author) and an American Catholic lecturer (John Haught) remains a matter for speculation. Certainly, Boyle had no warm feelings towards Catholicism: his lectureship was designed to explore the relationship between the new natural philosophy and the Christian religion, but it was a decidedly *Protestant* version of Christianity that he supported and confessed. Catholicism in late-seventeenth-century England was associated with political instability, even treachery. The last Catholic monarch, James II, had been deposed only four years earlier, and he and his immediate family continued to claim the thrones of England, Scotland and Ireland.

The religious climate of early twenty-first-century England has changed greatly since Boyle's day. Christianity is no longer actively supported by a majority of the population, and the issues which divide Protestant and Catholic Christians are much less important now than those which separate religious faith generally from the beliefs and values of society at large. The 2004 lecture also dealt with a branch of science – Darwinian evolution – which had been entirely unknown in the 1690s. Evolutionary ideas were certainly aired in the century following Boyle's death, but it was only with the publication of Charles Darwin's *Origin of Species* in 1859 that biological evolution found both an operative mechanism (natural selection) and also a prominent place in public consciousness. Some of the religious implications (real or imagined) of these evolutionary ideas have vexed Christian groups since Darwin's time. However Professor Haught's lecture, on 'Darwin, Design and the Promise of Nature', made the case that Darwinian evolution is in fact of real importance to contemporary ways of understanding the relationship between God and creation. Whatever the religious confession of the lecturer, Boyle would surely have approved of this discussion.

The ten lectures in this current volume emerged from the success of that evening in January 2004. Over the years since then these new Boyle Lectures have comprehensively explored how Christian theology relates to various scientific disciplines. This introductory chapter provides a brief account of Boyle's lectureship 'then and now' and looks in particular at the background and character of his original Trustees as well as their present-day descendants.

Robert Boyle was born in 1627, the fourteenth child and seventh son of Richard Boyle, 1st Earl of Cork, an adventurer who had gained vast lands from the Crown in the south and south-west of Ireland in the late sixteenth and early seventeenth centuries. His son Robert was schooled for a time at Eton, but much of his education was by private tuition. He embarked on a European tour at the age of 12 and was in Geneva when his father died in 1643. Returning to England, he lived for a time with his sister, Lady Ranelagh, to whom he remained close throughout his life, before settling at his own property, the manor of Stalbridge in Dorset. A trip to Ireland in 1652 allowed him to consolidate his estates there, the income from which enabled him to devote his life to the pursuit of the new natural philosophy then emerging.

From 1654 Boyle was based in Oxford, home of much of this new 'scientific' activity. He used an air pump – essentially a bell jar from which much of the air could be evacuated – to carry out a number of famous experiments, the results of which were published in his *New Experiments Physico-Mechanicall Touching the Spring of the Air* (1660). He was a founding fellow of the new Royal Society (1660) and was invited to become its president in 1680, but declined because of his unwillingness to swear the necessary oaths. Boyle's scientific interests were developed in parallel with his strong religious devotion. He was concerned that each of these aspects of his life should be mutually supporting, and when he died in 1691 he left a codicil to his will establishing a lectureship to further that endeavour.

The second half of the seventeenth century was a time of great political strain in England. The first half-century had seen the Civil Wars, the execution of the king in 1649, and a commonwealth under Oliver Cromwell, which lasted until the restoration of the monarchy in 1660. The restored king, Charles II, was succeeded in 1685 by his openly Catholic brother James II, who was ousted in 1688 in favour of his Protestant daughter Mary and her Dutch Protestant husband William of Orange. Affairs of both Church and State were tense and fraught during these years. In general – and the generalization is so crude that it must be treated with great care – Anglicanism existed as a series of theological and political factions. 'High' Anglicanism was generally associated with the Tory political interest and had difficulty accommodating itself to the fact that an anointed monarch (James II) had been deposed. 'Lower' forms of Anglicanism tended to be associated with the Whig political interest, which welcomed the removal of James and his replacement by William and Mary. The Whig interest dominated political life in the late seventeenth century until the accession of Queen Anne in 1702 revived Tory influence. The Tory ascendancy was again reversed when Anne died in 1714 and the Elector of Hanover came to the throne as George I.

The dissenting Protestant tradition, which had grown in strength in England in the early part of the seventeenth century, continued to flourish in the middle and later years of that century, despite the political impediments which prevented dissenters from enjoying full membership of civil society. The City of London contained a significant dissenting population with various styles of religious practice. The Act of Toleration of 1689 gave dissenters (or nonconformists, as they were otherwise known) some relief from the penalties that had previously attached to non-attendance at Anglican religious services, provided they were willing to take the oaths of allegiance and supremacy. Some dissenters were willing to do so, others were not. Still others engaged in acts of 'occasional conformity', which gave them some level of protection without the sense that they had betrayed their true religious identity. Roman Catholics and non-Trinitarians (as Isaac Newton was, but privately) were expressly excluded for the application of the Act.

The codicil to Boyle's will which established his posthumous lectureship was dated the 28th of July 1691. It stated his intention to provide £50 per annum for ever 'or at least for a considerable number of years' to create a salary for some 'learned divine or preaching minister to be elected and resident within the City or London, or circuit of the bills of mortality' to preach eight times a year

> for proving the Christian religion against notorious Infidels, viz. Atheists, Theists, Pagans, Jews, and Mahometans, not descending lower to any controversies, that are among Christians themselves; these lectures to be on the first Monday of the respective months of January, February, March, April, May, September, October and November, in such church as my trustees herein named shall from time to time appoint (Birch, 1999: Vol. 1, p. clxvi).

Boyle indicated that he had not yet bought land to fund this endowment, but left 'all my messuage or dwelling-house in St Michael's Crooked-Lane, London' for that purpose. Boyle's Trustees were named in the codicil as 'Sir John Rotherham, Serjeant at law; Sir Henry Ashurst, of London, Knt. and Bart.; Thomas Tenison, doctor in divinity; and John Evelyn, senior, Esquire'. Provision was also made for succession among the Trustees in that

> the survivor or survivors of them and such person or persons as the survivor of them appoint to succeed in the following trust, shall have the election and nomination of such lecturer, and also shall have and may continue and appoint him for any term not exceeding three years, and at the end of such term shall make a new election and appointment of the same or any other learned minister of the Gospel residing within the city of London, or extent of the bills of mortality, at their discretion (Birch, 1999: Vol. 1, p. clxviii).

In her controversial book *The Newtonians and the English Revolution 1689–1720*, Margaret Jacob argued that 'Restoration liberal churchmen ... provided a firm foundation upon which the second generation of low-churchmen built during the 1690s and beyond' (Jacob, 1976, p. 143). She suggested that these older churchmen, including Thomas Tenison, 'provided these younger colleagues with a special and prestigious podium, the Boyle lectureship, from which to reach the wealthiest and most influential congregations in London'. This was of vital importance (Jacob suggests) because

> only a broad natural theology, anchored on sound natural philosophy, could enable the church to propose an acceptable Protestantism suited to an open society wherein rival religious, political and social groups vied for ... their own power and self-interest ... [The Boyle] lectures provided a podium from which this moderate section of the church could express its concern over the post-Restoration order and in turn formulate a philosophical structure to support its own concept of a stable, religiously oriented society (Jacob, 1976, pp. 143–4).

For Jacob, these low churchmen (or to use a highly ambiguous phrase, 'latitudinarians') believed that the form of natural religion which they favoured could build on Newtonian principles to forge a consensus among Protestants in the face of aggressively secularist individualism where 'mechanical laws governed by material forces ... complemented a social world of competing interests dominated by the dictates of power and self-interest'. Jacob sees the Boyle lectureship as an important vehicle used by latitudinarian churchmen to build this Protestant consensus:

> The Boyle lectures created the Newtonian ideology as a justification for the pursuit of sober self-interest, for a Christianised capitalist ethic ... Newton's natural philosophy served as an underpinning for the social ideology developed by the church after the Revolution (Jacob, 1976, pp. 160, 177).

She argues that a number of the most prominent Boyle lecturers, including Bentley (1692 and 1694), Samuel Clarke (1704 and

1705) and William Derham (1711 and 1712), shared Boyle's conviction that the model presented by the Newtonian worldview provided a basis on which new ways of thinking about the nature of society and God's role in its workings could be developed. A viable natural religion which stressed the reasonableness of revelation in a Newtonian context could serve the related aims of proving God's existence, demonstrating his providential action in the universe and entrusting a key role to moderate Anglicanism in creating and enforcing social structures and conventions appropriate to the times.

Jacob's thesis has proved remarkably controversial, and the scholarly debate about it is not reviewed here. My immediate interest is in the identity and character of Boyle's Trustees. Here Jacob suggests that each of the four original Trustees of the lectureship was chosen because of his long friendship with Boyle. But this claim is robustly disputed by another author, Christopher Kenny, who has also provided the fullest biographies of the early Boyle Lecture Trustees. Kenny suggests that the Trustees' actions were *not* determined by any advanced 'ideology' of the kind suggested by Jacob, but purely by the practical constraints of Boyle's bequest. Boyle chose his four Trustees from a complex network of personal friendships and involvement in charitable pursuits, nominating people who shared his sense that there was an urgent need to restore the national community to the practice of holy living. It is notable that there had been little prior contact between Tenison, Evelyn, Ashurst and Rotherham before Boyle called them to service as Trustees of his lectureship, and that Boyle himself had *never* in fact personally met either Ashurst or Rotherham.

There was a significant dissenting presence (Ashurst and Rotherham) among the Trustees, indicative of Boyle's own orientation towards a simple and unified Christianity with a significant Puritan element. This is hardly the kind of all-controlling Anglicanism, latitudinarian or otherwise, that Jacob saw. Kenny further argues that the Trustees showed no particular favour towards the kind of mathematically and mechanically ordered universe that Newton had proposed. 'Whatever publicity Newton's views received from the performance by individual lecturers was achieved inadvertently, and was certainly not on the agenda of the Trustees' (Kenny, 1996, p. 76). Evelyn, the only member of the Royal Society in the group, had little interest in Newton's mathematics. Neither Ashurst nor Rotherham had any association at all with natural philosophy. Tenison, although he had published work on Francis Bacon, had little interest in (or time for) natural philosophy. As such, the suggestion that the Boyle Lectureship was associated with the kind of overt promotion of Newtonianism which Jacob suggests is, for Kenny, something of a fantasy.

Who, then, were these early Trustees? Thomas Tenison (1636–1715) was born at Cottingham in Cambridgeshire, where his father, a royalist, was the local curate. In 1653 Tenison was admitted to Corpus Christi Cambridge, where he was influenced by the Cambridge Platonists, especially Ralph Cudworth. He graduated BA in 1657 and was ordained in 1659. He was admitted MA in 1660, BD in 1667, and DD in 1680. He served as Rector of St Andrew the Great in Cambridge from 1662 to 1667, remaining at his post during the plague years of 1665–7, when many others (including Isaac Newton) left the university and took refuge at home.

By the 1690s Tenison was a busy man and his involvement with the Boyle Lectureship must have been a relatively minor part of his great range of activities. The bulk of his early writings had been devoted to a sustained campaign against the Roman Catholic Church, and he was firmly convinced of the need to build a scholarly and learned Anglican clergy to help achieve this. He founded the first public library in London in 1684, taking advice on the project from both John Evelyn and Sir Christopher Wren. From 1680 he was Vicar of the large and prestigious parish of St Martin-in-the-Fields (which perhaps explains why the first Boyle Lecture was held there). He was also rector of St James's Piccadilly from 1686 to 1692. His spirited opposition to Roman Catholicism led to St Martin's becoming known as the 'Anglican Bastion' following James II's accession in 1685. Tenison's duties as Vicar of St Martin's included attending at the execution of one of his most celebrated parishioners, the Duke of Monmouth, James's illegitimate half-brother, who was executed for treason in 1685.

Tenison became Archdeacon of London in 1689, an appointment which gave him direct jurisdiction over most of London's parishes. A leading advocate of comprehension (that is, of finding a way in which non-Anglican Protestants could be brought into membership of the Church of England), he was willing to accept the practice of occasional conformity in the interests of a longer-term Protestant reconciliation. By the time of Boyle's death on 30 December 1691, Tenison had been appointed Bishop of Lincoln by Queen Anne. He was offered the Archbishopric of Dublin in 1693, but declined the appointment. He became Archbishop of Canterbury in December 1694.

Tenison's chaplain was Edmund Gibson, later Bishop of London and from 1711 one of the 'second generation' of Boyle Lecture Trustees. Tenison's Whig politics led to something of a fall from favour when the more Tory-inclined Queen Anne succeeded to the throne in 1702. The only personal episcopal nomination that Tenison was able to have approved during Anne's reign was that of Charles Trimnell to Norwich in 1709: as we shall see, Trimnell, like Gibson, became a second-generation Boyle Lecture Trustee in 1711. Maintaining his vigorous anti-Catholicism to the end, Tenison had the satisfaction of outliving Anne: having crowned the new king, George I, he died at Lambeth in December 1715.

Tenison was responsible for ensuring the financial survival of the Boyle Lectures when the founder's original funding arrangements ran into difficulties. As his biographer Edward Carpenter writes:

For the remuneration of the lecturer, who was to be elected for a term not exceeding three years by the Archbishop and others, Boyle assigned the rent of his house in Crooked Lane. The fund, however, proved uncertain, and had it not been for Tenison's generosity, the scheme would have lapsed. The archbishop provided a yearly stipend of £50 per annum for ever, to be paid quarterly, charged on a farm in the parish of Brill in the county of Bucks (Carpenter, 1948, p. 34).

The second of the original Trustees, John Evelyn (1620–1706), is remembered mainly as a horticulturist and diarist. Evelyn was born at Wotton in Surrey, his father's 700-acre estate, which was worth the enormous sum of £4,000 per annum. He was admitted to the Middle Temple in 1637 and in the same year became a fellow-commoner of Balliol College Oxford. As was often the case with those of his social standing, he left the university without taking a degree: later in life, however, he received a DCL from Oxford. In 1652, he began to create the famous garden at Sayes Court, which he left in the hands of his son-in-law in 1694, returning to Wotton. He died in London 12 years later.

Kenny comments that 'Evelyn was the embodiment of what the Lectureship represented and for Boyle's purposes, the exemplary pious Christian' (Kenny, 1996, p. 88). It was this personal commitment to practical piety and charity that explains why Boyle appointed Evelyn as a Trustee. They were close friends for over 30 years, having first met in 1656 at Sayes Court. In 1659, Evelyn proposed to Boyle the establishment of an academy, a kind of monastic scholarly community, but this aim was not fulfilled; the Royal Society, which was founded in 1660, failed to show the religious character that Evelyn had originally hoped for. Nonetheless, Evelyn became a Fellow of the Royal Society in 1661 and acted as its secretary in 1672. He later had significant communication with Richard Bentley, the first Boyle Lecturer (1692).

Evelyn's scholarly interests were wide-ranging, from practical horticulture to statuary, numismatics and antiquarian scholarship. Despite being a convinced royalist, Evelyn was unwilling to become involved in public affairs, although he had an intense devotion to the Anglican Church. Kenny sees him as having attempted 'to express the true Ciceronian life, maintaining a balance between the public requirements of a *vita activa* and philosophical retirement [which was] not in contradiction with a strong Protestant sense of individual sin and the need for salvation'. This was a man who, on his 60th birthday in 1680, 'closeted himself away for a whole week to take a solemn survey of his life and sins and to make his peace with God' (Kenny, 1996, pp. 91, 98).

Evelyn has left us a number of diary entries that cast light on arrangements for the early Boyle Lectures. In early 1692 he wrote:

Went this morning to meet Bishop of Lincolne [Tenison], Sir Robt Ashwood [error for Sir Henry Ashurst], and Sergeant Roderith [error for Sir John Rotherham] so we made choice of one Mr Bentley, a Chaplain to the Bp of Worcester: Dr Stillingfleete for our first preacher; & that the first sermon should begin on the first Monday of March, at St Martin's Church, Westminster, & the 2nd on the first. Monday of Aprill, at Bow-Church in the Citty, & so *alternis vicibus* (Evelyn, 2000, 13 February 1692).

Richard Bentley, the first Boyle Lecturer, was born in 1662, ordained in 1690 and served as chaplain to Edward Stillingfleet, Dean of St Paul's from 1678 and Bishop of Worcester from 1689. He became a Fellow of the Royal Society in 1695 and was created DD in 1696, serving as Master of Trinity College Cambridge from 1700 to 1742. Margaret Jacob speculates that Newton himself could have been involved in the nomination of Bentley as the first lecturer, remarking that the 'evidence for Newton's direct involvement with the Boyle Lectures is highly suggestive, yet not conclusive' (Jacob, 1976, p. 151). Newton had apparently met the Trustees at Boyle's funeral in January 1692. In the following week, Newton is known to have met both Evelyn and Samuel Pepys who, for whatever reason, possessed a copy of the July 1691 codicil by which Boyle had established the lectures. Jacob speculates that Newton proposed Bentley to Evelyn at that meeting, but this remains a matter of unconfirmed speculation. Before Bentley published his lectures he is known to have consulted with Newton, who responded with one of the most famous declarations attributed to him:

When I wrote my treatise upon our Systeme I had an eye upon such Principles as might work with considering men for the beliefe of a Deity & nothing can rejoice me more than to find it usefull for that purpose (Manuel, 1968, p. 125).

There is no entry in Evelyn's diary dealing with the first of Bentley's lectures, but the following month he wrote:

Mr Bentley at St Mary-le-Bow, being the church appointed by us, every first Moneday of the Eight Monethes, for the Lecture establish'd by Mr Boyle (Evelyn, 2000, 4 April 1692).

Later that year we have a report of some dissent among the Trustees:

We did, with much reluctancy gratifie Sir Jo Rotherham, one of Mr Boyls Trustees, admit the Bishop of Bath & Wells [Richard Kidder, bishop from 1691 to 1703] to be Lecturer for the next yeare, instead of Mr Bently, who had so worthily acquitted himself. We resolved to take him in againe the next year (Evelyn, 2000, 14 December 1692).

A year later, we find Evelyn getting his way:

I came to Lond to give my voice for Mr Bently for proceeding on his former subject the following yeare; in Mr Boyls Lecture in which he had ben interrupted by the importunity of Sir Jo: Rotherham, that the Bishop of Chichester [note this is a mistake, Evelyn means 'Bath & Wells'] might be chosen the yeare before: to the greate dissatisfaction of the Bishop of Lincolne [Tenison] and my selfe, & so we chose Mr Bently againe for the yeare to come (Evelyn, 2000, 3 December 1693).

Margaret Jacob sees Evelyn as having been a 'weathervane of Latitudinarian thinking' (Jacob, 1976, p. 33). Kenny is wholly unconvinced of this, suggesting instead that Evelyn was much more representative of general classical humanism and Anglican piety. Of Jacob's assertion that in his role as a Trustee of the Boyle Lectures Evelyn was 'one of the most important guardians of church thinking and a promoter of natural religion based upon Newtonian principles', Kenny comments: 'the idea that Evelyn promoted a form of "natural religion" is so outrageous that it defies criticism' (Kenny, 1996, p. 93).

Compared to how much we know of Tenison and Evelyn, there is much less information available about the third and fourth Trustees, Sir Henry Ashurst (1645–1711) and Sir John Rotherham (1630–1708). Attempts to understand why Boyle chose them must therefore remain somewhat conjectural. The Ashursts were a family of London merchants with a strong tradition of Presbyterian nonconformity. Henry's father was a particular friend of the noted Presbyterian divine, Richard Baxter. They were active in the Levant trade, a stronghold of the Whig political interest in contrast to (and in practical competition with) the Tory-dominated East India Company. London had a particularly strong dissenting tradition, and despite semi-regular denunciations from Anglican pulpits in the City, dissenters were nonetheless socially respectable in London, and wealthy.

Born in Watling Street in a neighbouring parish to St Mary-le-Bow, Ashurst was apprenticed in the Merchant Taylors' Company. His family was established in Hackney and he became a commissioner of excise in 1689 and commissioner of hackney coaches in 1694. He was MP for Truro 1681–95 and for Wilton in Wiltshire 1698–1702. Knighted in 1688 and later created baronet, Ashurst also served as alderman of Vintry ward in the City. He was a Middlesex justice of the peace from 1689 to 1711, an Oxfordshire JP from 1701, a Deputy Lieutenant of Oxfordshire from the same year, and London agent of the assembly of Massachusetts from 1689. He bought the manor of Waterstock in Oxfordshire for £16,000 in 1691. When he died in 1711 Ashurst named Edmund Calamy and other Presbyterian clergy as trustees for the various advowsons which he controlled at that time.

Ashurst was one of the most influential Presbyterians of the late Stuart period. Kenny suggests that Jacob entirely fails to take account of the fact that such a strong dissenter was named by Boyle as one of his four Trustees. In part (he argues) this is because she fails to engage with Boyle's own relationship with dissenters and dissent. In 1662 Boyle became governor of the 'Company for the Propagation of the Gospel in New England and the Parts adjacent in America'. Although not dominated by dissenters, the Company had a strong dissenting membership and Boyle remained its governor until 1689. Boyle's moderation towards dissenters was also apparent from his participation in another related venture, the Council for Foreign Plantations, which 'kept a close eye on the affairs of the colonies, particularly those relating to the treatment of dissenters' (Kenny, 1996, p. 105). Dissent, for Boyle, was no enemy of Anglicanism: the real threat was posed by atheism, Catholicism and the non-Christian religions.

Ashurst was the only friend of Boyle's named both as a Trustee of his lectureship and as an executor of his will. He was added as an executor on 29 December 1691 following the death of Boyle's sister, Lady Ranelagh, who had previously been named in that capacity. The other two executors of Boyle's will were his eldest surviving brother, Richard, 1st Earl of Burlington and 2nd Earl of Cork, and John Warr, one of Boyle's servants. In 1693 Lord Burlington filed a bill of complaint against Ashurst and Warr: the matter was passed to the Attorney General and dealt with in the Court of Chancery in 1695. A study by R. E. W. Maddison in 1952 noted that

> [i]n 1697 the Attorney General filed yet another Bill of Complaint against the Executors in which, inter alia, he complained of the 'frivolous & vaine' reasons given for their failure to complete the negotiations to establish the income for the Boyle Lecture (Maddison, 1952, p. 27).

The least well known of the original Trustees is Sir John Rotherham (1630–96). His father was the Revd Thomas Atwood Rotherham, Vicar of Pirton in Hertfordshire and of Boreham in Essex. He was admitted to Lincoln College Oxford in 1648, graduating BA in 1649 and MA in 1652. He had been admitted to Gray's Inn in 1647 and was called to the Bar in 1655, where his clientele derived largely from London's Presbyterian community. Not only a dissenter but also suspected of having republican sympathies, Rotherham was knighted and made a Sergeant-at-law and Baron of the Exchequer by James II in 1688 as part of the programme of preferments offered to dissenters by the king at that time. These appointments were terminated on James's departure from England later that year. Rotherham died in 1708 after 16 years of service as a Trustee. In this regard, he is known only (as we have seen) for having objected to the re-appointment of Richard Bentley for a second year in 1693.

Rotherham and Boyle never met. It seems likely that Boyle thought that a legal presence among the Trustees would be a wise appointment and that Rotherham was proposed for the role by

Ashurst. This made the original Trustees a balanced group of two Anglicans (including one bishop) and two dissenters. For Kenny, this clearly indicates that 'Boyle's moderation towards dissenters was much greater than has hitherto been recognised' (Kenny, 1996, p. 113). Boyle's recent biographer, Michael Hunter, has suggested that Boyle was arguably closer to nonconformists than he was to latitudinarian Anglicanism (Hunter, 1994a, p. lxx). For Kenny, this 'must throw further doubt on [Jacob's theory of] the role of the Lectureship as an Anglican exercise in social control' (Kenny, 1996, p. 114).

By 1711, the lectureship was firmly established but three of the four Trustees had died. The only survivor of the original group, Tenison, was presumably too busy as Archbishop of Canterbury to attend very closely to the practicalities of the event. It seems (although the evidence is not wholly clear) that six new Trustees were appointed in that year. The Bishop of Norwich, Charles Trimnell (1663–1723), bolstered the Anglican episcopal presence among the group, in which role he was supported by White Kennett (1660–1728), then Dean and later to become Bishop of Peterborough. The third clerical appointee in the new group is of significant interest to what is now the Boyle Lectures' home church. The Revd Samuel Bradford (1652–1731) was born in the parish of St Ann Blackfriars in London in 1652. He was appointed Lecturer at St Mary-le-Bow and subsequently Rector in 1693, and was created DD by Queen Anne on her visit to Cambridge in April 1705, on the same day that Newton was knighted. In 1716 Bradford was elected Master of Corpus Christi Cambridge, and in 1718 he became Bishop of Carlisle in place of the deposed high churchman and Tory Francis Atterbury. He was translated to Rochester in 1723 and in the same year became Dean both of Westminster Abbey and of the Order of the Bath.

By far the most socially prominent of the new generation of Trustees was Richard Boyle, 3rd Earl of Burlington and 4th Earl of Cork (1694–1753). Born at Burlington House in Piccadilly, he became Lord Treasurer of Ireland in 1715 among his many other political appointments. In 1733 Burlington resigned all his public offices, having supported Sir Robert Walpole as Prime Minister until that time. Burlington had four major seats: Burlington

House in Piccadilly, Chiswick House in Middlesex, Londes-
borough in the East Riding of Yorkshire and Lismore Castle in
County Waterford. The latter property was on 42,000 acres and
had been bought by the 1st Earl of Cork from Sir Walter Raleigh
in 1602. The Lismore estate generated virtually all the wealth
which Burlington devoted to his various projects, though he never
actually visited Ireland. He is chiefly remembered for his extensive
architectural interests: he fostered and encouraged the Palladian
style in England, as seen in the villa at Chiswick and the York
Assembly Rooms. He established a hugely valuable art collection
and was a generous patron of music and literature.

The last of the new Trustees was Edmund Gibson (1669–1748).
His ordination in 1698 was at the hands of Archbishop Tenison, whose continuing patronage ensured Gibson's subsequent
appointments as Chaplain to the Archbishop of Canterbury,
Canon of Chichester Cathedral, Rector of Lambeth and Lecturer
at St Martin-in-the-Fields. Francis Atterbury's famous 1697 'Letter
to a Convocation Man' had marked the start of a high-church
campaign for a sitting convocation. Gibson led the low-church
response to Atterbury, an action which confirmed his Whig political allegiance. In 1715 he was appointed Bishop of Lincoln (the
largest diocese in England), becoming Dean of the Chapels Royal
in 1721 and Bishop of London in 1723. The following years
were the high point of Gibson's influence: he was known both
as 'Walpole's Pope' and the 'Church Minister'. He organized
the bishops in the House of Lords and as Bishop of London had
responsibility for the Anglican Church in the American colonies.
He became disillusioned with Walpole, however, and failed to
be appointed Archbishop of Canterbury in 1737. He returned to
favour following Walpole's resignation in 1742 and was offered
the Archbishoprics of York (1743) and Canterbury (1747), both
of which he declined due to ill health. With Gibson's death in
1748 and Lord Burlington's five years later, the last of the second
generation of Boyle Lecture Trustees had gone to their reward.

The new series of Boyle Lectures is also administered by a group
of distinguished Trustees. These individuals are drawn from backgrounds which bring together a number of contexts which were
of importance to the original lecture series and remain so to the

new one. The first of these 'contexts' is that of the Boyle family. Jonathan Boyle succeeded as 15th Earl of Cork and Orrery in 2003. He entered the Royal Navy through Dartmouth in 1963, where he served in submarines, leaving service in 1979 to join the City trading firm of E. D. & F. Man. Lord Cork is currently Life Governor of the Society for the Advancement of the Christian Faith, Chairman of the Trustees of the Chichester Cathedral Restoration and Redevelopment Trust and a Trustee of the charity MapAction.

Lord Cork's brother, the Hon. Robert Boyle, read law at Christ Church Oxford before qualifying as a chartered accountant with Coopers & Lybrand in 1972. He has been a non-executive director (and chairman of the audit committee) of a number of public companies and was previously a senior partner at Pricewater-houseCoopers (PwC), where he was responsible for the firm's relationships with a number of major institutions, including BSkyB and the BBC. His public sector and charitable work has included a secondment to the Civil Service, work with the BBC and serving as auditor of the Oxford University Press and the White Ensign Association.

A number of former Masters of City livery companies have served as Trustees, reflecting the Lectureship's association with the City of London. The Trustees have also benefited greatly from the service of a former Lord Mayor of the City of London, Sir Brian Jenkins, a Trustee from 2004 to 2011. Sir Brian was Prior of the Priory of England and the Islands in the Order of St John and chairman of St John Ambulance between 2004 and 2010. Previously Deputy Chairman of Barclays PLC, Chairman of the Woolwich and, for many years, a senior partner in Coopers & Lybrand (now PwC), Sir Brian also served as President of the Institute of Chartered Accountants in England and Wales, President of the British Computer Society, President of the London Chamber of Commerce and Industry and Chairman of the Charities Aid Foundation. He is also a past Master of the Merchant Taylors', Chartered Accountants' and Information Technologists' companies, and an honorary liveryman of the Cordwainers' Company. Educated at Tonbridge and Trinity College Oxford, he was commissioned in the Royal Artillery during national service.

David Vermont was born in 1931 and educated at Mercers' School and Christ's College Cambridge. He has been a member of the Honourable Artillery Company since 1949 and was with the Royal Horse Artillery for national service. He worked with the Sedgwick Group from 1955 to 1988 and was Master of the Mercers' Company 1981–2. He was Chairman of the Council of Gresham College 1988–93 and has been an Honorary Member of the Faculty of Divinity in the University of Cambridge since 1998. He was awarded the Cross of St Augustine by Archbishop Rowan Williams in 2005, co-authored *A Brief History of Gresham College* with another Boyle Trustee, Richard Chartres, in 1997, and is an Honorary Fellow of Gresham College.

Julian Tregoning is a London-based director of BNY Mellon with a wide 'ambassadorial' role for the US banking group in Europe. He is also a director of BNY Mellon International Asset Management Group, the holding company which owns the group's asset-management businesses outside the USA. After Harrow and BRNC Dartmouth, Julian Tregoning joined Save & Prosper Group, where he rose from being a trainee to Managing Director. In 1995 he was appointed a director of Robert Fleming & Co., with responsibility for developing the Fleming group's business in Latin America. From 1993 to 1995 he was Chairman of what is now the Investment Management Association (IMA), and in 1997–8 he served as President of Europe's investment funds trade body, the European Fund and Asset Management Association (EFAMA). He was Master of the Worshipful Company of Grocers in 2001–2. Since 2010 he has been Chairman of Governors of Oundle School and is also a trustee of six charities and of the City of London Club, where he was Chairman in 2000–3. He is also on the General Committee of Boodle's, a 250-year-old club in London's St James's Street.

The lectureship's connection to the Church of England is represented by four distinguished Trustees. The Rt Revd and Rt Hon. Dr Richard Chartres became the 132nd Bishop of London in November 1995. He read history at Trinity College Cambridge and was ordained in 1973, serving as a curate in St Andrew's Bedford. In 1975, he was appointed chaplain to Robert Runcie, then Bishop of St Albans, and from 1980 to 1984 he served as the Archbishop's chaplain at Lambeth and Canterbury. He moved to

St Stephen's Rochester Row in the Diocese of London in 1984:
during eight years in the parish he also served as Gresham Professor of Divinity. He was consecrated Bishop of Stepney on 22 May
1992 and was appointed Dean of HM Chapels Royal and a Privy
Counsellor in 1996. Bishop Chartres is an *ex officio* member of
the House of Lords and was appointed KCVO in 2010.

The Revd George R. Bush has been Rector of St Mary-le-Bow
since 2002. Educated at St John's College Cambridge, he trained
for ordination at Ripon College Cuddesdon and (briefly) at United
Theological College, Bangalore. He was ordained in 1985 to a
parish in inner-city Leeds and was subsequently Chaplain of St
John's College Cambridge before returning to London, first as
Vicar of St Anne's Hoxton and now as Rector of St Mary-le-Bow.
He is a past President of Sion College and trustee of a number of
charities. In 2011–12 he served as chaplain to the Lord Mayor.

The Revd Dr John Polkinghorne is a Fellow and former President of Queens' College Cambridge. He holds MA, PhD and ScD
degrees from Cambridge and held academic appointments as a
Lecturer in the University of Edinburgh (where he returned as Gifford Lecturer in 1993) and ultimately as Professor of Mathematical
Physics at Cambridge from 1968 to 1979. He resigned his chair
to study for the Anglican priesthood and was ordained deacon
in 1981 and priest in 1982. Dr Polkinghorne served as Vicar of
Blean in Kent from 1984 to 1986 before returning to Cambridge
as Fellow, Dean and Chaplain at Trinity Hall until his election as
President of Queens' in 1986. The author of over 20 books in the
field of theology-and-science, John Polkinghorne was appointed
KBE in 1997 and won the Templeton Prize in 2002.

Dr Russell Re Manning graduated BA from Oxford in 1998
and subsequently took MPhil and PhD degrees in divinity from
Cambridge. He was a Research Fellow at St Edmund's College
Cambridge from 2004 to 2011 and a University Lecturer and
Senior Research Associate in the Faculty of Divinity at Cambridge
from 2007 to 2011, at which time he took up a new appointment
as Lord Gifford Fellow in Natural Theology at the University
of Aberdeen. He joined the Boyle Lecture Trustees in 2010 as
co-convenor. Dr Re Manning has written many research papers,
book chapters and monographs, as well as editing *The Cambridge*

Companion to Paul Tillich (2009) and *The Oxford Handbook of Natural Theology* (2013).

Mention should also be made of a former Trustee who, with John Polkinghorne, is the second Boyle Lecture Trustee who is also a Fellow of the Royal Society. The Earl of Selborne, a Trustee from 2006 to 2009, was born in 1940 and is a working peer in the House of Lords. His main current role is as Chairman of Blackmoor Estate Ltd, a 1,000-hectare farming company in Hampshire. Lord Selborne was Managing Director of Blackmoor from 1962 to 2004. He holds or has held a large number of other appointments in the fields of agriculture and science and has chaired a number of House of Lords committees and been vice-patron of the Royal Agricultural Society of England since 1990. A member of the Court of Assistants of the Mercers' Company since 1984, he was Master of the Company in 1989–90. Lord Selborne also served as Chairman of Trustees at the Royal Botanic Gardens, Kew, from 2003 to 2009, as Chancellor of the University of Southampton 1996–2006, as President of the Royal Geographical Society 1997–2000 and as a non-executive director of the Lloyds TSB Group from 1995 to 2004. A Fellow of the Linnean Society of London, of the Society of Biology and of the Royal Society of Arts, Lord Selborne was appointed a Deputy Lieutenant of Hampshire in 1982, KBE in 1987 and GBE in 2011.

The lectures were reinstated in 2004 by the present author (Michael Byrne) and have been convened annually by him (jointly with Russell Re Manning from 2010) since then. Michael Byrne graduated in genetics from Trinity College Dublin in 1981. He holds postgraduate degrees in history and theology as well as a PhD in history of science from Birkbeck College. A chartered accountant, he has worked for a number of investment banks and as chief operating officer and managing partner of three City headhunting firms. He served on the governing body of Birkbeck from 2000 to 2008 and of Heythrop College from 2009 to 2011. He is also a magistrate (JP) in west London and a Fellow of Birkbeck. With George R. Bush he co-edited an extensive history of St Mary-le-Bow published in 2007.

The new Boyle Lectures have benefited greatly from the service of these Trustees, as did the original series in a very different time and intellectual climate. The first 'Boyles' lasted for 40 years and made an impressive and lasting contribution to the dialogue between theology and the sciences at the dawn of the modern era. We hope for no less from the new series and, as the remaining essays in this volume amply demonstrate, we believe we have made an encouraging start to that project.

Introduction

Science and Religion in the Twenty-First Century

RUSSELL RE MANNING

This book collects together the first ten in the revived series of Boyle Lectures delivered between 2004 and 2013. The lectures explore issues at the interface of science and religion and the Boyle Lecturers are all distinguished scholars working in a wide variety of areas in the so-called 'science-and-religion field'. This Introduction locates these lectures within the wider context of the development of the discipline of 'science-and-religion' up to the early years of the twenty-first century. In what follows, I outline the 'pre-history' of the science-and-religion field before surveying some key controversies in the recent history of this area. In conclusion, I briefly note some of the future directions for work in science-and-religion as this century proceeds.

Science and religion before 'science-and-religion'

Reflection on the core issues in science-and-religion long pre-dates the 'founding' of the specific field of academic study devoted to the relationship between science and religion. Indeed such reflection pre-dates the rise of the distinctly modern understanding of science (and also the distinctly modern notion of religion). Where this interest was explicitly focused on the relationship of the 'scientific' and the 'religious', much of it was within the domain of what has traditionally been known as 'natural theology' (Re Manning, 2013).

It was natural theology that was the primary context for

reflection on the relationship between science and religion in pre-modern thought, and it had a powerful influence on Patristic and Medieval theology, as well as on developments within Aristotelian natural philosophy. It was not specifically concerned to relate the two disciplines of science and religion, largely because divisions between these two disciplines were not (yet) firmly entrenched. Rather, most pre-modern natural theology sought to refine further the synthetic worldview of pre-modern Christendom (indeed, with important exceptions, this was predominantly a Christian enterprise). At times, this involved developing and defending arguments to prove the existence and nature of God against heretical alternatives and to prove the theological view of the world as created, fallen and redeemed (against, for example, the pure Aristotelian view of the world as eternal). At other times, science and religion coalesced in a constructive and creative synthesis, with theologians and philosophers drawing on each others' ideas in the development of the scholastic consensus that dominated intellectual and practical life in Europe up until the emergence in the sixteenth and seventeenth centuries of the distinctive worldview of modern empirical science.

Here is not the place to reflect upon the difficulties of defining the shift to modern science – one prominent historian of science began an influential account as follows: 'There was no such thing as the Scientific Revolution, and this is a book about it' (Shapin, 1996, p. 1). What is clear, however, is that something fundamental did alter in our conception of the natural world with the emergence of what came to be called modern science, and this had a profound and lasting impact on the enterprise of natural theology – and on thinking about the relationship between science and religion more generally. Robert Boyle was, of course, right at the heart of this tumult, and in the lecture series that bears his name we can see something of the dramatic transformation that thinking in the 'science-and-religion field' underwent through the course of the Scientific Revolution and beyond.

The major new characteristic of modern scientific natural theology was a specific emphasis on the question of the relationship between the two spheres of knowledge. Of course, the idea of a distinction between knowledge from and of God and knowledge from and of the world is hardly a specifically modern one, and the image of the 'two books' – the Bible as the book of God's words and the world as the book of God's works – has a long and complex history. However, with the emergence of modern science the question of how to relate the methods and findings of scientific enquiry into the world to those of religious life and thought became particularly urgent. Partly this was because of a perceived threat to religious doctrines; partly it was because of precisely the opposite – because natural theologians felt that the new science gave support to their religious views, which encouraged them to search for ways to bring their science and their religion together. More important was the subtle shift in epistemic authority that occurred during this period. In ways that are still far from fully clear even to professional historians, Western Europe shifted towards 'the gradual assimilation of all cognitive values to scientific ones' (Gaukroger, 2006, p. 11). In a way unprecedented elsewhere, science not only emerged in early modern Europe (there have been spontaneous flourishings of science in many other cultural situations), but stuck and became self-perpetuating. The values of science became the values of modern culture to such an extent that the idea of a return to pre-scientific life is simply unthinkable.

This shift in the contextual background of science can be well illustrated simply by comparing the titles of prominent works that engage 'science-and-religion' at roughly hundred-year intervals over the last four centuries: Richard Bentley's *The Confutation of Atheism. From the Origin and Frame of the World* (1692), William Paley's *Natural Theology. Evidences of the Existence and Attributes of the Deity* (1802), Andrew Dickson White's *A History of the Warfare of Science with Theology in Christendom* (1896), and Richard Dawkins' *The God Delusion* (2006). Not only is there a clear movement from a scientific rejection of atheism to a scientific defence of it, the scholarly backgrounds of the authors of these works themselves are significantly divergent. Both Bentley and Paley were ordained Christian clergymen with wide-ranging scholarly interests in the classics and moral philosophy, whereas White was a prominent politician, ambassador and educational reformer – as the inaugural President of Cornell University he was determined that it become 'an asylum for science'. Before taking up his position with a mandate to advance the popular understanding of science, Dawkins was a zoologist. All wrote from and to their times, both reflecting and helping to nurture a background context within which work on the relationship between science and religion took place. All this has helped bring about a fundamental change over the last four centuries of the modern era: from an assumption that science confirms or bolsters religious claims to an emerging consensus that there exists a fundamental conflict between science and religion, with the burden of proof now shifted firmly on to the shoulders of the religious.

The emergence of the science-and-religion field

Richard Dawkins' *The God Delusion* is just one book out of hundreds published every year in what is now established as the science-and-religion field. This area of academic and public debate is a vibrant, dynamic and exciting one in the early years of the twenty-first century. In his recent *Cambridge Companion to Science and Religion* (2010), the historian of science-and-religion Peter Harrison cites the observation made in 1939 by the Cambridge philosopher C. D. Broad that discussions of science and religion had 'acquired something of the repulsiveness of half-cold mutton in half-congealed gravy' (Harrison, 2010, p. 1). By contrast, contemporary work in the science-and-religion field is a far more appetizing prospect. All major academic publishers have prominent book series and journals devoted to new research in science-and-religion and new textbooks, introductions and collaborative volumes appear almost daily. There are major international research centres, scholarly societies and degree programmes devoted to the study of science-and-religion, as well as an increasing number of academic appointments in the area, many of which are supported by substantial philanthropic endowments. The prestige of the Gifford Lecture series remains undimmed and the popular appeal of the writings of such scientist-theologians as John Polkinghorne and Alister McGrath demonstrates that this academic vitality is not locked up within ivory towers but reaches out to a receptive wider public. The revival of the Boyle Lectures in 2004, celebrated in this book, is itself part of this resurgence.

And yet things were not always thus. Leaving aside Broad and his gravy, and notwithstanding the substantial mid-twentieth-century works aiming to reconcile science and religion, it was not until the 1960s that the discipline of science-and-religion as such came into being (Bowler, 2001). At this time a number of scholars began to focus explicitly and more systematically on the relationship of science to religion, broadening the discussion from isolated specialist accounts of themes and topics to a more comprehensive overview of the subject. By far the most important single work, credited with creating the science-and-religion field as a distinctive area of enquiry, was Ian Barbour's *Issues in Science and Religion* (1966). Barbour organized discussion of the relationship between religion and science into engagements between religion and the history, method and theory of science, and developed an influential typology of the relationship between science and religion.

Three characteristics of Barbour's approach to science-and-religion are particularly noteworthy. The first is Barbour's insistence that serious work in science-and-religion requires a thorough grounding in historical and philosophical study. Even when not explicitly focused on historical or philosophical perspectives on science-and-religion, all work in this field must (Barbour affirms) be aware that the component parts of its enquiry are unavoidably mediated both historically and philosophically. Already an inherently inter-disciplinary subject, the science-and-religion field requires further multi-disciplinary mediation to avoid clumsy one-to-one correspondences and overly simplistic conclusions. In other words, the 'and' in science-and-religion is crucial. Second, Barbour's book is typical of much work in the field in the way that it sets up the science-and-religion relationship asymmetrically: it is religion that is responsive to the developments (theoretical and practical) in the sciences, not vice versa. In effect this prioritizes the cognitive authority of science, which remains substantially unaffected by the engagement in a way that is not the case for the religious component. This asymmetry is present in the third characteristic – the preferred biography of the practitioners of science-and-religion.

Barbour, along with his fellow pioneers of science-and-religion, Arthur Peacocke and John Polkinghorne, was a practising scientist before re-training in theology. This once again promotes the idea that 'science-and-religion' is primarily undertaken to broaden their religious outlook by those who have a scientific background. As a result the 'science-and-religion' relationship is frequently one-sided, with the religious element in effect secondary to the scientific. Here, perhaps, is the root of a still unresolved tension within much contemporary work in science-and-religion: is it primarily a disinterested critical study of the relationship between science and religion in their various forms and contexts, or is it that part of theology that seeks to undertake constructive theological work in engagement with science? Both are, of course, important and legitimate aspects of academic work, but they should be distinguished, and it is not always clear within much writing in science-and-religion where one ceases and the other begins.

Barbour's influential typology identifies four broad-brush approaches to the relationship of science and religion: conflict, independence, dialogue and integration. While the conflict model is that which dominates the public perception of science-and-religion, it has relatively few defenders within the field, beyond the usual nineteenth-century suspects of Dickson White, Draper and the 1860 Huxley–Wilberforce debate. Of course, those identified as 'new atheists' endorse a strong version of the conflict model, but many of the leading figures in that movement tend to eschew participation in the science-and-religion field, which they identify as inherently apologetic. The independence model seeks instead to separate science and religion and keep the two safely apart from one another. Rooted in Kant's strict separation of fact from value, the most common version of this approach identifies science with fact and religion with value; it then affirms that the two are neither in conflict nor in accord – they are simply different ways of talking about different aspects of reality. This position is most famously associated with Stephen Jay Gould, who defended a version in his model of what he called 'non-overlapping magisterial' or 'NOMA'. It was also developed by the influential American liberal theologian Langdon Gilkey, who used it as the basis of his testimony at the 1981 McLean vs Arkansas lawsuit against an Arkansas state law mandating the teaching of creationism in schools (Gould, 2001; Gilkey, 1985).

The dialogue position has become, at least rhetorically, practically the default stance for those working in the science-and-religion field who wish to affirm that the engagement is a truly two-way one and that both science and religion must be affected by the encounter. Indeed, in some cases 'dialogue' was simply synonymous with the coming together of science and religion and, as was the case with the ecumenical and inter-religious movements, the staging of a dialogue was held as an end in itself. As with these movements, however, the dialogue approach has waned in recent years, with many recognizing something close to unidirectionality in what was intended to be a more genuinely two-way conversation.

Barbour's final approach – integration – is perhaps the most controversial. While analytically this position seems to be simply the polar opposite of the conflict type – rather than conflicting, science and religion are mutually reinforcing and aim at a single unified discourse – in practice much work that can be identified with this approach falls somewhat short of a full-blown claim to integration. For example, the recent work of the British Reformed theologian Alister McGrath aims at an integrative 'scientific theology' or 'natural theology' within the wider enterprise of Christian dogmatics (McGrath, 2008). Following the lead of the Scottish theologian Thomas F. Torrance, McGrath aims to reverse the tendency within Reformed thought towards versions of the conflict or independence models of science-and-religion to affirm the constructive place for the sciences within a Christian systematic theology. However, a not uncommon tension arises here: if, as he claims, McGrath's project is one of natural theology, then scientific understanding of the world and of God must be capable of taking place informatively *outside* the orbit of dogmatic theology; if, on the other hand, the only location for religiously relevant science is *within* Christian dogmatics, then McGrath's is better considered a 'theology of nature'. In neither case are essential elements of the integration model adequately realized: in the former, science is accorded too great an autonomy; in the latter, there is not enough autonomy to enable genuine integration as opposed to absorption. The possibility of a genuinely integrative approach to science-and-religion remains an open question.

Barbour's typology has been enormously important in the development of the science-and-religion field and has brought a great deal of clarity to some often quite murky waters. It has also perhaps now served its time, having been amended and added to so many times that its original analytical precision has been lost. The relationship between science and religion is divergent, dynamic and particular; in truth, there is no such thing as 'science-and-religion' (and this is a book about it). Instead, as is increasingly recognized in both theory and in practice, there are thousands of related engagements between sciences and religions taking place within the overall field of science-and-religion. As such, one-size-fits-all typologies are of only very limited use. In a sense, of course, this is a sign of Barbour's success: by enabling the emergence of the specific discipline of science-and-religion, he has equally enabled its diversification into myriad sub-disciplines and specialisms.

Beyond the conflict thesis: historical perspectives in science-and-religion

Ian Barbour began *Issues in Science and Religion* with an account tracing the historical development of the relationship between science and religion from the emergence of modern science in the seventeenth century. Subsequent work has made the sub-discipline of the history of the relationship between science and history one of the most vibrant areas of research in the science-and-religion field. Indisputably, the greatest single contribution to this area has been John Hedley Brooke's patient dismantling of the so-called 'conflict thesis', according to which the history of the relationship between science and religion is inevitably one of antagonism. Brooke's work has instead consistently sought to expose the complexities of the relationship between science and religion in particular contexts, and to unmask the ideological presumptions that tend to animate much historical work in this area. As a result the historical sub-discipline of science-and-religion has moved beyond the conflict thesis and anachronistic debates about

xlvi

the anti-religious origins of modern science. By focusing on key mythologized moments, such as the Galileo affair, Darwin, and the 1860 Oxford debate, historians have emphasized the interpenetration of scientific and religious ideas historically (and into the present day!) and have redrawn the genealogy of both modern science and religion as a series of complex local negotiations and short-lived conflicts and solutions.

In keeping with the 'complexity thesis' it is difficult to summarize such a diverse body of work, but the case of Darwin is an interesting one, given his prominence within the science-and-religion debates. For a long time, opinions about Darwin were polarized: either a clear-sighted visionary and secular saint who followed the scientific facts through to their conclusion even at the cost of his own religious faith – the Darwin of the famous 'devil's chaplain' quotation adopted by Richard Dawkins – or a profoundly religious man who saw evolution by natural selection as a natural theological theory able to account for the long, slow work of divine providence – the Darwin of the famous 'tangled bank' conclusion of the *Origin*. In fact, the story is far more subtle, and Darwin's own religious journey and reflections on the theological significance of his science – and the scientific significance of his theology – is a good example of the complex situation of the mid-nineteenth century, a time that was both the heyday of scientifically informed natural theology and that also saw the emergence of the professional scientist (the term itself was coined in 1833 by the Cambridge polymath and natural theologian William Whewell). As John Hedley Brooke memorably puts it: 'on reflection it would be surprising if the man who showed us that we cannot pigeon-hole pigeons could be pigeon-holed himself' (Brooke, 2003, p. 199).

Rationality, realism and the quiet revolution: philosophical perspectives on science-and-religion

In the same way that much work in the science-and-religion field has been mediated by history, so too philosophy has played a crucial role in developing the discipline. Again, in sharp contradistinction to binary 'either/or' approaches, much work in the philosophy of science-and-religion has sought to highlight the complexity of both components. Drawing together work from both the philosophy of religion and the philosophy of science generates some interesting creative encounters. Work in this sub-discipline has tended to focus on the two major themes of rationality and realism in science-and-religion. In both cases, the starting point has been relatively simple: rebutting the claim that while science is rational and realist religion is neither. Drawing on the work of a number of leading authors in the philosophy of science, notably Thomas Kuhn, Bas van Fraasen, Michael Polyani and Hilary Putnam, those working on philosophical perspectives in science-and-religion have stressed the importance of nuanced understandings of rationality and realism in science. Similarly influenced by philosophers of religion such as Richard Swinburne, Alvin Plantinga and William Alston, many have sought to engage with the faith–reason dichotomy in religion. These are deep waters and discussions do have a tendency towards the technical, but one thing is clear: Dawkins' claim that 'scientific beliefs are supported by evidence, and they get results. Myths and faiths are not and do not' simply does not stand up to philosophical scrutiny (Dawkins, 1995, p. 33).

More recent work in the philosophy of science-and-religion has focused on substantive philosophical issues. While the impact of once fashionable postmodernism has now waned, a more subtle 'quiet revolution' has been taking place in the philosophy of science, with profound implications for science-and-religion. Central to this revisionary moment are two related philosophical dissatisfactions with received scientific orthodoxy. The first is the so-called 're-emergence of emergence' as a key concept within scientific metaphysics; the second is the rejection of the regnant understanding of the laws of nature as universal and exceptionless regularities. Both are themselves arguably instances of a wider philosophical re-evaluation of the idea of 'naturalism' and a reassessment of the importance of reductionism to the natural sciences.

In contrast to the 'nothing buttery' of reductive naturalism that opposes the 'spooky' supernaturalism of religious superstition, more recent naturalist philosophies have stressed the breadth, complexity and richness of the natural and have soundly rejected the reductive aspirations of some scientists to boil it all down to a theory of everything. From the analytical philosopher John McDowell's rejection of what he calls 'bald naturalism' to the recent interest by philosophers of the continental tradition in so-called 'speculative realism', there is now an increasing recognition that the realism/idealism disjunction is no longer compelling and that the task of a truly 'critical' philosophy must be taken up with renewed vigour (McDowell, 1996; Bryant, Harman and Srnicek, 2011). At the heart of these 'new naturalisms' is the insistence that much modern philosophy has been mistaken in equating the natural sciences with a reductive naturalist metaphysics. These new movements have no desire to reinstate the 'ghost in the machine'; rather their aim is to reject the purely mechanistic conception of nature in the first place.

Such grand philosophical ambitions can be seen in the two specific areas of philosophy of science referred to above: emergence and the laws of nature. Across a range of sciences and in a variety of different contexts, there has been a remarkable resurgence in the use of the concept of emergence in recent years (Clayton, 2004; Clayton and Davies, 2006; Re Manning, 2007). The concept is not a new one and there is no consensus regarding its precise meaning and application, and yet its importance is clear: reductionist one-way models of causation and scientific understanding seem no longer compelling. From debates about divine action and God's changelessness, to Christology and claims about the emergence of spirit, work at the interface of science and religion has been greatly affected by this shifting philosophical consensus, and more careful work on the varieties of emergence and their uses (and abuses) by theologians is now required.

While ideas of emergence challenge the claim that science reduces the world to a single set of basic constitutive ingredients, recent philosophical work on the laws of nature has upset the prevailing wisdom that insisted upon the universality and exceptionlessness of those laws. Again across a wide range of scientific disciplines this orthodoxy has been questioned and been shown up as an ideological invention of a particular period in the philosophy of science, largely driven by the need to replace outmoded Aristotelian models of the coherence of nature (Watkins, 2013).

The result has been that the picture of a uniform world susceptible, at base, to the laws of physics has been replaced with that
of a 'dappled world' in which the boundaries of the kingdom of
'queen physics' have been radically redrawn (Cartwright, 1999;
Cartwright and Martin, 2013). Again the implications for those
working in the science-and-religion field are striking: from the
historical issue of the importance of theology in the creation of
modern science to the vexed question of divine action and determinism (Murphy and Brown, 2007).

As numerous as the stars in the sky: topics in science-and-religion

When we turn from the historical and philosophical sub-disciplines
of the science-and-religion field to particular scientific theories
themselves it will not be possible to give more than a fleeting
overview of the various areas of engagement. There are active sub-
disciplines of science-and-religion in all the major fields of scientific
research, including physics, biology, chemistry, psychology, artificial intelligence, mathematics and ecology. Other strands of work
focus on religious or theological *topoi*, such as belief formation,
ritual practices, and doctrinal topics including creation, divine
action, religious experience, *imago dei* and eschatology. There are
various flourishing sub-disciplines within the scientific study of
religion – primarily adopting perspectives from anthropology, psychology, sociology and economics to analyse and explain religious
beliefs and practices. Equally, and often overlooked in discussions of the science-and-religion field, is the significant work of
(primarily religious) scholars analysing and advising on the ethical
and social aspects of scientific developments; from the impact of
technology in general to specific issues such as stem-cell research,
genetic modification, and various aspects of science-and-religion
in healthcare and warfare. Instead of attempting to give a full survey of this diverse body of work, in what follows I will focus on
three key issues in contemporary science-and-religion: evolution,
cosmology and the cognitive science of religion.

1

Beyond the evolution wars?

Unsurprisingly, it has been biology, and particularly its central theory of evolution by natural selection, that has been the most active area of debate in the science-and-religion field. To some extent this reflects the prominence in the public eye of Dawkins himself, but it has also been driven by other, related factors, particularly the virtual beatification of Charles Darwin and the controversies surrounding intelligent design theory (Jenkins, 2009). Unsurprisingly, given the sharp demarcation of the dividing lines between science and religion as put forward by Dawkins (science = fact; religion = delusion), attention has focused on those who attempt to defend a theological alternative to evolution, such as so-called creationists and intelligent design theorists. While not all critics of the scientific and philosophical cogency of 'Darwinism' are religiously motivated, most are (Fodor and Piatelli-Palmarini, 2010; Behe, 1996). Further, as Conor Cunningham makes clear, both the atheist neo-Darwinians and the religious anti-Darwinians share a common evangelical zeal to provide a fully comprehensive explanation of biological phenomena (Cunningham, 2010). For the neo-Darwinists, the answer lies in the all-encompassing theory of evolution; for the religious anti-Darwinians, it is to be found in the designing intelligence's unique capability of instigating so-called 'irreducible complexity'. So polarized and bad tempered has this argument become that one recent introductory textbook to science-and-religion had to resort to a fictionalized debate between 'a theist' and 'a naturalist' to set out the issues at stake (Clayton, 2012).

Fortunately however, although this discussion unavoidably takes precedence in any consideration of science-and-religion in relation to biology, it is increasingly clear that this is a starting point that can safely be left behind, along with all its unproductive name-calling. Instead, as the philosopher Michael Ruse has carefully argued in response to the question 'Can a Darwinian be a Christian?' the important issue is not *whether* evolution and religion are compatible, but *how* (Ruse, 2000). Serious and fruitful discussions in this area of science-and-religion turn not on the compatibility of Darwinian and religious ideas, but on ways in which they mutually inform one another and on the further consequences of their conjunction for both disciplines. For example, recent work has emphasized the importance of the influence of natural theology on the formation of Darwin's ideas and, from the 'other direction', work by Christian theologians has turned to Darwin in order to engage with specifically theological questions, such as the problem of evil (Brooke, 2009a; Southgate, 2008).

As science-and-religion in the twenty-first century moves beyond the unhelpful 'evolution wars' of the late twentieth century, an exciting new chapter can open up in the history of the engagements between religion and biology. In this context, it will be possible to retrieve some of the more substantial questions raised by the encounter that have been obscured in recent years by all the hullabaloo surrounding Darwinism and creationism. These include a fresh focus on the question of 'design' and on the concepts of direction and purpose in what is still sometimes called 'natural history'. Here the idea of 'convergence' in the work of the 2005 Boyle Lecturer Simon Conway Morris is central, as well as work on social selection and cooperation (Conway Morris, 2003; Wilson, 2012; Nowak, 2006a). Importantly, all these developments call into question not Darwin's central thesis of evolution by natural selection, but the development of that position into the genetic imperialism of neo-Darwinism, encapsulated in Dawkins' brilliant metaphor of the 'selfish gene'. Once the stranglehold of genetic determinism is loosened, constructive work integrating Darwinian biology and religious thought can once again be developed, rather as it was in the years immediately following the publication of Darwin's original writings, such as the much neglected writings of *Lux Mundi* (1889).

Lighting the blue touch paper: God and cosmology

If the headlines from the encounters between biology and religion are predominantly antagonistic, those from the engagements between the physical sciences and religion tend to be less shrill. Notwithstanding Stephen Hawking's recent pronouncements about the death of God, there is a surprising academic and popular consensus that dialogues concerning physics and religion can be meaningful and productive – if a little hard to follow! (Hawking and Mlodinow, 2010). For all his prominence as a scholar and public intellectual, Hawking's denial of the need to invoke God to explain the spontaneous generation of the universe has hardly lit the blue touch paper of the public imagination in the way that Dawkins' polemic has.

And yet we should not let this apparent modesty obscure the seriousness of the challenge to religion that Hawking's position entails. In effect a scientific updating of Bertrand Russell's famous claim in his 1948 radio debate with the Catholic philosopher Frederick Copleston that 'the universe is just there, and that's all', the claim to the self-sufficiency of the universe cuts against the very foundations of religious doctrines relating to the creation and sustenance of the world by God. At issue is a modern version of the cosmological argument between materialists, who hold that the universe is simply matter in motion, and creationists (in the proper sense), for whom the fact that there is anything at all requires that there be a God (of some form or another) responsible for its coming to be and staying in existence.

For too long now the convenient solution of the serendipitous compatibility of Big Bang cosmology with the religious doctrine of creation has remained unchallenged. Here the central (religious) claim is that scientific cosmology concurs with religious accounts of creation (at least the *ex nihilo* interpretation of the Genesis narrative) by demonstrating both that science points towards a single originary moment and that science itself can never provide an explanation of that origin. Unfortunately, however, this confidence is misplaced for at least two reasons. First, the apparently happy resemblance between the biblical account of creation in the specific act of God and the scientific account of the origins of the universe in the Big Bang should be far from surprising once the theological underpinning of the cosmology becomes clear. As is well known, it was the Belgian Catholic physicist and priest Georges Lemaître (1894–1966) who first proposed the theory of what he called the 'primeval atom', and the narrative of Big Bang theory, even in its secular forms, unavoidably 'performs an uncanny recapitulation of Christian creation theology'

(Rubenstein, 2012, p. 485). As such, it is hardly surprising and equally hardly informative that Big Bang cosmology preserves a ring-fenced inviolability around a creator God, such that even avowedly atheistic forms of Big Bang creation out of nothing end up affirming the sovereignty of absolute power, even when this is referred to as 'nothing' rather than 'God'.

Second, it is by no means obvious that a religious cosmology of creation need be committed to the idea of *creatio ex nihilo*. It is a commonplace of discussions of creation and cosmology to insist that the religious account of creation is about dependence and not origination – the Genesis narrative, for instance, tells of God's love for his creation and identifies certain liturgical obligations, whereas the scientific account tells of the mechanics of what happened at the very beginning of the universe. There is, of course, some truth in this distinction, but in order for it to be more than simply a lazy affirmation of the 'how/why' disjunction (science tells us how/religion tells us why) we must be careful to recognize that both the religious and the scientific accounts unavoidably include elements of both how and why: any account of the very origins of the universe itself must combine both the factual and the speculative. To talk of the origins of the universe at all is to talk of the point at which the knowable and the unknowable coincide. In the terms of French philosopher Quentin Meillassoux, our 'ancestrality' is strictly speaking inaccessible to us; we simply cannot imagine the unimaginable reality 'before' the universe (Meillassoux, 2008). In other words, both religious and scientific accounts of the origin of the universe need not – indeed in strict terms, cannot – be committed to an idea of creation out of nothing as such 'pure' substantive nothingness is quite literally unthinkable.

Opening the black box of the brain

In the distant future I see open fields for far more important researches. Psychology will be based on a new foundation ... Light will be thrown on the origin of man and his history. (Darwin, 1859: p. 458)

Darwin's prediction has undoubtedly come true and recent years have seen an explosion of new developments in our understanding of the human mind. Through a combination of technological advances and innovative theoretical models of cognition, neuropsychology has made great progress in helping us to understand the workings of the brain. Moreover, not only has scientific research mapped and analysed the hardware of our grey matter to an unprecedented extent, so too the mysteries of human cognition are being unravelled, including how we form and communicate religious beliefs. The previously unadaptive (in evolutionary terms) beliefs and practices of religion are now 'explained' by a new discipline, the cognitive science of religion, which has emerged to make sense of these explanations and their consequences (Boyer, 2001; Newberg, d'Aquili and Rause, 2001; Visala, 2011).

Two key questions arise from this revolution in our understanding of the human mind for work in science-and-religion. First, does the scientific evidence supporting the 'naturalness' of religion serve to confirm or deny the truth of religion? On the one hand, the demonstration that religious beliefs and practices can be explained in perfectly normal terms as an accountable phenomenon alongside others, such as the emergence of language, music and even science itself, seems precisely to normalize religion. As such, there is no need to reach for complicated Freudian, Marxist or Nietzschean theories about the origins and development of religion; instead we should accept religion as a normal part of human life.

At the same time, however, this normalization seems to conceal a more subtle attack on religion. By explaining the origin and development of religion in 'purely natural' terms, neuroscience and the cognitive science of religion in effect reduce it to merely a human phenomenon. Indeed, some of the core concepts of the cognitive science of religion seem to support this interpretation, such as Justin Barrett's 'hyperactive agency detection device (HADD)', even when they are used to argue for precisely the opposite (Barrett, 2004). For all Barrett's conviction that natural religion equates to true religion – our minds being how they are in order to track what is the case in the 'outside world' – the suspicion remains that a natural explanation all too easily slides into a reductive one, according to which there is nothing more to religious belief and practice than a picturesque memory-aid for survival techniques. Of course, as should be clear, the facts alone cannot settle this dispute, and both 'reductionist' and 'religionist' interpretations depend more on background metaphysical assumptions than they do on scientific evidence. Just as with the 'God-spot' debates in the neuroscience of religion, so here the key issue is not which religious conclusions are required by the scientific data, but rather how the 'pure science' and the 'pure theology' are brought together. What new discoveries in the psychological sciences reveal more than anything else are the perils of rushing to theological conclusions (both theistic and atheistic) and the need for careful reflection on the character of, and patient application of, the mediating discourse of philosophy.

The second key question raised by work in neuroscience and cognitive science of religion concerns the understanding of religion in much of the literature. To put the question in its bluntest form: Does 'religion' as it is discussed in the science-and-religion field bear any relation to the beliefs and practices of the faithful worldwide and to the developed reflection on religion that characterizes mainstream theology? All too frequently, the answer to both parts of this question is 'no', and this is well illustrated by recent discussions in the cognitive science of religion. On the one hand, these studies tend to take an overly broad and indiscriminatingly inclusive view of religious beliefs and practices, drawing very little distinction between religious, spiritual, magical, mythical and supernaturalist beliefs and practices. Not only is this simply too wide a range of phenomena to be helpfully explained by a common account, it introduces an uncomfortable tension between religion as an aspect of human cultural life and religion as a distinctive phenomenon. The interest (and sales-power) of most such scientific accounts of religion depends on the specificity of religion and yet that specificity is systematically undermined by the under-theorized definition of religion operative in this work.

The flip-side of such uncritical inclusivism is that there is a tendency for work in this area to operate with a somewhat attenuated theology, or indeed a suspicion of theology. Again, Barrett's work is informative; while drawing 'religionist' conclusions from the naturalness of religion, Barrett insists that it is religion – and not theology – that is natural. Indeed, for Barrett religion is 'intuitive' (which he carefully glosses as 'maturationally natural') from childhood, whereas theology – along with atheism and science – needs to be learnt (of course, once acquired it can become 'second nature' but such naturalness is known as 'practised' as opposed to 'maturational') (Barrett, 2010). For all its emphasis on the cognitive architecture of the religious imagination, such an approach prioritizes a more literalist understanding of religion consistent with its 'folk' origin and neglects the rich potential to be opened up were theological and not just religious cognition to be investigated. In this, however, the latest work in cognitive science of religion simply reflects the lowly status of theology within the science-and-religion field more widely.

The future of science-and-religion

Identifying the contours of the contemporary landscape of an area of study is always a controversial undertaking, especially with such a wide-ranging and inherently inter-disciplinary one such as science-and-religion. Even more so when peering into the future. Nonetheless, in what follows I point towards three further areas likely to be of future interest as discussions of science-and-religion proceed into the twenty-first century.

Sciences–and-religions

In truth there is no such thing as 'the' science-and-religion discipline, just as there is no single such thing as 'science' or 'religion'. Instead, historically and conceptually, these must be particularized and the plurality of disciplines – and debates – within the area must be recognized. In particular, in light of the breakdown of monolithic models within the philosophy of science, a more variegated approach can now be developed, in which the different special sciences can and must be considered in their own unique encounters with religion. What may hold, for example, within discussions of physics and religion ought not to be simply carried over into discussions of biology and religion. Similarly, the distinctions within scientific disciplines should be recognized, as well as the full range of scientific disciplines – why focus solely on the 'hard sciences' at the expense of the wider strands of scientific thinking in the social and cultural sciences? That said, as with any complexification strategy, care must be taken not simply to explode the discussions into a thousand incommensurable dialects. It is here, again, that the role of philosophy is so crucial, acting not simply to mediate 'horizontally' between science and religion but also 'vertically' within the sciences themselves.

Likewise, just as there should no longer be a single discipline of *science*-and-religion, so too should the plurality of religions and religious traditions needs to be recognized. As with similar disciplines such as the philosophy of religion, some initial steps have been taken in this direction, but it is now crucial to acknowledge that discussions of science and religion have too frequently simply assumed a privileged position for Christianity within such debates (Clayton and Simpson, 2006). To some extent, of course, the prevalence of Christianity is justified historically and conceptually: 'science itself' is not a universal concept or practice and the question of why the particular form of empiricism took root and established its authority when and where it did within the context of European Christianity is still a topic of fascinating discussion. That said, the increasingly inter-related and globalized character of twenty-first century life and the rich diversity of scientific and religious traditions surely require a wider set of perspectives for work in this area in the future.

The practices of science and religion

As it has developed from the framework first set out in the 1960s by Ian Barbour, the science-and-religion field has been dominated by theoretical issues, especially the impact of various scientific perspectives on the status of various religious beliefs. However, as was noted earlier, alongside this emphasis on science and religion as theoretical discourses with core propositional claims that need to be brought into constructive engagement, some important work has also been undertaken on *practical* issues, and this aspect of the science-and-religion field will surely become more important as the twenty-first century progresses. Both science and religion are as much practices as they are theories, and both have enormous practical impacts on our lives. These impacts stretch beyond the canonical topics of 'applied science-and-religion' such as stem-cell research and end-of-life issues for which we are most likely to expect the formation of an 'ethics panel' with an obligatory religious representative. Far more striking are the everyday impacts of, for example, communications technology, medicine, and food production and distribution. These issues, and many more, may not immediately strike as central topics for the science-and-religion field – and they may be more politically sensitive than the ideal of a neutral academic discipline can stomach – but they are nonetheless of crucial importance to our lives as citizens of both a scientific and a religious culture.

The environmental crisis

It seems likely that the definitive context for the further development of science-and-religion in the twenty-first century will be the slow-burning crisis of climate change and ecological destruction. In the face of the predictions of catastrophic transformations to our environment on a global level, much is uncertain (including the predictions). As politicians and activists move from one crisis summit to another and philosophers seriously question the ethics and rationality of both climate change and preventative action, those in the science-and-religion area cannot remain silent about this issue.

Ever since Lynn Townsend White's controversial paper 'The Historical Roots of Our Ecologic Crisis' (1967), the debate within science-and-religion discussions has tended to focus on the question of responsibility and on models of nature and of religious dominion over nature. These are, of course, important historical questions, but the increasing urgency of the ecological crisis calls especially for constructive work in which the vital matrix of science and religion will be crucial. From being simply one topic among others, there is now surely a case to be made that this issue should be given a privileged position in framing all work within the science-and-religion field.

Conclusion

Not all of the issues I raise here are addressed by the Boyle Lectures collected together in this book, and by no means all the Boyle Lecturers would endorse all that I have suggested here about the wider context within which their lectures are situated. The field of science-and-religion is a dynamic one and, like any vibrant area of research, full of controversies and debate. What is clear, though, is that the lectures collected here offer a compelling snapshot of the current state of the field of scholarship at the interface of science and religion in the twenty-first century, and one that will surely inspire further important work in this area.

I

Darwin, Design and the Promise of Nature

JOHN F. HAUGHT

The religious world in general and the Christian world in particular have had a very difficult time coming to grips with the Darwinian portrait of life on Earth. The main issue for theists, now as always, is that of how to reconcile evolution with the idea of divine providence. After Darwin, what does it mean to say that God 'provides' or cares for the world? Prior to the age of science, of course, suffering and evil had already raised weighty questions about God's care for the world, but our new awareness of evolution has amplified them considerably. What then does providence mean if life comes about and diversifies on Earth in the manner proposed by Darwin and his neo-Darwinian descendants?

The pre-scientific cosmos, at least at first sight, seems more congenial to belief in divine providence. The dominant world-picture in Western thought after Plato generally consisted of a ladder of distinct levels, a Great Chain of Being, running from lowly matter at the bottom to divine creative wisdom at the top (Lovejoy, 1965). The intervals between matter and God were taken up by plants, animals, humans and angelic beings, all contributing to a rich vertical plenitude of creation, wherein every being had its divinely assigned station. And, most notably, the ontological discontinuity differentiating the contiguous levels allowed humans to think that they were radically distinct from other living beings and perhaps cared for in a special way by God.

However, let us compare this venerable hierarchical cosmology with the picture of the universe that the natural sciences have recently drawn up. Imagine 30 large volumes on a bookshelf, each tome 450 pages long, and every page standing for one million years. Let this set of books represent the scientific story of a 13.7-billion-year-old universe. Our narrative begins with the Big Bang on page one of volume one, but the first 21 books show no overt signs of life at all. The Earth-story begins in volume 21, 4.5 billion years ago, but life still doesn't appear until volume 22, about 3.8 billion years ago. Even then, living organisms do not become particularly interesting, at least in human terms, until almost the end of volume 29. There the famous Cambrian explosion occurs, when the patterns of life suddenly burst out into an unprecedented array of complexity and morphological diversity. Dinosaurs come in around the middle of volume 30, but are wiped out on page 385. Only during the last 65 pages of volume 30 does most mammalian life come into existence. Our hominid ancestors begin to show up several pages from the end of volume 30, but modern humans don't appear until the bottom of the final page. The history of human intelligence, ethics, religious aspiration and scientific method takes up only the last few lines on the last page of the last volume of the story.

Can we ever hope to rewind the providential vine that clung for centuries to the vertical, hierarchical cosmology around the new 30-volume horizontal narrative of a world still in process? Can the religious sensibilities and aspirations pruned in the context of ancient and medieval cosmologies survive and find new life in the radically different picture of the cosmos now emerging? If so, in what sense would they still be continuous with religious tradition? And again, what can the doctrine of divine providence mean in light of the Darwinian chapters of the new cosmic story (Haught, 2000)?

The 'temporalizing' of the Great Chain of Being that began to take place even prior to Darwin is not by itself necessarily a threat to the providential understanding of nature. The principle of plenitude, which holds that every step in the hierarchy of being must be occupied by some proportionate mode of being, could in principle be satisfied by a providential 'programme' for the gradual unfolding of creation (Gillispie, 1996, p. 18). But what most perplexes theology is the Darwinian recipe for the evolution of life over the last four billion years. Evolution's ingredients can be reduced to three generic features: (1) *contingent events* such as the accidents involved in the spontaneous origin of life, random genetic variations (mutations) that constitute the raw material of evolutionary diversity, and undirected occurrences in natural history, such as climatic changes or meteorite impacts, that shape the pathways of evolution in unpredictable ways; (2) *natural selection*, which weeds out mercilessly all nonadaptive forms of life; and (3) *deep cosmic time*, the billions of years that the universe has made available to evolution for its plentiful experiments with life.

The major question for theology, now as in the years immediately subsequent to the publication of Darwin's *Origin of Species*, is that of how to reconcile the brute impersonality and blindness of the three items in evolution's recipe with trust in divine providence (Gillispie, 1996, p. 220). Of course, there is more to evolution than the struggle and predation that Darwinians typically highlight. Evolution is not all competition and waste, but also symbiosis and cooperation. Still, as scientific information of natural history has accumulated after Darwin, the ideas of providence and evolution have not become any easier to tie together (Bowler, 2001). Life's long journey, as we now realize, has left such a wide trail of loss and pain that many sensitive people have given up trying to make religious sense of it at all. For some, the Darwinian account of life stretches the persistent problem of theodicy far beyond the breaking point. The idea of divine providence has generally been associated closely with a divine 'plan', 'purpose' or 'design', but there seems to be little in the Darwinian charting of life's journey that corresponds to such cosy concepts. Cataloguing signs of divine design was the backbone of Robert Boyle's natural theology and the famous lectures he endowed (Boyle, 1772; Hedley Brooke, 1991). But were he here with us today, Boyle himself might agree that after Darwin any natural theology built solely or primarily on the notion of design is hardly destined to prosper.

The Boyle Lectures, which took place between 1692 and 1732 in defence of the rationality of Christianity, make it evident that scientifically-minded religious thinkers at that time were much more impressed than most scientists are today by the purpose-

3

ful ordering of nature, especially the adaptive design in living phenomena (Ruse, 2003). But the claim that nature's designs can lead the mind directly to God, or that reason without the help of revelation can confidently affirm the existence of a providential divine plan for nature, is no longer easy to defend, at least among the scientifically educated. Most biologists today are convinced, in any case, that purely natural evolutionary mechanisms are sufficient to account for the adaptive design that nests organisms in their specific environments. Moreover, Darwinians now interpret the 'design' in life as only apparent. The eye, for example, may seem to be the product of intelligent contrivance, but it is really the unintended outcome of a process of blind natural selection. The adaptive complexity in the life-world today stands at the end of an unimaginably protracted period of time during which the 'struggle for existence' has led to the 'selection' of some species and organisms while washing out most others along the way. Should we be surprised, then, when the renowned biologist George Williams calls nature 'a wicked old witch' (Williams, 1995)?

Does evolution rule out divine providence?

As for Charles Darwin himself, the excessive amount of pain constitutive of the life-world ruined his earlier belief in divine oversight of the world. But he and Williams are not alone among great scientists scandalized by the way life processes work. To give just one other example, Sir Charles Sherrington, in his 1940 Gifford Lectures (*Man on His Nature*), expresses similar dismay at the disproportionate amount of suffering caused by parasites:

> There is a small worm (Redia) in our ponds. With its tongue-head, it bores into the lung of the water-snail. There it turns into a bag and grows at the expense of the snail's blood. The cyst in the snail's lung is full of Redia. They bore their way out and wander about the body of the snail. They live on the body of the snail, on its less vital parts for so it lasts the longer; to kill it would cut their sojourn short before they could breed. They breed and reproduce. The young wander within the sick snail. After a time, they bore their way out of the dying snail and

4

make their way to the wet grass at the pond-edge. There amid the green leaves, they encyst themselves and wait. A browsing sheep or ox comes cropping the moist grass. The cyst is eaten. The stomach of the sheep dissolves the cyst and sets free the fluke-worms within it. The worm is now within the body of its second prey. It swims from the stomach to the liver. There it sucks blood and grows, causing the disease called 'sheep rot'.

The worms then lay eggs that make their way down the animal's liver duct and finally exit into the wet pasture. 'Thence as free larvae they reach the meadow-pond to look for another water snail. So the implacable cycle rebegins.'

What does all of this mean? Sherrington has no idea:

It is a story of securing existence to a worm at cost of lives superior to it in the scale of life as humanly reckoned. Life's prize is given to the aggressive and inferior of life, destructive of other lives at the expense of suffering in them, and, sad as it may seem to us, suffering in proportion as they are lives high in life's scale. The example taken is a fair sample of almost count-less many (Sherrington, 1951, p. 266).

Even if liver flukes exhibit a mesmerizing inventiveness, it is not easy to attribute their ingenuity to beneficent divine design. There can be no edifying religious message at least on this page of the book of nature. Prior to Darwin, a prevalent justification of belief in providence was the display of adaptive living design that the Boyle Lectures and, later, William Paley had highlighted. However, Darwin apparently provided an adequate account of the design in living beings without resorting to theology at all. Natural selection of random variations could explain life's design, provided that there is enough time. And time there has been in abundance. Even before Darwin, geologists had already demon-strated that Earth's life-journey had taken at least some millions of years. And Darwin had no idea that life actually originated as long as 3.8 billion years ago, leaving more than enough opportun-ity for even the most improbable instances of adaptive design to come about gradually, in a purely natural way. The vast amount of time in which change can occur randomly and piecemeal in evolutionary history eliminates the need for ad hoc interventions by supernatural engineering (Dawkins, 1996). Thus, any return today to a natural theology built around the notion of divine design in living beings will seem unreasonable to those who are fully aware of deep time and Darwinian evolution.

A new natural theology?

Nevertheless, natural theology, as Robert Boyle might be satisfied to find out, has not gone away completely. Instead of looking closely and minutely at living organisms and their exquisite adaptivity as the primary evidence of a designing deity, a revived natural theology today gazes out more expansively at the larger cosmic context in which the life-story is embedded. Life, as scientists today see more clearly than only half a century ago, cannot be understood apart from its larger cosmic context and the history of the whole universe (Rees, 2000). In light of contemporary astrophysics, the original and fundamental cosmic conditions that made for a life-bearing universe appear themselves host to a providential fine-tuning (Polkinghorne, 1987). A more sweeping view of nature than that provided by evolutionary biology now provides an alluring opportunity for natural theology to exhibit evidence of divine intelligence in nature after all (Davies, 1992). Even those theologians who spurn natural theology can no longer be too dismissive of this proposal. After all, if life had been intended by God to emerge and evolve in our universe, it would not be surprising if we discovered that the conditions for such an adventure had been built into the physical foundations of nature from the very start.

Even if this is so, however, the Darwinian character of evolution remains an enigma – and a serious challenge to natural theology. The randomness, waste and suffering that accompany biological evolution still raise questions about divine providence conceived of as design. Knowledge of evolution may even lead sensitive souls to curse those finely tuned cosmic conditions that made possible the excessive suffering that many living beings must endure. Cosmic design, as the authors of Job and *The Brothers*

Karamazov timelessly admonish us, is little comfort to those who wonder why life on Earth has been so prone to pain and perishing.

Is blind trust enough?

What justification, then, could there possibly be for trusting in divine providence amid the darkness of evolution? One response is that of blind, unconditional trust in God in spite of apparent absurdity. Not being able to make theological sense of the Darwinian recipe should not prevent the devout from still trusting that there may be a hidden meaning in evolution, one that it would be presumptuous to try to access. Maybe 'contingent', 'accidental', 'random' and 'wasteful' are terms that we ignorant mortals attach to evolution only because of our abysmal ignorance of God's wider vision for the universe. Whenever anything takes place that falls outside our own sense of appropriate order, we tend to refer to it as an accident or absurdity, but perhaps it is *really* part of a wider and eminently wise divine plan to which we are not privy, and into which we should not pry.

If we take this posture of pure trust, we might conjecture that what appears to be absurd contingency from a human perspective could be the tangled underside of a tapestry that, from God's vantage point on the other side, is a tightly woven pattern. As for the struggle, cruelty, waste and pain in evolution – evidence, at least to many, of a universe beyond the pale of providence – Darwin's recipe has absolutely nothing qualitatively new to add to the perennial challenges to faith. Genuine piety by its very nature is already quite fully appraised of the realities of evil and suffering, but it trusts *in spite of* all apparent absurdity. Indeed, too much intellectual self-confidence may even deaden a faith that arrives at authenticity only by embracing, not removing, radical uncertainty. Thus, a contemporary awareness of life's evolutionary struggle may pose no more of an obstacle to trust in divine providence than suffering and evil have ever done.

Many deeply religious people, including some scientists and neo-orthodox theologians, are quite content to take this approach to evolution. They confess that they cannot reconcile the cruelty of Darwin's recipe with their own belief in divine providence. But they allow that their own human (including scientific) perspectives are finite, and that they are simply not in any position to declare the Darwinian universe essentially indifferent or evil.

Providence as Darwinian pedagogy?

The strictly fideist perspective, however, can at best tolerate, it can never celebrate, evolution, or attempt seriously to integrate it deeply into a theological vision. It remains essentially a defence against Darwinism, even though there may be no formal attempt to refute evolutionary biology in the aggressive manner of contemporary creationism and what has come to be called intelligent design theory (Dembski and Ruse, 2004). Of course, to some degree every theological interpretation of evolution has to partake of faith's encouragement to trust. But theology is also obliged to give reasons for its hope, and this imperative must lead to bolder speculation about the possible meaning of the Darwinian recipe than we have just seen. Blind trust in God is not the only option available to scientifically enlightened religious believers. This is why a reasonable theology need never dispense completely with natural theology as a component of its quest to understand the ways of God.

One interesting attempt to make providential sense of evolution is a variation on the ancient religious intuition that Earth was set up by God as a school for life, and indeed a 'soul school' for humans. Perhaps nature's severe Darwinian curriculum is providentially justifiable if it makes life strive for more life. After all, how could organisms, from bacteria to humans, ever really be alive – much less thrive – without having to struggle? And how anaemic of soul would humans be if the terrain over which their own lives travelled were devoid of obstacles and dead ends? If Earth were a totally accommodating abode, our lives would languish for lack of enticement.

Perhaps then the Darwinian domain was crafted deliberately by God especially to prepare human beings for the attainment of eternal life (Hick, 1978, pp. 255–61; 318–36). Once humans

8

emerged in life's Darwinian curriculum, the formula that gave rise to so much abundance and diversity of life beforehand could now function as the pedagogical context for moulding human character. What more fitting environment for soul-making could any of us have conjured up than the one that Darwin laid out a century and a half ago? Guy Murchie, in his colourful book *The Seven Mysteries of Life*, elaborates on this hypothesis. Earth, in all its evolutionary ruthlessness, he argues, may best be thought of as a 'soul school'. Try to imagine that you are the Creator, Murchie proposes. Then what kind of a world would you create? Would it be one in which we could all luxuriate in blissful and undisturbed tranquillity and hedonistic enjoyment? Not at all:

> Honestly now, if you were God, could you possibly dream up any more educational, contrasty, thrilling, beautiful, tantalizing world than Earth to develop spirit in? ... Would you, in other words, try to make the world nice and safe – or would you let it be provocative, dangerous and exciting? In actual fact, if it ever came to that, I'm sure you would find it impossible to make a better world than God has already created (Murchie 1978, pp. 621–2).

So this is the best of all possible worlds, after all, and divine providence is manifest in the rigour as well as the creativity of evolution.

The idea that God is a practitioner of tough love can be found scattered throughout the Bible, and especially in Hebrews 12.5–13. But it is not hard to imagine how such an outlook on suffering could at times build resentment and even hatred of God for making the world so unnecessarily severe. Moreover, a soul-making theodicy tends at times to interpret the entirety of creation as serving only the goal of human salvation. Its approach to providence renders the story of the universe ultimately inconsequential except as a stage for the human drama of salvation. Thus, the evolution-as-curriculum proposal can easily seem excessively anthropocentric or too Earth-centred for refined ecozoic and cosmic tastes. Even if human suffering were a proportionate punishment for our guilt, we would still have cause to wonder, along with Darwin, about the excessiveness of pain experienced by other living beings. Why do they have to go to 'school' with us? The soul-making theodicy may be a small part of a larger set of truths, but I am convinced that theology must look for deeper ways of thinking about providence in a post-Darwinian context.

Providence in cosmic directionality?

Perhaps then the works of Teilhard de Chardin (1881–1955) and Alfred North Whitehead (1861–1946), who discern a less soul-centred and more cosmic directionality in evolution, can provide a vision of nature compatible with both science and trust in providence (Teilhard de Chardin, 1964). For example, those who look deeply into Teilhard's writings may actually come to 'see' quite clearly that there are meaningful trends in cosmic process usually overlooked by evolutionary materialists and cosmic pessimists (Teilhard de Chardin, 1999). Doesn't the fact that the universe unfolds from simplicity to complexity, that it evolves from mindless materiality through life to conscious self-awareness, justify a religious suspicion that a nurturing divine sponsorship somehow shepherds such a remarkable adventure?

Along with a general trend towards increasing complexity-consciousness, one may also observe, with the famous Jesuit palaeontologist, that there has been an increasing 'centration' at the heart of the cosmic and evolutionary process (Teilhard de Chardin, 1970, pp. 31–5; 99–127). From the beginning, 'matter' has had a tendency to congeal around centres that function as attractors towards more complex and emergent levels of being. A progressively richer nucleation occurs in the atom, the eukaryotic cell, the central nervous systems of vertebrates, and most obviously human subjectivity. And now that humans have become the dominant terrestrial species in evolution, the habitual cosmic 'search for a centre' expresses itself in a novel way in Earth's religious traditions. Religions fit comfortably into cosmic evolution as characteristic ways in which the universe continues, at the human stage of becoming, its ageless search for a transcendent centre. Instead of interpreting religious trust in a providential centre as incompatible with evolution, the Teilhardian vision portrays such trust as absolutely indispensable to the ongoing creation of the universe (Teilhard de Chardin, 1970). Even our own search, here and now, for the meaning of providence in an age of evolution is an integral part of the process of evolution itself.

In brief, the fact that the universe has converged from the fragmentary atomic simplicity of its origins to higher degrees of complexity – consciousness – centration is for Teilhard a hint that at a very deep level, perhaps inaccessible to science, nature has been graced all along by a providential influence. But what about all the messiness and suffering in evolution? For Teilhard, these tragic realities are not the consequence of a primordial human fault, nor are they essentially divine pedagogy – even though *per accidens* they may prove to be instructive at times. Rather, such evils are the dark side of an unfinished universe. An incomplete cosmos by definition is one that has not yet been brought to perfection, and it is in the inevitable darkness of its present incompleteness that excessive suffering, physical evil, and sin too, can gain a foothold.

Why inevitable darkness? Because any creation that is all light from the outset, completely unblemished by any shortcomings, would be already finished. And such a creation could really never become distinct from its maker. If it were perfect from the start, the world would have no autonomy, no narrative self-identity and no 'otherness' vis-à-vis its maker. In other words, it would not be a world at all but a simple appendage to deity. Thus, Teilhard seems to be saying, a God who truly cares for the universe must suffer the pangs of allowing it only gradually and experimentally to become itself. The alternative would be no real creation at all (Teilhard de Chardin, 1969). Providence makes no sense apart from a gradually emerging universe. And the appropriate religious response to suffering and evil is not to make legitimate room for them in the world by way of a theodicy-based on guilt and punishment, but to hope for a future of new creation in which God will decisively conquer them.

A similar conjunction of providence and creative process is implied in the cosmological vision of the great mathematician and philosopher Alfred North Whitehead. Whitehead's expansive vision weaves life's evolution into an overall cosmic process whose general orientation is that of bringing about intense beauty. Beauty is a difficult notion to define, but it implies, at the very least, a 'harmony of contrasts' or an 'ordering of novelty'. Without the novelty of contrast there would be only bland order. But without order the elements of novelty and contrast would dissolve into chaos. Beauty is a delicate balance of coherence and complexity, unity and diversity. It embraces local shades of disharmony, bringing them to aesthetic resolution within an ever widening cosmic vision (Whitehead, 1967, pp. 252–96; 1978, pp. 62, 183–5, 255; 1968, pp. 8–104; Hartshorne, 1941, pp. 212–9).

It is towards composing more expansive and more intense beauty, according to Whitehead, that our universe has always been aiming. It has not always succeeded in this objective, but overall the natural world has in fact made its way from simplicity to complexity, from triviality to more intense versions of ordered novelty – that is, beauty (Whitehead, 1978, p. 265). In its aiming towards beauty, the most sublime of all values, the universe shows itself, therefore, to be something more than mindless meandering. It is not rash to suspect that from its beginning the cosmos has manifested at least this 'loose' kind of teleology.

Darwinian evolution, in all its waywardness, fits quite comfortably into this generous cosmology. Although Darwinian process leads towards the intensification of beauty in ways that may not conform to our usual human standards of conduct, this need not obscure the fact that the universe, at least in a generally directional way, is in the business of enlarging the sway of beauty. But why does the universe have this urge to move beyond the status quo at all? Why the impetus for so much novelty, contrast and diversity? And why is the cosmic making of beauty spread out over so many billions of years? Why has there been so much evolutionary drama, including not only the bringing of beauty into being, but also an exorbitant amount of tragedy and loss? And why did life have to take so long to complexify to the point of becoming endowed with consciousness and the capacity for goodness and worship?

Whitehead's aesthetic cosmology would consider all of these puzzling features of the cosmos, including Darwin's recipe, to be consistent with the notion of a God whose 'design' for the universe is the *maximizing of beauty* (Cobb and Griffin, 1976, pp. 123–4). And if God is also thought of as infinite love, then this love would act most effectively not by forcing its will on to the cosmos but by allowing the universe to unfold spontaneously, according to its own cadence, though always within the context of relevant metaphysical constraints. Moreover, Whitehead thinks of God as a compassionately empathetic redeemer, able to heal – in ways that we cannot fathom – all the tragedy and suffering that occur in the cosmic process. In this Whiteheadian vision, the sometimes troubling Darwinian picture of life turns out to be consonant with a providential God whose power consists essentially of persuasive love. Since genuine love by its very nature cannot be dictatorial, a God who loves and cares for the world's autonomy would not force the universe to reach the fullness of perfection in the magic of a single momentary act of institution, but would leave space and time for the universe to emerge as its own distinct reality – and at its own pace.

Consequently, the piecemeal, experimental and profligate way in which the cosmos and life evolve should come as no major surprise to those who believe in a God of love. It is not unreasonable to speculate that by gently presenting to the world relevant new possibilities for 'becoming itself', a persuasive God would provide a much sounder metaphysical explanation of the evolutionary story of life than pre-scientific versions of theism, mechanistic materialism or intelligent design theory could ever hope to offer. Such an explanation would in no way contradict Darwin's science, but would instead provide a cosmological and theological context that can make very good sense of it.

Providence and the promise of nature

However, acknowledging the general cosmic directionality that both Teilhard and Whitehead – each in his own way – articulate is still not enough to constitute a theology of evolution. From a Christian theological point of view, it must also be demonstrated that both the processive character of the cosmos overall, and the troubling Darwinian recipe in particular, are precisely what we should expect if the world is both grounded in and ultimately saved by the God revealed in Jesus Christ.

Without contradicting the Teilhardian and Whiteheadian attempts to interpret the cosmos and evolution in generally religious terms, Christian theology must reflect on evolution more explicitly in the light of its own revolutionary understanding of God. If, as Christians believe, the roots of our tradition lie in the story of Jesus, the one whom we take to be the visible face of the invisible God, and in whom the fullness of the Godhead dwells bodily, then a theology of evolution must make this teaching its very point of departure. It must then show that a Christian understanding of God in some *systematic* way embraces and brings intelligibility to the life-world as science now understands it.

This task may not be easy, for Christians believe that divine providence is actively, personally and passionately involved in life, whereas Darwinism understands life in terms of purely natural causes. If the cosmos itself is able to bring about life and its diversity in a purely blind and natural manner, how might theology provide any deeper illumination? Furthermore, since Christians believe that God cares for the weak and the poor, why is the process of natural selection permitted to eliminate so ruthlessly all incompetent, maladaptive forms of life? And if Christians believe that God is eager to create goodness and to redeem all suffering, why is the creative process drawn out for so long a time inconclusively?

I believe theology may effectively display the theological harmoniousness of divine providence with Darwinian evolution, if it takes as its starting point only two standout features of the image of God, which emerge from our revelatory sources. The first of these is the theme of the 'descent of God' (Hallman, 1991). The second, a motif that permeates the biblical literature, is that of the God who opens up the future by making promises and dependably keeping them. I believe that on these two closely allied pillars of faith theology may construct a plausible theology of evolution.

The descent of God

In Philippians 2.5–11, Jesus is pictured as being in the form of God, but, not clinging to that status, he empties himself and becomes a slave. Theological reflection has often taken this intuition by nascent Christianity (possibly derived from an early liturgical hymn) to entail that what is being emptied out is really the very being of God. But the notion of divine emptying (*kenosis* in Greek) does not depend solely on a single text from Philippians. It is Jesus' entire life and death on the cross that reveal to Christians the astounding notion that God is essentially humble, self-emptying love that gives itself away unreservedly to the entirety of creation. In fact, in the light of God's self-revelation in Christ, the entire body of biblical narrative, sometimes hesitantly, strains to tell the story of the humble descent of the infinite God into the domain of creaturehood.

As theologian Donald Dawe writes:

> God accepted the limitations of human life, its suffering and death, but in doing this, he had not ceased being God. God the Creator had chosen to live as a creature. God, who in his eternity stood forever beyond the limitations of human life, had fully accepted these limitations. The Creator had come under the power of his creation. This the Christian faith has declared in various ways from its beginning (Dawe, 1963, p. x).

However, Dawe continues, 'the audacity of this belief in the divine kenosis has often been lost by long familiarity with it. The familiar phrases "he emptied himself [*heauton ekenosen*], taking the form of a servant," "though he was rich, yet for your sake he became poor", have come to seem commonplace. Yet this belief in the divine self-emptying epitomizes the radically new message of Christian faith about God and his relation to man' (Dawe, 1963; Moltmann, 1974; von Balthasar, 1990a). Here, I believe, the doctrines of creation and incarnation allow us to go beyond Dawe's anthropocentric language and speak of God's kenotic relationship to the entirety of nature.

Theologian John Macquarrie, echoing Dawe, notes how radical the transformation of the God-image has been in Christianity:

That God should come into history, that he should come in humility, helplessness and poverty – this contradicted everything – this contradicted everything that people had believed about the gods. It was the end of the power of deities, the Marduks, the Jupiters ... yes, and even of Yahweh, to the extent that he had been misconstrued on the same model. The life that began in a cave ended on the cross, and there was the final conflict between power and love, the idols and the true God, false religion and true religion (Macquarrie, 1978, p. 34).

Our question, then, is what this revolution in the understanding of God – and hence of divine providence – has to do with the evolution of life. An evolutionary theology, I would suggest, must picture God's descent as entering into the deepest layers of the evolutionary process, embracing and suffering along with the entire cosmic story, not just with the recent human chapters. The Spirit of God stretches the divine compassion out across the totality of creation, enfolding and healing not only human struggles and suffering but also the epochs of evolutionary travail that preceded our emergence. In spite of its endless diversity, there is a fundamental unity to the life process; and all of life is linked, throughout its evolution, to the eternal ground that we may call life-itself. There is an ontological coherence – rooted in the very being of God – that ties together the striving, achieving and failing of all shades and stages of life. The continuous biological drama of striving, failing and achieving connects our own lives even to the most archaic instances of metabolism. Providence, therefore, must be thought of not only as divine care for humans and our history, but as God's care for the totality of life and the cosmic process that sponsors life.

Redemption must mean, then, at the very least, that the whole story of the universe and life streams into the everlasting bosom of divine compassion. While incorporating our human stories into the divine being, the God revealed in Christ assimilates into the divine eternity, and hence into ultimate redemptive bliss, the whole story of life on Earth (and life elsewhere in the universe if it exists there). And since the entire physical history of the universe, as recent astrophysics has made clear, is tied into the existence of life everywhere, we can no longer separate our human hope for ultimate deliverance from the larger cosmic course of events. Because of the divine omnipresence, nothing in the universe-story or in life's evolution can occur outside of God's own experience. If Jesus is truly the Incarnation of God, then his experience of the Cross is God's own suffering. By virtue of life's unbroken historical unity, we may be so bold as to assume also that the eons of evolutionary suffering in the universe are also God's own suffering. And this would mean that the whole of nature in some way participates in the promise of resurrection as well.

But how does the theme of the divine descent help us understand why life, in the first place, has unfolded on Earth in the ragged manner that evolutionary science has depicted? Why are struggle and death constitutive of the ongoing creation of life? Why does God's creation, once life comes about, no longer follow the path of pure design that natural theologians and intelligent-design proponents would prefer?

There is a great mystery here, but once again a kenotic theology of creation may be enlightening (Moltmann, 1985, p. 88). For if theology remains true to its revelatory sources, it must also envisage the divine descent as the ground of creation itself. That is, even as a condition of there being any world distinct from God at all, the omnipotent and omnipresent Creator must be humble and self-effacing enough to allow for both the existence of something other than God, and a relationship to that other. If this other is to be truly other, and not just an accessory attached to God's own being, then the divine omnipotence and omnipresence must become small enough to allow room for what is truly distinct from God. It is out of the divine humility, therefore, that the otherness of the world is 'longed' into being by God. Creation is God's 'letting be' of the world, a release that makes possible a dialogical relationship (and hence a more intimate communion) of God with the finite, created 'other'.

Once God's 'other', a world fashioned in accordance with the eternal Logos, has begun to emerge as a fundamentally historical reality, it can sustain its otherness only by becoming more, not less, differentiated from its Creator (Teilhard de Chardin, 1999, pp. 186–7). And once life emerges spontaneously within the history of this other, it need not forfeit the seeds of autonomy allowed to take root in it by the other-regarding providence of its maker. It is ultimately for this reason that the Darwinian recipe consists of its three ingredients: contingency, law and time.

Contingency, for instance, may be troubling to those fixated on the need for design in nature, but it is absolutely essential for creation's autonomy and aliveness. The alternative would be a world so stiffened by lawful necessity that everything in it would be determined and dead – ordered perhaps, but dead. At the same time, the remorseless and impersonal invariance of the laws of nature, including natural selection (the second ingredient of the Darwinian recipe), may be essential if the world is to have any degree of autonomy or self-reliance vis-à-vis its Creator. The alternative, once again, is unimaginable: a construct in which every event would be directly caused by divine action – in other words, not really a world at all, but a puppet.

Finally, if nature is allowed to be distinct from the God who calls it into being, it must be granted sufficient temporal amplitude for life-evolving experiments with the wide variety of possibilities made available to it by the infinite resourcefulness of its Creator. Once we understand divine care as inseparable from the eternal divine descent, we may appreciate more readily why the creation of the world does not take place instantaneously but instead unfolds across billions of years. The God revealed in Jesus and his cross allows the world enough scope to become ever more distinct from – and thereby able all the more intensely able to relate to – its creative ground. A mature theology of providence may come to realize that God 'descends' from all eternity so as to permit the self-actualizing of the universe. Thus evolution, including all the aspects of it that send us scurrying for signs of design, is consistent with any world whose emergent freedom eventually allows for the intimate relationship with the self-humbling God that Christian faith perceives to be transparent in the divine incarnation.

Providence as promise

The evolution of life on Earth has required a nearly unimaginable expanse of time. In fact, it appears to some evolutionists that time, when there is an abundant amount of it available, is so creative that it renders God completely superfluous in the crafting of the many kinds of life. Nevertheless, even if evolutionists at times – inappropriately in my view – attribute a kind of causal efficacy to the immensity of time, evolutionary biology cannot give an adequate account of time itself. Darwinism neither asks nor answers the question of why the universe has been endowed with an irreversible temporal character at all. Obviously, irreversible time is a prerequisite for evolution, but evolutionary science does not ground or explain it. So any truly penetrating account of time's creativity in evolution must ask what gives the natural world the character of temporal becoming in the first place.

Evolutionists, unlike physicists and philosophers, seldom dwell on the cosmological conditions of temporality, even though without time, evolution by natural selection would be inconceivable. Given enough time, they rightly point out, even the most improbable things can happen. But time must first be given! Why then is the universe temporal at all? The various sciences may try to answer this question at their own levels of inquiry, but a biblically guided theological search for the deepest conditions of time, and hence of evolution, could argue that it is *the coming of the future* that pushes the present into the past and permits a linear sequence of events to occur. In other words, it is not the blind movement of the past towards the future that endows the universe with its temporal character, but the constant arrival of a new future.

Theologically speaking, however, the 'coming of the future' is ultimately the coming of God, whose self-revelation occurs inseparably from promises that open up the world to an unprecedented horizon of newness. Indeed, it may not be inappropriate to say that in its ultimate depths the fathomless future is one of the things we mean when we use the word 'God' in a Christian setting (Moltmann, 1975; Rahner, 1969; Pannenberg, 1977; Peters, 1992).

The arrival of the future in the mode of promise explains in an ultimate way not only the fact of time, but also the other two

ingredients of evolution's recipe: contingency and lawful predictability. The contingency in natural history, even when accompanied
by pain and loss, is essential to any world open to the coming of
the future. Try to imagine what nature would be like, were it
completely devoid of undirected, accidental events. It would be so
frozen and rigid that it could never become new, but would persist in endless cycles of sameness. Nature could carry no promise
or openness to creative renewal.

Likewise, the predictable constraints in nature that we call
laws, including natural selection, are essential to the promissory
bearing of nature. If it were devoid of the reliable and recurrent
routines faithfully operative in its unfolding, the universe could
have no narrative continuity from one stage to the next. At every
moment, it would crumble into disconnected droplets of disarray.

In the depths of Darwin's recipe, it seems to me, there resides
what we may be so bold as to call the 'promise of nature' (Haught,
1993). This promissory interpretation of nature, a synthesis of
science and a biblical reading of reality, is not only consistent with
evolution by natural selection, but it also sets forth an ultimate
explanation of the contingency, necessity and temporal openness
that permit evolution to take hold in nature in the first place. Our
theological approach does not compete with the natural sciences,
but digs beneath their regional inquiries into the subsoil of a cosmic narrative graced throughout with an inherent openness to
the future. Providence here takes the form not so much of design
and fine-tuning as the perpetual dawning of a new future for the
world. That the story of the Big Bang universe will itself eventually
come to a physical end – freeze or fry – should not be disturbing
to those who trust in God's promise of redemption. An infinitely
compassionate and resourceful future can be the ultimate redemptive repository of the entire series of cosmic occurrences no less
than of those episodes that make up our individual lives.

Finally, although I cannot develop the point here, I would suggest that our search for the deep cosmic conditions of evolution
may also provide a way in which the tradition of natural theology
featured by the Boyle Lectures may undergo a renewal today.
Instead of focusing only on the fact of living design, which can
be accounted for scientifically in terms of the Darwinian recipe,

a revived natural theology will focus on nature's openness to the future. In my view, the fact that the universe possesses a narrative character made possible by its inherent openness to the future is the greatest of wonders. It is a wonder that we generally take for granted, but it runs much deeper into nature than does design. The theme of 'nature as promise' harmonizes nicely with the eschatological orientation of biblical religion. Darwin's recipe itself may not provide suitable soil for a natural theology centred on intelligent design, but it may very well provide the entry to a natural theology based on nature's narrative openness to the promise of an ever-renewing future. Perhaps Robert Boyle himself – deeply Christian thinker that he was – would not be averse to such a reconfiguration of natural theology after Darwin.

2

Darwin's Compass: How Evolution Discovers the Song of Creation

SIMON CONWAY MORRIS

It was G. K. Chesterton who trenchantly reminded us that, if one was going to preach, then it was more sensible to expend one's energies on addressing the converted rather than the unconverted (Chesterton, 1913, p. 31). It was the former, after all, who were – and even more so are – in constant danger of missing the point and sliding away from the Faith into some vague sort of syncretistic, gnostic, gobbledygook. Chesterton, as ever, was right, and should you think this is just another of his tiresome paradoxes, may I urge you to re-read him: his prescience concerning our present situation and, worse, where we are heading, is astounding. Yet it might seem a little odd in a lecture devoted to the ancient and ongoing debate between science and religion to invoke at its onset the name of Chesterton. Well, no, I don't think so. First, as Stanley Jaki has reminded us, it is over-simplistic to regard Chesterton as anti-science (Jaki, 1986). What Chesterton regarded with the deepest alarm was not science, but its misuse. Indeed, long before the time of Chesterton, others already saw the dangers of unprincipled meddling where hubris and ignorance marched hand-in-hand. Robert Boyle was one such.

Indeed, from the time of Boyle we should ask how far we have come. So far as the science–religion debate is concerned the linearity of history looks curiously circular. What exactly has changed? In Boyle's time, we see science, albeit in nascent form, already beginning to grasp limitless possibilities in knowledge, while at the same time the drumbeat of Hobbesian materialism is clearly heard. As Reijer Hooykaas has remarked, the reductionists were abroad, and among the atomists there were leanings towards naturalism, if not atheism (Hooykaas, 1997). Somewhat mysteriously, the barriers between science and religion, if not already in place, certainly were in the process of construction. And today? Who hasn't met the scientist who boomingly – and they always boom – declares that those who believe in the deity are unavoidably crazy, 'cracked', as my dear father would have said, although I should add that I have every reason to believe he was – and now hope is – on the side of the angels. Conversely, the religious reaction was, and remains, to shy away from the implications of science. Better to doubt evolution, the age of the Earth, even the world itself, than imperil one's soul. The devout Boyle remained confident that this divide was false and pernicious. Yet even in his time Boyle's vigorous faith and orthodoxy, rather than simple observance of the customary pieties, was perhaps more unusual than we realize. Of Boyle himself it was written that he is 'said to be a learned and witty man of science *in spite* of his religious convictions' (Hooykaas 1997, p. 59). If that raised eyebrows in the time of Charles II, today the same sentiments are likely to provoke mute astonishment.

It is surely telling that the apparent disagreements between science and religion are so often treated with a bluntness and unsubtlety that in any normal discourse would be dismissed as juvenile. Hear the sounds of debate? Then sure enough within minutes we will be reminded of Galileo before the Inquisition or Bishop Wilberforce being mangled by T. H. Huxley. So often the terms of reference are condescending and dismissive, with the supposedly losing side being equated with flat-earthers. If at all possible, the additional sins against political correctness are also heaped against the doors of religious discourse. This is bad enough, but the discussion is usually based on a chronic chronological snobbery that supposes individuals dead for many years, if not centuries, were singularly unfortunate not to have lived in our times among people who not only know but are *right*. It would also be a mistake to overlook the fact that the undoubted continued hostility between science and religion in no small part is exacerbated by the sleight-of-hand whereby a materialist philosophy is illicitly imported to bolster a particular worldview of science. It remains an astonishing piece of window-dressing: meaning is smuggled into a world that by definition lacks meaning. Boyle himself knew the enemy. He was more than prepared, in the words of Hooykaas, to be the one who 'unmasks their pride ... exposes their narrow mindedness [and] ... shows up their arrogance' (Hooykaas, 1997, p. 58).

So how are we to be true heirs of Robert Boyle, legitimate scientists but inspired by faith, willing not only to conduct the debate, but win it? The present-day auguries are hardly auspicious. Too often our arguments, our world-picture, even our data, are cringingly presented, in a combination of nervousness and accommodation. Do I really have to remind you of our opponents' visceral aversion to religious thought and practice? To be labelled as the credulous believers in fairy tales, bottomless receptacles for wish-fulfilment, blind to the undoubted evils of the world, are common enough jibes. So too is our opponents' almost limitless degree of patronizing. Think of Daniel Dennett's parody of religious thought in the form of his 'Skyhooks' (Dennett, 1995). Is he so naïve as to imagine the orthogonal intersection of our world with other realities is akin to some sort of elevator or a London Underground escalator? Nor should we forget that the attitude of our opponents is not one of benign disdain, but a deep-seated animus. Nor are they reluctant to pronounce on matters, such as reproductive technology or genetically modified food, with a conviction and assurance that in other contexts they would despise as symptomatic as the worst of dogmatic interference by the Pope or similar. These things matter, and as Peter Kreeft reminds us, they not only matter, they matter absolutely.

Polemic and rhetoric have their places, but we are here not only to honour Boyle but to re-examine how science and religion not only must co-exist – and I hope nobody here has fallen for Stephen Jay Gould's reckless canard of science and religion defining independent magisteria of influence (and by way of further parenthesis, should they toy with this superficially appealing idea be warned they face logical incoherence) – but far more importantly how science reveals unexpected depths to Creation, while religion informs us what on Earth (literally) we are going to do about it (Gould, 2001). From this perspective, the impoverished world-picture that the Western world has been busy painting with a meagre palette of predominantly browns and greys on a scruffy piece of hardboard (rescued from the attic) might not only be re-illuminated, but in this new blaze of light the wonder might become deeper – and the risks clearer.

I think it almost goes without saying that of all the areas of science concerned with this dialogue, that of organic evolution is the most sensitive, in some ways the most vulnerable. This is hardly surprising: the stakes are the highest, because where we humans came from and what we are must be questions of central importance. In other areas of science, on the other hand, the temperature of engagement is lower, and even in quiet corners scenes of cordiality may be witnessed. Such is most obvious in terms of the astounding developments in physics. Not only with the evidence for an instantiation of Creation – the Big Bang, if you prefer – but even more powerfully the now famous evidence for cosmological fine-tuning and the implication this has for an Anthropic Universe (Rees, 2000). So peculiar and so finely balanced do the key physical constants appear to be that it is hardly surprising that many physicists have embraced the concept of not just one universe but a gadzillion of them tucked away behind black holes or hidden in other dimensions, ever present but ever invisible. And out of that gadzillion, well, we are the lucky ones where everything turned out to be just, precisely right.

Should we choose to be parochial and stick to just one, 14-billion-year-old universe with its physical constants just so to ensure habitability, then we are not necessarily clear of the woods. Neil Manson has emphasized that, if we can accept fine-tuning, we still have no notion of why the numbers are what they are, nor how they could all be systematically different yet still be combined to provide a habitable universe (Manson, 2000). Yet we must also acknowledge Howard van Till's point that it is the interdependence of each value as much as the fine-tuning of any one that is so remarkable (Till, 2000). All this smacks of design: physicists are rightly wary and the invisible host of multiverses remains ever popular.

Somewhere, and even more mysteriously somehow, out of physics and chemistry life emerged. By natural processes surely, but by routes and in an environment of which we have no secure knowledge. Despite its physical substrate the processes of evolution, and indeed their bewildering complexity of products, seem to find no echo in any anthropic principle, no sense of particular rules analogous to the gravitational constant or nuclear strong force. The paradox of this view is that it is nevertheless just these evolutionary processes that have led – in the view of some inexorably – to a species that strangely can find meaning in such physical concepts. Some find it distinctly strange that just one species has stumbled on facts that not only inform us about the cosmos but in a deep fashion define its comprehensibility. From an evolutionary point of view, paradox or irony notwithstanding, this view in turn verges on the incomprehensible. This is because if there is a consensus among neo-Darwinists it is that evolution is an open-ended and indeterminate process. It cannot be over-emphasized how pervasive is this view. Organisms must be fit for purpose, but 'purpose' in only a relative sense. A widely agreed corollary is just as humans are an evolutionary accident, as interesting in their own way as a duck-billed platypus or for that matter watercress, so too is human intelligence. More than one investigator has pointed out that if indeed this is true then the SETI project, that is the Search for Extraterrestrial Intelligence, is at best quixotic and more likely based on a massive delusion. A profound irony: the one species capable of understanding the Anthropic Principle can only share his discovery with – a gerbil.

Intelligent design?

Yet even if we were to espouse this view of evolution as being utterly indeterminate, everything a fluke of history and circumstance, the organisms themselves never cease to amaze us, be it a bacterium living in the boiling water of a volcanic pool, an albatross circumnavigating the Southern Ocean, or a spider spinning its web of silk. As is repeatedly pointed out, to talk about organisms as designed may indeed be a metaphor, but the integration of function, their unbelievable complexity not least at the level of biochemistry, their emergent sophistications be they in terms of navigation, exquisite sensory perception or intelligence, indeed their sheer poise, should leave us stunned. Organisms *are* astonishing, and it is our common failing that this is too often lost sight of in the attempt to depict biology as a subject only to be conducted in an atmosphere of steely rationalism. The latter is no doubt the necessary procedure for investigation so long as it is never forgotten that the things we study are *alive*. In unguarded moments, some biologists will gladly admit that the way an organism is put together is remarkable. It is not the point that we understand that biochemical cycle, a certain enzyme, or that hormone, it is the way systems interact and have a dynamic interdependence that is – unless one has lost all sense of wonder – quite awe-inspiring. Nor should we dismiss this as an unworthy emotion. From this perspective, it is easy to appreciate the intellectual attraction of the quasi-scientific/quasi-theological movement known as intelligent design (ID). In my opinion, intelligent design is a false and misleading attraction. Here there would be little point in reiterating the many objections raised against intelligent design, especially those made by the scientific colleagues (but opponents) of Michael Behe and Bill Demski, two of the principal proponents of intelligent design. Rather it seems to me that intelligent design has a more interesting failing, a theological failing. Consider how in our culture it is the worshippers of the machine and the computer model, those admirers of organized efficiency who might be the ones to end up with a warped view of the Creator. Here is a deity identified as the engineer of the bacterial flagellar motor (or whatever your favourite case-study of ID might be) who rather than being encumbered with a large white beard is now transmuted into the very model of scientific efficiency. Let God don a very large white laboratory coat. ID is surely the deist's option, and one that turns its back not only on the richness and beauty of creation but, as importantly, its limitless possibilities. It is a theology for control freaks.

What is life?

My enthusiasm for life surely needs no reiteration. Let us also recall, however, how little of it we really understand. It is pretty clear that organisms are not blobs of malleable protoplasm buffeted by environmental circumstance. First, there is some intriguing evidence that at least in some circumstances organisms are predisposed – I won't use the word designed – to evolve. That is somewhat less surprising when we consider such evolvability in the context of the complexity of the developmental systems. Among the many oddities of life is the fact that first there is no detailed instruction manual – and in this context, we can effect-ively ignore the genetic code – but these systems, if prodded or disrupted, are remarkably adept at self-repair. Not foolproof, of course, otherwise we would never catch a cold or, for that mat-ter, die. Yet remarkable nonetheless. So too, however neglected it may be because of its sheer familiarity, we too easily forget the remarkable homeostasis of living organisms, that is their internal balance and capacity for adjustment whatever the external envi-ronment. In any computer room, along with the banks of hard disks, screens and printers there will be the steady hum of air con-ditioning, extracting the excess heat. Noisy and inefficient; now compare it with the temperature regulation of your brain. Not only is the integrity and integration of living systems quite aston-ishing, but attempts to employ machine-like analogies soon run into difficulties (Barham, 2004). To be sure we refer to motors, switches, transport mechanisms, fluid flow, pumps and electricity, but the reality is that organisms have a subtlety and efficiency far beyond any machine we can build. Again and again, we discover that even in apparently straightforward functions there is an exactness to purpose that is eerily precise. The fact remains that we have no idea of what it is about life that, although obviously made of atoms no different than you find in a stone, combines to form such a dynamic entity, culminating in the entirely surpris-ing ability to become conscious. But consider even the cell. Here jostling together are innumerable chemical compounds involved in extraordinary biochemical cycles, including reactions that may be accelerated a billion times by protein catalysts – the enzymes –

and all depending not only on carefully transmitted instructions – again depending on a truly baroque arrangement – but instructions that can be appropriately modified long after transcription from the original genetic code. We are left in the rather extraordinary position of describing things that at one level we hardly understand. Given the remarkable advances in our understanding of biochemistry, molecular biology and evolution as a whole, it is all the more strange we have failed to develop concepts, ideas, even a language that could capture this dance of life. Or is it so surprising? We forget at our peril that language presupposes deep assumptions about the way the world is. If we decide it is arid, machine-like and meaningless then it will be all the less odd that its richness will slip through our nets.

World-pictures

A world-picture that encompasses science but also the deep wisdom of theology may help us to explain how it is we can think, how we discover the extraordinary, but so too it may warn us of present dangers and future catastrophes. Not only that, but it can instruct us as to what may be the limits of desirable knowledge and risks of unbridled curiosity. This world-picture could also show that far from being a series of mindless accidents, history has directions and conceivably end-points. And the other world-picture, one based not just on science but wedded to a scientistic programme? Well, you know it as well as I do. Here all is ultimately meaningless. The metaphorical sparrow in the storm may still enter the warm and well-lit mead-hall, but its return to the violent night outside erases all memories and obligations.

Such views presuppose a world-picture very alien to many scientists and philosophers today. Theirs is ultimately a council of despair. One species, on one tiny planet, in a vast and ancient universe. There are several responses to this view. First, who are we to decide what is or is not appropriate? What metric do we use? One can observe that at least in terms of size, perhaps oddly, we are just in the centre, the mid-point between the unimaginably small and the cosmically vast. Next, what if we stand on an immensity of time? Leaving aside what time is, would it make any practical difference if the beginning was a million years ago, as against the believed value of 13 billion, let alone even 100 billion years? Did the innumerable brachiopods (or whatever is your favourite fossil organism) drum their metaphorical fingers and glance at their watches, wishing the Palaeozoic would slip by just a bit more quickly? Maybe the 13 billion years is the time we need, for carbon to form, for life not only to evolve but to find itself in a neck of galactic woods that is stable enough not to frighten the horses with rogue black holes, gamma ray bursts and titanic supernovae.

Suppose this approach has some merit. Metric-sized animals that are the end-result of many billions of years of prior stellar and biological evolution may be the only way to allow at least one species to begin its encounter with God. But you may well riposte: let us reconsider organic evolution. Isn't it an open-ended process, to be sure showing an inherent evolvability, but to evolve to what? To be able to function, to reproduce, of course, but to produce in the fullness of time a very strange species, capable of great good but also terrible evil, sensitive to hidden dimensions but also credulous, able to measure the span of the universe but also allow the Flat Earth Society? As has already been made clear, the viewpoint within orthodox Darwinism is agreed and uncontroversial: humans are an accident of evolution, because *everything* produced by evolution is strictly incidental to the process.

Accordingly humans are as fortuitous as a tapeworm, and by implication ultimately no more – or less – interesting. I have already suggested that if we are hardly able to define life, this alone should give us pause for thought. I would further argue that the study of evolution itself already hints that to reduce all to the accidental and incidental may turn out to be a serious misreading of the evidence. In terms of evolution, the clear evidence for organismal simplification, not to mention the repeated move to parasitism, does not negate the realities of evolutionary progress and the emergence of irreversibly complex states. More particularly the view that evolution is open-ended, without predictabilities and indeterminate in terms of outcomes is negated by the ubiquity of evolutionary convergence (Conway Morris, 2003). The central

point is that because organisms arrive repeatedly at the same biological solution, the camera-eyes of vertebrates and cephalopods
perhaps being the most famous example, this provides not only a
degree of predictability, but more intriguingly points to a deeper
structure to life, a metaphorical landscape across which evolution
must necessarily navigate.

Converging on convergence

Concerning evolutionary convergence, I could give you innumerable examples, but the central aim of this chapter is to show
that the evidence now strongly suggests humans to be an evolutionary inevitability. On this basis, some time-honoured
theological questions may be re-addressed. What is it then concerning evolutionary convergence that can inform us about both
the definition and emergence of humanness? This is a large and
complex area, and in passing I will only note that there are a number of key features, such as complex vocalizations, tool-making
and cultural transmission, that are both vital to the general argument and are patently evolutionarily convergent. Not only have
they evolved independently a number of times, but as importantly
this indicates that these features are real biological properties,
defined entities that are necessary prerequisites for the evolution
of humans.

For reasons of time and also relative importance, it is pardon-
able, I trust, if I choose to focus on the emergence of complex
intelligence and mentality. Briefly, it is now clear that an intelligence equivalent to the primates has evolved independently at
least twice, that is in the dolphins and corvids (or crows) (Marino,
1996; Clayton and Emery, 2004). In fact, the figure is probably
substantially higher, but any estimate depends on questions of
phylogenetic relationships and continuing debates about levels
of intelligence, for example among the cetaceans (Clayton and
Emery, 2004; Marino et al., 2004; Rendell and Whitehead, 2001).
Even so, within at least the dolphins and crows the similarities
are indeed very striking. And there is good reason for such surprise. First, this primate-like intelligence has emerged in strikingly

different contexts. Sitting in trees and laying eggs is one thing, living in an ocean is another, and both contrast with the evolution of the apes in jungle and savannah. Second, and even more importantly, even though dolphins are also mammals, their brain structure differs markedly from that of the apes, while that of the crows is even more distinct.

Thus from radically different neural substrates the same type of mind emerges. This is surely startling, for at least two reasons. First, it reinforces our view that mind is not some sort of epiphenomenon, a simple by-product of chemistry and electrical activity in a squishy organ that happens to be located in the skull. If it was, why should it be so similar? Second, as Ed Oakes has pointed out to me, if wings (also convergent) need air to fly, perhaps brains require an equivalent 'mental atmosphere' to operate.

Recall that so far as the hominid fossil record can be relied upon concerning such intangibles as awareness, language and empathy, let alone an almost universal religious instinct, the transition to full humanness was evidently a gradual process (and a process that is still arguably incomplete). This in turn has two very interesting implications. First, if consciousness was hovering in the wings of the theatre of evolution with its fully fledged emergence only a matter of time, then why us as against some other species still grunting in the undergrowth? Simply an accident of circumstance, being first on the block? Possibly so, but we should remember that belief in a personal God implies choice, both on our part and more importantly God's. Is the history of the Jewish nation a sort of analogy? Chosen, prodded by their true prophets, and despite diversions and disasters leading the rest of us by a route nobody expected to the Incarnation? Tricky, and possibly a dangerous argument, because of course the story doesn't stop there. Either way, the plea of 'Why us?' takes us towards new and different dimensions, but ones of which our materialist colleagues will, I fear, be blissfully oblivious.

Second, and I very much fear treading on even more problematic – but in fact related – ground, suppose that there were other species on this planet even closer in sentience to humans than either dolphins or crows? How should we treat them? Larder, zoo, nature reserve, or an invitation to tea? I suspect strongly that would be our dilemma if, for whatever reason, the Neanderthals had not disappeared. A similar question is asked by the American writer, Harry Turtledove, in one of his stimulating science fiction novels based on a counter-factual world (Turtledove, 1988). In his book *A Different Flesh*, we are asked to imagine a North America that is the abode of australopithecines but otherwise uninhabited by hominids, that is until the arrival of the Europeans. His story stretches over several centuries, but a central theme is how we should treat our very near cousins, creatures he calls the 'sims'. That question stretches from initial contacts finally to medical trials involving the deliberate infection of the 'sims' with HIV. Hypothetically with the 'sims' and probably actually with the Neanderthals, these represent species that are so close to us that any Socratic dialogue would beg agonizing questions of moral decision. In either case, humanness is in the last stages of emergence, a consciousness that is already grasping realities beyond immediate vision. We might be grateful that such a dilemma cannot arise with either the extinct Neanderthals or hypothetical 'sims', until we recall that just such an emergence of mind almost certainly occurs within a few weeks of conception in the human foetus (Vining, 2004).

Far from being a series of curious accidents, the study of evolution poses some deep and awkward questions. I suggest, moreover, that it may illuminate in other ways who we are and our place in the world. I have already mentioned that evolutionary convergence hints at a prior 'landscape' that predetermines, albeit in an extraordinarily rich way, the outcomes of the process, not least human intelligence and by implication the inevitability of contact with a different sort of Mind, an encounter with God. I want to argue that this is more than a powerful metaphor, and in doing so I now move to the heart of this Boyle Lecture. Consider music.

A universal music?

In a fascinating essay, Patricia Gray and colleagues remark on the many similarities between our music and that of animals (Gray et al., 2002). That gap between them and humans is obvious enough:

no bird in a tree astonishes us with Tallis' 40-part motet, *Spem in alium*, but the basics of harmonics, melody, invention, inversion, duetting and even riff sessions are all shared. Like consciousness, evidently the symphony orchestra is also waiting in the wings of the theatre of evolution. Music is, therefore, a splendid example of convergence. As such, one can certainly propose scientific explanations, both in terms of the physics of sound production and the biology of function such as sexual matters or territoriality. The plausibility of such assumptions, not least in the famous songs of the male humpback whales, need not detain us. This is because Gray et al. go on to make a much more interesting argument. Suppose, they suggest, there is a Universal Music, and the reason why all earthly song is so similar is because all are gaining access to an Ideal, a reality both 'out there' but also intimately close, in a 'dimension' discovered by evolution, familiar but also one that defies simple categorization. Such a view has equal applicability to intelligence, mentality and discovery of the other 'invisibles' that together define our continuing search for Truth.

There is, moreover, an intriguing analogy to the discovery of music that has even more interesting theological implications. I alluded above to the mysterious origins of language. We can, of course, simply take a biological stance, and in the context, say, of predator warnings or the demands of reproduction so an analysis of the howls, screeches, chattering and whistles will lead to fruitful insights. Does it apply to language? As with music there are other approaches, other dimensions that touch wider and more remote shores. Here, I have in mind J. R. R. Tolkien's fascination with words and the origins of language. His creation, or more strictly sub-creation, of Elvish might owe much to his interests in Welsh and Finnish, but it is also clear that his immense creativity and the invocation of the beautiful, mysterious and almost painfully real Middle Earth, was founded on a deep appreciation and love for languages. In some strange way, the articulation of Elvish and the other languages of Middle Earth were the catalysis for the rest of his mythos. It is also evident that Tolkien, already a master philologist, was fundamentally influenced by another of the Inklings, Owen Barfield, and especially his book *Poetic Diction* (Barfield, 1952). In essence, and as compellingly explored by

Vernon Flieger, Barfield and thereby Tolkien believed that from its source language had become fragmented: Flieger's metaphor is 'splintered light' (Flieger, 2002). Originally, certain words, in 'primitive' times, carried an immensity of meanings that importantly touched on the unseen and mythical, if not the sacred. With the elapse of time these meanings subdivided, precision (of a sort) was gained, but also much was lost. Paradoxically, reality was blurred and disenchantment spread.

The implications of this are not difficult to grasp, but they seem to me to be extraordinarily fruitful. The sense that there are other realities, orthogonal to everyday experience, is certainly familiar: who has not entered zones of timelessness, had prescient dreams, compelling hunches or odd synchronicities? It is not my assumption that these realities are either exclusive or incompatible. In fact, there is every reason to think that individually but obliquely they collectively touch on much deeper matters, but in our present state they can be deeply disconcerting. Potentially, however, they open portals to new perspectives and possibilities. Who is not familiar with the metaphor of hearing the harmony of spheres or engaging in speech with animals? Literally these are either fanciful or folk tales, but if the New Testament tells us anything, it is, as Tolkien finally persuaded C. S. Lewis in their celebrated night-time walk in Magdalen College, that point when myth became true and real.

Evolution beyond the horizon

My work on evolutionary convergence, with its claims that the roads of evolution are constrained, that not all is possible (in fact the reverse is the case: nearly all is impossible), and that the outcomes of evolution are thereby effectively inevitable, frequently provokes the question along the lines of, 'Fine, so what's next?' A fair question, and one that not only generates interesting responses but again touches directly on theological issues. Some predictions are pessimistic and well-rehearsed. We simply destroy ourselves, be it by global warming, pandemic, bio-terrorism, nuclear warfare: exit is inevitable, whether by a bang or more probably by a whimper. Other prognostications I find even more chilling. Maybe we are too clever for our own good, but not clever enough to realize that serving as a handmaiden to machine-intelligence we are sealing our fate and embarking on the construction of a terrible world, joyless and cripplingly uninteresting, arid in all but computation. To many, and as with so much else we see around us, there is in this gloomy view a grinding sense of inevitability. In our heart of hearts, it is not what we want, 'but then you can't stop progress, can you? Shame really. N'other cup of tea?'

Perhaps, however, what is construed as 'progress' is better viewed as the wrong road that if not swiftly abandoned will lead to a destination that we understand but one over which one day we will have no control. Such thinking, of choices, decisions and acknowledgement of fault (repentance, if you prefer), is of course very germane to theological thinking. Indeed, theology may end up making some absolute and very surprising claims. Let us reconsider the rhetorical question, 'Fine, so what's next?' In contrast to the musings of science the view of orthodox Christianity is, I think, fairly straightforward, even if its implications are not. If Adam is metaphorically the first man, then Jesus as Christ is the last. In one sense, there is no more future. Evolution did have an end-point, it was us, and now with the Incarnation it is time to move on. To the non-theist this perspective will no doubt seem not warped, but simply mad. Robert Boyle emphatically would not have been so minded, and it is now time to see not so much whether science and religion have any relation but rather to suggest that they are intimately linked in a way that actually promises great goodness but from our present stance seems to be much more problematic.

A Faustian compact?

It would be otiose to suppose that science, along with medicine and technology, has not delivered extraordinary benefits and gifts. Nor is it disputed that there are side effects and unforeseen consequences that can undo at least some of the good done. As a group scientists, even under existing pressures, generally maintain a high degree of integrity and are genuinely interested in what is true as against what is popular or expedient. Yet the darker side is never very far away. Discoveries and inventions, even those apparently innocuous, in the wrong hands may lead either to distortion of societies or ways of delivering death yet more widely and efficiently. So too the dangers of monopoly power and the manipulation of the market place may benefit the few and impoverish the many. The risks are most obvious in biotechnology, but in fact no area of science is free of risk. To many, the benefits of science appear to be gained at the increasing expense of a Faustian compact.

Theologians have not been silent on these issues, but I suspect that we are not going to make much headway when the aim is blatantly scientistic and deeply manipulative. Here, the ultimate aim is of controlling the world in a way ostensibly for the best but in fact wedded to a naturalistic programme, that is to see no arbiter outside human agency, or worse whim. To such ears talk of the Fall, the realities of radical evil, even the danger of damnation will seem quaint, risible and medieval; nothing that is to do with the real world. Robert Boyle, in his time, was not so sure. He was deeply concerned that some areas, notably of magic and astrology, might lead into very dangerous territory where malevolence would be made manifest. The point is not whether magic and astrology are in any sense true, but to act as if they might well be. So too today we are unwilling to concede either the possibility of what Roger Shattuck calls 'Forbidden Knowledge' or that we might be 'assisted' by those who do not have our long-term interests at heart (Shattuck, 1997). As long as we view the world as an accidental happenstance, to be treated as a utilitarian object, we not only lose sight of Creation, but also ourselves and our place in it. Well, that is a debate that is still with us, and was as familiar to Robert Boyle.

An evolutionary eschatology?

So is this the end of the matter? There is one final aspect of Creation that in my view we would do very well not to overlook. Science certainly informs us about the integrity and complexity of the world around us, and thereby are we the better equipped to appreciate its beauty. Yet whatever else it might be, just as with our own all-too-short lives so the visible world, and so far as we can ascertain the entire universe, cannot be permanent, at least in any recognizable form. The standard view is that given the expansion of the universe, and the new evidence that on a cosmic scale this process is accelerating, our future in the long term is not too bright. Fairly early on, the Earth itself will become uninhabitable as the Sun enters old age and swells up. Present estimates indicate that within a billion years the oceans will have boiled away, and if those estimates are wrong the death of our planet would not be much postponed beyond that. Other local excitement will be the projected collision between our galaxy and the nearby Andromeda galaxy. Again, it is in the distant future, but in the cosmic scale of things may get a few lines on page 10 of the *Universal Herald*. But these are all views from the parish pump. This is because as expansion of the universe continues, so galaxy after galaxy will slip away over the horizon of visibility. Whereas today billions of galaxies are visible, in the distant future all will be receding from us so fast, so far away, that none of their light will ever reach us. Beyond our galaxy, there will be nothing to see. So too the stars will dim, and later still, even the stars will cease to exist.

There is, however, another view. It will not, I warn you, be popular. Yet consider: let us assume the universe is genuinely *ex nihilo*, made out of nothing by the good grace of God. That is certainly part of the Christian orthodoxy, and so far as I can see neither the size nor the age of the universe makes any difference to this assumption. It also appears to be consistent with the evidence from the Big Bang. We should, however, be wary about such concordism, this apparently happy marriage between cosmology and revealed religion. Not that concordance is out of the question, far from it. Just that one should be wary because scientific evidence is always provisional. Apparently, irrefutable data or hypotheses have a curious habit of turning out to be gloriously, wonderfully wrong. From our present stance, it is difficult to see what data could more satisfactorily explain many cosmological observations than the Big Bang, but we should be cautious of two things. First, that the Big Bang is the same as God's Creation, and second, to fool ourselves that Creation *ex nihilo* is actually in any useful way open to comprehension. What surely matters, however, is that what can be brought out of nothing might be either returned to nothing or otherwise utterly transformed.

Let me conclude with one small observation. I have, uncertainly and with little skill, tried to show that Robert Boyle's concerns and beliefs remain as valid and pertinent today as they did in his time. A common complaint against such people as Boyle, or indeed any of his antecedents, is that they simply knew less, so no wonder they were the more credulous. This, however, is to fall simply into the scientistic trap, and neglects the likelihood that if some areas of worthwhile human endeavour have flourished, others have unnecessarily withered, to our common detriment. Moreover, this view turns its back on eternal verities that were as true in Boyle's, or Pontius Pilate's, times as they are in ours. That such verities are presently widely dismissed as social constructs, power games or whatever will most likely serve to erode the good and impoverish the many, but at least allow the intellectuals to dream the more easily in their many beds. Nor am I sure, despite the best efforts of such people as C. S. Lewis, Peter Kreeft and many other brilliant apologists, how these ventures would be successfully recaptured. Science when it treats creation as a true Creation, and thereby faces up to its responsibilities, may well be important. I expect Boyle would have agreed. It seems ultimately, however, that it is the knowledge and experience of the Incarnation, the wisdom and warnings given by Jesus in the Gospels, and not least the Resurrection that in the final analysis are all that matters. Again, I expect Robert Boyle would have agreed.

My thanks to Vivien Brown for adroit manuscript preparation, and the organizers of the Boyle Lectures (especially Michael Byrne) for their invitation to submit this edited version.

3

The Emergence of Spirit: From Complexity to Anthropology to Theology?

PHILIP CLAYTON

Introduction

The difficulties of natural theology: Boyle the naturalist and Boyle the apologist

This particular Boyle Lecture interweaves a complex quintet of fields: science, philosophy of science, anthropology, metaphysics and theology. So as not to waste your time, I shall state my thesis right at the start: the contemporary naturalist should be pulled in two directions by the growth of science. On the one hand, the sciences suggest nature's self-sufficiency as a closed and coherent system; on the other, they hint at what we may credibly view as a transcendent source for nature. The idea of a transcendent source does not negate science, but it does undercut claims on behalf of science's self-sufficiency.

Clearly, some of the arguments of Robert Boyle, the early modern apologist, will simply not serve us in today's context. In particular, one thinks of the various proofs from design, the repeated and detailed attempts to move from complex natural systems to divine providence, which we post-Darwinians can no longer endorse. Boyle believed that 'a virtuoso, or modern naturalist, who is versed in a way of philosophizing, will discern himself, and discover to others, a great many signatures and impresses of the divine attributes, not taken note of, or not reflected on by the ancient, nor by merely book learned spectators, even of this age' (Boyle, 1690–1: 2nd part, p. 714). And he claimed, more boldly, that 'the Christian virtuoso, to whom God has vouchsafed more than ordinary degrees of knowledge by the help of anatomy, astronomy, chemistry, hydrostaticks, dioptricks, etc. will be able to discover many wonderful things about the fabric and uses of many creatures, that by unskillful, or inattentive, or lazy pursuers, are altogether either unperceived, or unheeded' (Boyle, 1690–1: 2nd part, p. 715).

But these over-ambitious claims may have obscured a more enduring side of Boyle's natural theology, which I now wish to recommend to your attention. Rose-Mary Sargent rightly calls Boyle 'the diffident naturalist' in her eponymous book on his 'philosophy of experiment' (Sargent, 1995). All but one of Boyle's theological works were printed in London, whereas natural philosophical works were printed in Oxford and London, leading one to wonder whether Boyle despaired of convincing the cultured despisers in Oxford but was more optimistic of reaching the masses in London (Hunter and Davis, 1999). Remember also Boyle's insistence that 'natural religion' is necessary but not sufficient for faith:

> Natural Religion, is the first that is embraced by the mind, so it is the foundation, upon which revealed religion ought to be superstructe ... as it were the stock, upon which Christianity might be ingrafted. For I readily acknowledge natural religion to be insufficient, yet I think it very necessary (Boyle, 1690–1: 2nd part, pp. 685–6).

My task is to place an apologetic argument before you. But apologetics will only be taken seriously, if it in turn takes scientific naturalism seriously; and on this point Boyle can still be our teacher. As a naturalist and exemplary experimentalist, Boyle retained the highest respect for natural order: 'it more sets off the wisdom of God in the fabric of the universe, that he can make so vast a machine perform all those many things ... *by the mere contrivance of brute matter managed by certain laws of local motion* and upheld by his ordinary and general concourse, than if he employed from time to time an intelligent overseer, such as nature is fancied to be, to regulate, assist, and control the motions of the parts' (Hall, 1965, p. 151; Wojcik, 1997, pp. 161–2). If studying the natural order meant dispensing with physical miracles, Boyle concluded, so be it. God brings about whatever be the divine intentions 'without ... acting otherwise than according to the catholic laws of motion' (Hall, 1965, p. 151). Never compromise on the quality of your science, Boyle insists; and I offer his words as a standard for what follows: 'a naturalist, who would deserve that name, must not let the search for knowledge of final causes make him neglect the industrious indagation of efficients' (Hall, 1965, p. 154).

Boyle's unrelenting naturalism, however, left his theology untouched, whereas the more radical naturalism of our day ascends even to the lofty pulpits of our most prestigious churches – for better or worse. How shall we proceed with this conundrum?

I suggest that, the intelligent design movement notwithstanding, there is no place within science for purely empirical proofs of the existence of God or God's purposes within evolutionary history. Yet it is fascinating to reflect philosophically and theologically on the biological data and what they might portend. Here, I undertake that speculative task, controlling the results as much as possible through scientific insights without claiming scientific warrant for all the conclusions. I take my lead from emergence theory, the study of emergent complexity in natural history.

Emergence in nature

Overview

There are numerous reasons for biologists to be cautious about talk of purpose in evolution. Unfortunately, these reasons have sometimes produced a reticence to acknowledge the significance of teleological systems within the biosphere. Recent years have brought renewed study of purposive systems and behaviours, however, and it is now not uncommon to find treatments detailing macro-evolutionary patterns. Many biologists now speak of a 'directionality' to evolution, frequently correlating it with the increase in biological complexity.

The natural theology to be defended here proceeds in three steps. First, analogies between various cases of emergent complexity are strong enough to support emergence over reduction as the more adequate interpretation of science and as a fundamental characteristic of natural history to date. Second, the development of symbolic language in *Homo sapiens* sets in motion a new level of evolution, cultural evolution, which requires forms of explanation that are different from and not reducible to biological explanation. Finally, I will argue that this emergentist understanding of humanity is fully consistent with a theistic worldview and, as I shall argue, appears to be better explained by theism than by its competitors.

A working definition of emergence and the case for emergent complexity

Emergence is linked to the sciences of complexity, that is, to the principles of self-organization and the formation of complex systems. Complexity theory asks, 'What are the steps and the processes that lead from the elementary particle to the thinking organism, the (present!) entity of highest complexity?' (Lehn, 2002). Complexity is inherently a systemic function; it involves the interaction between many components of various kinds and the principles that affect their correlation, coupling and feedback relationships. The goal of the sciences of complexity, writes Jean-Marie Lehn, is 'to progressively discover, understand, and implement the rules that govern [matter's] evolution from inanimate to animate and beyond, to ultimately acquire the ability to create new forms of complex matter' (Lehn, 2002, pp. 476–8). Emergent complexity spans the entire spectrum of cosmic history, 'from divided to condensed matter then to organized and adaptive matter, on to living matter and thinking matter, up the ladder of complexity' (ibid.).

So what, in the simplest possible terms, is emergence? It is the hypothesis that reduction, or 'reductionism', is false. An emergentist theory of human thought and action, for example, argues that the reduction of the human sciences to biology or physics is false. A non-reductive theory of religious belief argues that the reduction of religious belief to its psycho-social functions is false.

43

That's the negative pole of emergence theory; what are its positive assertions? Three general claims undergird emergence theory in the philosophy of science. First, empirical reality divides naturally into multiple levels. Over the course of natural history, new emergent levels evolve. Second, emergent wholes that are more than the sum of their parts require new types of explanation adequate to each new level of phenomena. Third, such emergent wholes manifest new types of causal interaction. Biological systems are not 'nothing more than' microphysical interactions; they include irreducibly biological interactions and must be explained in biological terms. Nor are the mental experiences that you are having right now 'nothing but' complicated brain states. In a real and important sense, one mental state can indeed cause another.

Entire books have been devoted to the recent evidence on behalf of these emergentist claims (Clayton and Davies, 2006). The emergence of living organisms and the emergence of mental experience are often listed as the standard intuitive examples of such phenomena. But emergence is not manifested only at the level of life or mind; it is evident even at the very earliest stages of cosmic evolution. Classical physics has been described as emergent out of quantum physics (Zurek, 2002, p. 14; 1991). Even quantum phenomena may themselves be emergent (Adler, 2004). In an influential book, physics Nobel Laureate Robert Laughlin has recently argued that scientific reduction is a dogma and that many of the key features of his field, condensed matter physics, can be explained only within the paradigm of emergence (Laughlin, 2005; Anderson, 2005). Among Laughlin's examples of emergent phenomena are superconductivity, the quantum Hall effect, phase transitions, crystallization, collective instabilities and hydrodynamics.

In defence of strong emergence

One finds in the literature an ongoing battle between weaker and stronger versions of emergence theory. The more robust version, which I have labelled 'strong emergence' and defended in my work, makes two claims. First, new things emerge in natural history, not just new properties of some fundamental things or stuff; and second, these emergent things exercise their own specific forms of causal power. Such 'downward causation' occurs at many different levels in nature. Strong emergence is a thesis about the nature of natural evolution.

As you know, interpretations of evolution are fraught with controversy. If evolution is really 'all about the genes', as Richard Dawkins seeks to convince us, then all evolved structures are nothing more than expressions of this same fundamental dynamic. However rich and staggeringly diverse are these manifestations, they should be understood in fundamentally the same conceptual terms. If, on the other hand, the dualists are right, then at some point one encounters a radical break. In this sense, dualists remain at heart Cartesians: one can study the entire physical world from atoms to chimpanzees with the same set of mechanistic explanatory tools; but as soon as one turns to man and woman, who alone possess *res cogitans*, a new explanatory tool box is required, consisting instead of souls and the eternal Laws of Thought.

In contrast to both views, emergence claims that the story of evolution is one of continuity and discontinuity. Continuity first: everything in the natural world is composed of the same 'stuff' of matter and energy, and no new substances are added along the way. When one pursues the scientific project, one seeks to develop a continuity of understanding to the greatest possible extent. But sharing the scientist's 'natural piety' for the world as it actually expresses itself empirically also means that one works with whatever explanatory framework best explains the data at present – as long as it is testable and can demonstrate its explanatory superiority over its rivals.

Practising this natural piety – this commitment to study the world in whatever ways it presents itself to us – means that we are not merely biologists *simplicatur*, much less geneticists only. We are cytologists, systems biologists, botanists, zoologists, primatologists. We are not only molecular biologists and geneticists, but also population biologists and ecosystem theorists. We are interested in the large and complex as much as in the small, in emergent phenomena as well as reducible phenomena. This, I suggest, was the mindset that lay behind Charles Darwin's great breakthroughs.

PHILIP CLAYTON

Anthropology

What does this commitment to the data as they present themselves say about the animal in whom we are most interested, *Homo sapiens*? Emergentists pursue every bit of common ground that they can discover between humans and other animals – from the common chemical composition and structure of DNA through the mechanisms of cell communication and regeneration to the development of a central nervous system and brain to behavioural similarities to physiological responses. Nerve-cell similarities, for example, point out commonalities with the electrochemical responses in electric eels; brain plasticity is similar in frogs and humans; we learn about our own social nature from mirror cells and from the rudimentary theory of other minds in chimpanzees. Reconciling behaviours among the great apes and mutual care-taking among bonobos help us to understand our own inter-dependencies more fully. All these continuities are for the good from a scientific perspective.

Yet humans are also discontinuous with our animal cousins. The significantly larger frontal cortex and more complex anatomy of our brains has produced a mental life and corresponding behaviours that are qualitatively different from our closest animal relatives. Our disproportionately large brains give rise to more varied language use and linguistic play; and more complex language use in turn produces anatomical changes, such as larger language areas, greater brain plasticity and more complex inter-relationships among the brain regions (Durham, 1991).

Quantitative increases in complexity eventually lead to quali-tative differences, the emergence of new types of systems with correspondingly new causal properties. The evolution of human culture is startlingly different from the patterns of evolutionary dynamics that preceded it. To put the differences bluntly, cultural evolution is not only Darwinian but also Lamarckian; that is, it allows for the heritability of acquired traits. When you learn to use email – or shall we say, when you become enslaved to your email accounts – you can pass this knowledge on to your children (poor things). Most of what is important to us – our language, our knowledge of proper ways to behave, our beliefs about the existence or non-existence of God – is transmitted across generations in this fashion.

So far, we have spoken of empirical facts, but now things become somewhat more speculative. For we must ask: What is the nature of human persons, who emerge through the complex interaction of (Darwinian) biological evolution and (Lamarckian) cultural evolution? A word of caution from Boyle's *The Christian Virtuoso* frames the discussion: 'the very notion we have of spirits in general, is, to me, no small argument how little we really and particularly know of them' (Boyle, 1690–1: 2nd part, p. 707).

In the social world, events without significance are rare; virtually everything we do either has, or *fails* to have, an underlying valence of meaning. We do not merely grow older; we pass through a series of rites of passage. We do not merely use words and encounter objects; we fashion signs in our language and transform objects into symbols of deep judgements about the world (the cross, the flag, even the colour of our scarves). The famous sociologist of religion Peter Berger writes, 'Man, biologically denied the ordering mechanisms with which other animals are endowed, is *compelled to impose his own order* on experience. Man's sociality presupposes the collective character of this ordering of reality' (Berger, 1967, p. 19).

If this quest for meaning fails, 'not only will the individual ... begin to lose his moral bearings, with disastrous psychological consequences, but he will become uncertain about his cognitive bearings as well' (Berger, 1967, p. 22). Of course, building worlds of meaning is not just an individual task. 'Society', Berger notes, 'is the guardian of social order and meaning, not only objectively, in its institutional structures, but subjectively as well, in its structuring of individual consciousness' (Berger, 1967, p. 21).

The importance of this quest for meaning for anthropology cannot be overstated: *The construction of meaning is ubiquitous; it plays a role in all that humans do and think.* Nor is it limited to human contexts; one must also find one's sense of self within the natural world as well. As you know, this is no easy task. Friedrich Nietzsche has most clearly expressed the tension faced by individuals in a dark universe:

Once upon a time, in a distant corner of this universe with its countless flickering solar systems, there was a planet, and on this planet some intelligent animals discovered knowledge. It was the most noble and most mendacious minute in the history of the universe – but only a minute. After Nature had breathed a few times their star burned out, and the intelligent animals had to die (Nietzsche, 1973: Pt 3, vol. 2, p. 369).

Nietzsche's nihilism reveals the urgency of this highest and broadest human task: to make sense of our existence as a whole. The trouble is, whatever inferences we may seek to draw, conclusions from the physical sciences – whether it's the Big Bang or the emergence of complexity – do not directly prove the existence of God or an intelligent designer or any other metaphysical conclusions about ultimate reality. Still, the quest for meaning does unavoidably confront us with the question: Can one defend an account of this physical world that uses irreducibly religious or spiritual terms? Can one develop a rational theology of nature? Can the term 'God' still do real work, or should we conclude with Pierre-Simon Laplace, 'I have no need of that hypothesis'?

Religious belief conceives the entire universe as being humanly significant (Berger, 1967, p. 28). Religion strives for 'the establishment ... of an all-embracing sacred order ... a sacred cosmos that will be capable of maintaining itself in the ever-present face of chaos'. Berger continues: 'Every human society is, in the last resort, [persons] banded together in the face of death. The power of religion depends, in the last resort, upon the credibility of the banners it puts in the hands of [men and women] as they stand before death, or more accurately, as they walk, inevitably, toward it' (Berger, 1967, p. 51).

What then of the ideas and beliefs that are an intrinsic part of this process of religious meaning-making? Are social communities, for example, merely fictional constructions of this process, since what really exists are the individuals, the atoms of the whole process? Are the ideals that humans strive for – love, justice, compassion – all fictions? Or are some metaphysical beliefs actually true of the world? Do the sciences prove that we are alone in a hostile universe, as Nietzsche thought? Or do they offer clues about another possibility: that humans are pervasively preoccupied with religious symbols and practices because we live in a universe that is open towards transcendence, a universe that is the product of a cosmic order or designer – one who is not *less* intelligent and conscious than we are, and one whose existence is hinted at in the physical world, in cosmic history, and in the inner life of the subjects studied by psychologists, sociologists, artists and novelists (Berger, 1969)? Could not something of the divine be revealed by studying that animal that struggles with the question of God: ourselves?

Theology

The emergentist view of human nature and existence that we have come to is certainly religiously significant. It shows that human religiosity is not an absurd reaction to our existence or a sign of infantile irrationality, as some have claimed. Instead, the religious response is intrinsic to human existence to the world.

But now the question arises: Can we know whether any of these religious responses are true? For obviously, humans do not just have emotional and aesthetical responses to the universe and to the question of its ultimate meaning. Our attempts to construct meaning often come in the form of rather specific beliefs about the universe, about its ultimate origins and final destiny. Are all such beliefs mere projections on to a cold universe, bereft of meaning, by an animal all too hungry for some sense of cosmic purpose? Or are we justified in our hope and belief that some ultimate significance may underlie the process of emergence of which we ourselves are a part?

Agnosticism, atheism and intelligent design

Of course, one response to this question is agnosticism. We are inevitably and unavoidably driven to formulate hypotheses about the 'Before' and the 'After', as David Hume puts it. Yet according to the agnostic, no beliefs of this type have any 'traction' in the real world. And if none are testable, he continues, none are rational. Psychologically interesting, perhaps, but of no interest to seekers after Truth.

This tragic view of our human fate is widespread and popular, especially in this age of science. It became increasingly attractive in the modern period, perhaps because of its Byronic tone. Steven Weinberg writes famously, 'The more the universe seems comprehensible, the more it also seems pointless.' Jacques Monod's view is even more bleak:

> Chance *alone* is at the source of every innovation, of all creation in the biosphere. Pure chance, absolutely free but blind, at the very root of the stupendous edifice of evolution: this central concept of biology ... is today the *sole* conceivable hypothesis, the only one compatible with observed and tested fact. All forms of life are the product of chance ... (Monod, 1971, pp. 112–13).

One can't help but admire the existentialist's courage. Yet courage does not, by itself, make a position true. From another standpoint, the agnostic's pessimistic rejection of all metaphysical reflection also represents a form of betting against oneself. How will we ever *know* whether it's possible to evaluate hypotheses that go beyond the strictly scientific, unless we engage in rigorous and critical debate on these topics?

Unfortunately, the cultural prejudice of our day militates against even the attempt to debate the issues critically. In a recent BBC programme, a certain Oxford professor of the 'public understanding of science' argued that all religious belief is hopelessly superficial and anti-intellectual. Yet scholarly theologians were noticeably absent from the broadcast, and no serious philosophical debate of the topics took place.

Of course, debate-blocking measures occur from the other side as well. The American intelligent-design theorist Michael Behe argues that the functions of haemoglobin *could never* be biologically explained. 'Each of the steps of the [blood] clotting cascade', he asserts, 'is irreducibly complex ... [T]he clotting cascade was not produced by natural selection ... That is why I conclude that the cascade is a product of design' (Behe, 1997; 1996). Some American members of the so-called 'ID' movement go even further: 'Every fact of creation drips with evidence of God as the creator', writes Terry Gray, and 'Every time we think or speak about a fact of creation it is either acknowledging God as the creator or denying him' (Gray, 1996).

But surely there must be a region between the cavalier dismissal of religious reflection and direct inferences to God from what scientists do not know. In between these two responses is a third realm of discourse, one in which religious truth claims can be calmly and rationally assessed. Until we actually engage in the process of examining our ultimate beliefs as carefully as possible – including their consistency with science – a priori claims about what can and cannot be rationally decided are otiose. Is it not better to wager for the human quest for knowledge, in the broadest sense of this term, than against our own desire to know?

So what happens when one tries? I shall argue in the final few pages that the emergentist understanding of nature and humanity supports the idea of a metaphysical reality that is not less than personal, a ground of our existence to which agency may also be ascribed. My argument proceeds in three steps.

Emergent spiritual properties

I have argued that emergent complexity is a significant theoretical commonality shared across the sciences and a genuine macro-pattern manifested in natural history. If each stage of the evolutionary process produces new levels of emergent phenomena, then is it not likely that the level of human culture will produce (or has produced) yet another level? Let's call this the level of spirituality, the emergence of spiritual predicates.

Is this argument sufficient for a doctrine of God? Some theorists have attempted to understand the divine directly in terms of the arrow of emergence. According to what I have called *radically emergentist theism*, the divine itself becomes yet another emergent property in natural history – and indeed, presumably, the final one (Clayton, 2004). This is the route taken, most famously, by Samuel Alexander in his famous Gifford Lectures of 1918–19, published as *Space, Time and Deity*:

As actual, God does not possess the quality of deity but *is the universe as tending to that quality* ... Thus there is no actual infinite being with the quality of deity; but there is an actual infinite, the whole universe, with a nisus to deity; and this is the God of the religious consciousness, though that consciousness habitually forecasts the divinity of its object as actually realised in an individual form ... (Alexander, 1920: ii, pp. 361–2; 364).

What humans call 'God' is just the emergent property of spirituality in the universe. And 'God' is simply the universe becoming aware of itself.

But, I suggest, this sort of immediate connection between emergent patterns in nature and metaphysics is too direct. Alexander obviously assumes that emergence is both necessary *and sufficient* for doing metaphysics and theology. But there are reasons to be sceptical of such straight-line extrapolations from science to metaphysics. Here I follow Boyle over Alexander. Recall the Boyle text quoted above: scientific results may be necessary for theological conclusions, but they are not sufficient. When one introduces the level of metaphysics – that is, questions of the ultimate source or origin – other conceptual resources are required.

One thing we can learn from Alexander: once one has granted the ongoing advent of new emergent patterns, it is arbitrary to stop the progression with mental predicates. There may well be further levels of emergence – either qualities that we humans have some inkling of, or qualities utterly unknown to us. The Alexander case for viewing emergence as open-ended thus represents an important ally against reductionism; that is, against the limitation of emergence to the level of human mentality. We should embrace this argument, which effectively undercuts attempts to limit reality to the earlier stages of natural history.

The divine is not less than personal

If we are to reach the next level of reflection, we must pause to consider for a moment what it means for some of these higher-order properties, such as personhood, to emerge.

Science – and here I mean to include the social sciences – does not warrant the introduction of souls or other non-natural entities in the world. But even if soul-language is problematic, it is surely justified to move from the emergence of mental predicates and personal qualities to language of persons acting in the world. Indeed, would it not be arbitrary to acknowledge the emergence of the sort of psychological and intentional predicates that characterize the human person while refusing to acknowledge that form of agency that we all know as the activities of persons? I well remember a major international scientific congress a few years ago, at which a panel of neuroscientists was chiding philosophers of mind for their doubts about whether humans are really conscious and whether consciousness does anything in the world. 'Ascribing consciousness to persons is basic to the practice of neurology in medicine', one neurologist argued. 'When a patient shows rapidly decreasing awareness and cognitive functioning, that's a key sign for us that medical intervention is justified.' Of course, the physicians insisted, medicine cannot resolve the question of whether their patients have, or are, spiritual souls. But, they argued, to be experts in neuroscience in no way undercuts the belief that one's patients are persons; to the contrary!

How then shall we view persons, if they are more than Humean bundles of mental and psychological predicates on the one hand, yet less than substantial souls or hylomorphic entities on the other? I suggest that language of personhood serves an indispensable function in comprehending human actions and interactions. When we examine the neural correlates of consciousness, we can research only isolated mental attributes such as the state of arousal or fear or uncertainty. Electrode stimulation of a particular cortical region may correlate each time only with specific behaviours or memories. But surely, any adequate social scientific account will have to include theories about the agent – her wishes, her goals and her intentions both conscious and unconscious. At the very least, one would be forced to interpret person language as a sort of Kantian regulative ideal – an unavoidable way of speaking if one is to conceptualize the persons and their attributes that we encounter in the world. But a bit more reflection on our own experience as agents in the world is enough to justify a rather more robust account of the existence of human agents and their causal powers.

Now combine this conclusion with the previous one and notice what results. In Step 1 of the argument I defended the emergent level of mental properties – the properties of persons in the world – as well as an emergent level of spiritual properties. Here's the question: Why should we now deny of the spiritual level what we are willing to affirm of humans? If humans can be conceived as persons, why are we so certain that the divine can be no more than a series or bundle of spiritual properties – no more than the world as a whole 'deising' itself, as Samuel Alexander put it? Is it not much more natural and reasonable to postulate such spiritual properties as being unified in a being or agent?

Some caution is called for here. We cannot be flat-footed literalists; there is no reason to limit this conception to an agency identical to the finite human and animal agents we encounter in the world. A wide variety of metaphysical models is available. Patristic beliefs about the Trinitarian God, with their reliance on the Greek notion of substance, are not identical to theologies of emanation or to perennial philosophies or to 'Ground of Being' theologies. Classical philosophical theism is not identical to panentheism, the belief that the world is located within the divine although God is also more than the world. But what all of these models share in common is conceiving the religious object as more than merely a bundle of emergent properties; and surely they are right to do so.

So if emergence leads us to speak of a higher kind of agency than our own, what kind of agency might it be? In some traditions, the spiritual level is conceived as less than personal. Think for example of the metaphysics of *karma*, which is understood as a force that works more like a natural law rather than as personal agent. But surely, once we have granted that natural history has produced personal agency of the sort we know in our own actions, we should not expect that the next higher level, the level of spiritual properties, would be characterized by a lower form of causality, a causality analogous to natural law. Is it not more reasonable to conceive the religious object, the divine, as everything that human persons are – and presumably much more?

In short, the irreducibility of person language, combined with the open-ended nature of the emergence hierarchy, induces us to use language for the divine that is not-less-than personal. It suggests a deity who is not less agent than humans are, yet also infinitely more – a creative God, hence a God of intentions and plans, and hence, perhaps, a providential God as well.

Religious experience, revelation and the established religions

Boyle was right: science is not sufficient for metaphysics or theology. Yet, he insisted, some inferences can be drawn. We have so far discovered two. First, if there are emergent mental properties, it makes sense to speak of the persons who have these properties and of the personality or character that produces the patterns that we detect in their actions. Second, as we saw, if there are emergent spiritual properties it also makes sense to speak of the nature of the reality or being that produces the patterns that we detect. Since it is incoherent to imagine that the ultimate Ground or spiritual reality is less than what it has produced, and it clearly isn't merely a human person, we are justified in conceiving it as supra-personal. In short, we have discovered reasons to make the transition from finite agency to transcendent agency, at least in this carefully circumscribed sense. In the argument's third and final step, I shall argue for an analogous transition from metaphysics to theology.

Imagine that you are now inclined to conceive the metaphysical ultimate as not-less-than-personal. Like Boyle, I am sceptical of divine incursions into the physical order, and hence of physical miracles as traditionally conceived. Yet a world that is 'upwardly open', in the way that emergence theory describes it to be, might at its most complex levels manifest something of the influence of the divine. If any sign of more-than-personal divine activity exists, where might it be recognizable as such? Two possibilities come immediately to mind: individual religious experience, and the revelations of the divine that believers claim are recorded in the sacred scriptures of the great world religious traditions. Let's consider the first. In the experience of mystics through the ages lie shared observations and insights that, as Wordsworth put it, 'disturb [us] with the joy/ Of elevated thoughts; a sense sublime/ Of something far more deeply interfused ...' Given the vagaries of human experience and the fallibility of subjective reports of which we are only too aware, the philosophical force of these 'intimations of transcendence' may be limited. Still, if a self-revealing divine agent exists, it is hard to dismiss the possibility that some effects of the presence of this divine being may be manifest in the inner life.

What of the second route – the scriptures after which so many have moulded their lives and the traditions of reflection to which they have given rise? Of course, the hypothesis of a not-less-than-personal divine can be explored in a purely philosophical manner; we can enquire whether it is consistent, coherent and better justified than its rivals. But it can also be explored historically; we can study the documents that claim to be the histories of divine self-revelation, the records of the putative interaction of God and humanity (Pannenberg, 1991). In this new enquiry, a wealth of non-philosophical terms, narratives and symbols become relevant, terms more reminiscent of theological debate and religious practice – terms such as Spirit, pre-existence, self-revelation, creation, providence; terms such as grace, sin and salvation; but also terms such as Atman and Brahman, *moksha*, *sunyata* and co-dependent origination.

I do not share the optimism of the well-known Oxford professor Richard Swinburne, whose many books attempt to construct a ladder of reasoning step by unbroken step from purely philosophical considerations to Christian theological conclusions. Instead, I have argued that it is also reasonable to look for the locus, or loci, of divine self-revelation through history and across cultures. If so, it makes sense to look to the sacred texts and practices of the world's religious traditions to see what patterns may emerge there. If the conceptual arguments of the metaphysicians regarding the divine nature are to be taken seriously, as I have sought to show, then the records that claim to record the self-revelation of God may serve as important sources of material as well. Especially in cases where patterns of belief and value emerge across these traditions, they merit our close attention.

Beyond this point, I fear, reason begins to falter. It is a tall mountain that we have ascended, and one must sound a note of caution. Unaided reflection starts to lose its bearings, and the ascending path of speculation begins to disappear into the clouds. At some point one runs out of objective data the way a climber runs out of oxygen. Just consider the difficulties one now faces: the claims of the various religious traditions conflict; the primary sources are heavily redacted by later communities; even *within* the various traditions more specific beliefs are contested; cultural and historical differences threaten incommensurability; and subjective factors increasingly colour one's own assessment of the data. Rationality begins to lose its footing, and even metaphysicians must proceed onward with caution, if at all.

One may have strong reasons to locate oneself within a particular tradition of religious practice, as I locate myself within the Christian tradition. But the obscurity of the claims and the depths of the disagreements between religious traditions call for a certain humility. Boldness, a quality needed when we left the relatively safe fields of accepted science and began the ascent of metaphysical reflection, can now become a liability. In particular, when it comes to beliefs contested between Jews, Christians and Muslims, even more caution is required. Christians in particular – the boldness of whose truth claims in the past has produced crusades, inquisitions and pogroms – would do well to emphasize the present limitations on knowledge. We hope for a culmination of humanity's quest for knowledge of God, rather than a sort of sacred agnosticism; we hope for confirmation of our sense that we are not alone in the universe. Yet the hope for future confirmation cannot become the battering ram of religious apologetics, knocking down the walls of opposing religious traditions. 'Now we know only in part; then we will know fully, even as we have been fully known' (1 Corinthians 13.12).

Conclusion

I have sketched a major movement in contemporary science and the philosophy of science. Emergence theory not only sheds new light on natural history and the relationships between different levels of phenomena in the world; it also encourages us to think the uniqueness of human beings without denying our closeness to our animal cousins. The ladder of natural emergence first led us to speculate about the emergence of spiritual properties and then, taking the metaphysical leap, to postulate a not-less-than-personal spiritual reality or ground. Following in Boyle's footsteps, I argued that the results are fully consistent with a theistic worldview and may even be better explained by theism than by its competitors.

Science therefore does not undercut the belief that this rich and diverse natural order may reflect an intentional act of creation. Science certainly constrains our beliefs about divine action, but it does not eliminate the possibility that a Creator is engaged at least with humanity, and perhaps elsewhere in the universe as well. Thus, it turns out, it is dogmatism, not science, to claim that personal agency and meaningfulness are foreign to this universe. One is fully justified in looking to the resources of the existing religious traditions as one seeks to understand the upwardly open process of emergence as manifested both in the natural world and in the cultural realms of art, literature and philosophy. Perhaps we are, after all, at home in the universe (Clayton and Knapp, 2011).

I am grateful to Michael Byrne and Russell Re Manning for criticisms of earlier drafts. Important portions of the argument also reflect the influence of my long-time collaborator, Professor Steven Knapp of Johns Hopkins University.

4

Cosmology of Ultimate Concern

JOHN D. BARROW

The years 1691 and 1692 were very eventful and significant for the subject of natural theology and for the entwinement of theology and the natural sciences. Of course, in 1691, Robert Boyle died, and his will provided for the series of sermons and lectures that we now call the Boyle Lectures. The first of those was given by the young Richard Bentley in 1692 at the age of 29. But also in those two years, two very influential volumes were being published by John Ray, based on lectures that he gave in Cambridge on natural theology, and so the subject was very much in the intellectual air, of interest to scientists and theologians. It was only five years after Newton's *Principia* had appeared in 1687, and what Bentley decided to do created a sea-change in the way that natural theology was presented and fashioned.

Previously, the focus of natural theologians had been upon the multiplicity of the outcomes of the laws of nature, the fortuitous coincidences between many of those outcomes that appeared to create and sustain an environment tailor-made for life. But what Bentley decided to do was to take information that he had gleaned from more informal versions of Newton's *Principia* to create a version of the design argument in natural theology that was based not upon the outcomes of the laws of nature but upon the forms of those laws. Newton was the first scientist to create a system of universal laws of nature. Bentley engaged in correspondence with Newton in order to understand more clearly what Newton's views were about the issues he intended to raise in his lectures. Newton seemed to approve of this enterprise, and the famous *Letters to Bentley* are among the most interesting pieces of informal scientific reasoning that exist from that period.

Bentley recognized the scope of Newton's work for his own enterprise. He was a notable classical scholar. Later, he would go on to become Master of Trinity College, like Lord Rees; fortunately Lord Rees is a much more enlightened Master of Trinity College than Bentley ever was, and certainly will not be following the course of action that Bentley embarked upon in his engagement with the Fellows. They failed over many years to have him removed and, to their chagrin, he eventually died in his bed in the College. Well, they were probably pleased he died … but not in the College! Bentley took his cue from, in effect, new physics of his time, and we are going to do the same: we are going to look at what some modern ideas in cosmology have to say about our place in the universe.

Like Bentley, we know that the universe is big, but what Bentley did not know, and we do, is that it is also getting bigger. Since the late-1920s, we have known that the universe is expanding; that distant clusters of galaxies are receding away from one another at ever-increasing speeds. That introduces into cosmology a complexion of the universe that we might call an evolutionary one; that things are in a state of change. The universe is not like a watch in the sense that Paley once tried to persuade us in his *Natural Theology* of 1802 – it is not like a watch, because it is not finished. It is still changing, it is still developing, and it is still exploring the landscape of complexity that is available to it.

We can measure the size of the universe by means of the distance between receding objects, as it expands against time in billions of years. That historical trajectory means that at different times, conditions are different. When the universe is small, it is hot and dense, and too hot in its first quarter of a million years for any atoms to exist. Today, it is relatively cool and sparse, just a few degrees above absolute zero. As it cooled, it first allowed simple hydrogen atoms to form, then molecules, then great islands of material condensed out to form what we now call galaxies and, within them, stars, planets – and ultimately people arose by a complicated sequence of events.

In the future, the long-range forecast looks rather bleak. The Sun will undergo an irrevocable energy crisis. If our descendants wish to survive, they had better move elsewhere; but ultimately any other star they migrate to will suffer the same fate, and the long-range forecast of the universe is bleak for habitation and for life. Similarly, if you look back early enough, the universe is not able to support life. There is a short interval of cosmic history, a niche of time during which conditions allow life as we know it, or complexity in any chemical form, to exist. The fact that we live within that habitable niche is of course no coincidence. We live about 13.7 billion years after the apparent beginning of the universe's expansion. Those enormous periods of time seem very strange. A few years ago, I was shopping in my supermarket, and I discovered that these vast ages had even infiltrated the commercial world of Sainsbury's. On the shelf, there was a sachet of salt, and it had written on the side, 'This salt is over 200 million years old. Extracted from the mountain ranges of Germany. Best before April 4th 2003.'

This unfolding trajectory of evolution in the universe is linked to our own existence in unexpected ways. The elements of chemistry that you need for any type of complexity are elements heavier than helium and hydrogen gases. They do not appear ready-made in the universe; they do not come from the apparent Big Bang beginning. They are made in the stars by a sequence of nuclear reactions that are long and slow, that combine two nuclei of helium to make beryllium, then beryllium with helium to make carbon, and carbon with helium to make oxygen and so on. When stars reach the end of their lifetime and explode and die, these life-supporting elements are dispersed around space, and ultimately find their way into rocks and debris and planets and you and me. So all the carbon nuclei in your bodies have, at some stage, been through a star, perhaps more than once.

But this long process takes time, lots of time: nearly ten billion years of time is required to produce the building blocks of living complexity, and so we begin to understand why it is no accident that we find the universe to be so old. We need to live in a universe that is enormously old in order that it has had enough time to make the building blocks of any living complexity. A universe that was significantly younger than we find ourselves in today could not create the basic building blocks of life and mind of any sort. You might have thought a universe the size of our Milky Way galaxy, with its hundred billion stars and maybe as many planetary systems, would be a pretty good economy-sized universe, but a universe the size of that Milky Way galaxy with its hundred billion stars would be little more than a month old, barely enough time to pay off your credit card bill, let alone evolve complexity and life. So we should not be surprised by the enormous antiquity of the universe and those times spanning billions of years; we could not exist in a universe that was significantly younger.

Because the universe is also expanding, its age is inextricably bound up with its size. The enormous size of the universe is seen at once to be another consequence of its great antiquity: a universe that has to be billions of years old has to be billions of light years in size. Paradoxically, we could not exist in a universe that was significantly smaller than the one in which we find ourselves. This is a consequence of the link between age and size created by the expansion. So although the enormous size of the universe may raise the chance that life exists elsewhere, the universe would have to be pretty much as big as it is to support just one lonely outpost of life on Earth.

Philosophers of the past, such as Russell in the early twentieth century, always regarded the vastness of the universe as an indicator of its antithesis to the development and support of life. Modern astronomy turns this judgement on its head. We see that the vastness of the universe is the necessary condition for the development of life within it.

The great age and therefore size of the universe that we need, for these reasons, also gives it another very strange property: the universe is almost empty. There is almost nothing in it to speak of. It is just empty space. If you take any ball of material and you expand it greatly, its contents become more and more sparse, less and less dense, as it becomes larger. If you took all the material in the universe, smoothed it out into a uniform sea of atoms, there would be only about one atom in every cubic metre of space. No physics laboratory in the world could make a vacuum that is anywhere near as empty as that. So to a first approximation, the universe is mostly just empty space. You and I, and everything else within it, from that perspective, are just a minute trace element.

If we decide to lump that density together in more interesting combinations, instead of having an atom in every cubic metre, we would run into a planet like the Earth every ten light years, a star like the Sun every thousand light years, and a galaxy like the Milky Way every ten million light years. So you begin to see why extraterrestrials are not queuing up on our doorstep. The enormous distances between planets, between stars, between galaxies, the insulation of different sites where life can develop from each other, is a consequence of the tiny density of material in the universe, which is further consequence of its enormous age that is needed for life and complexity to develop.

Another property that follows is that our universe is cool. If you expand a lot, you will cool down a lot. So the very low temperature of our universe today is a reflection of the enormous amount of expansion that has taken place over nearly 14 billion years. This low temperature has one especially dramatic consequence.

I have a picture of our next-door-neighbour galaxy, M81, taken by the Spitzer Telescope. Our own galaxy would look rather similar if we were to see it from outside. What is most interesting about this picture, if you are a cosmologist, is not the galaxy but the black, dark night sky all around.

The dark night sky is the first interesting cosmological observation that was ever made, and its significance was first recognized by Edmond Halley at a time close to the inauguration of these lectures. Halley asked the question, 'Why is the sky dark at night?' At first, you might tell him, 'Well, you need to get out more. You need to talk to people. Notice the Sun.' But the answer to the question is profound. Halley could not find the answer. It has nothing to do with the Sun. If you look out into the forest, for example, your line of sight everywhere ends on the trunk of a tree. Halley wondered why it was not the same when he looked out into the universe. Why did his line of sight not end everywhere on the surface of a star? Surely, there are enough of them – maybe even an infinite number of them. The whole of the sky should look like the surface of the Sun all the time. The sky should never be dark!

We only found the answer to this question after astronomers discovered the expansion of the universe. The enormous expansion and consequent cooling of matter and radiation as it expands to fill an ever larger volume means that there is too little energy in the universe today to illuminate the night sky. If we turned all the matter in the universe into radiation just like that, all that would happen is the temperature would rise from three degrees above absolute zero to about 15 degrees above absolute zero, and nobody would notice. There was a time when the sky was bright, but it was a long time ago: when the universe was just a quarter of a million years old, greatly more compressed than today, when the temperature was a thousand times greater, and then the whole sky was illuminated like the surface of the Sun. But today, because of the age and the size needed for our universe to contain life, we are guaranteed to find the night sky to be dark.

So we have discovered, through the eyes of modern cosmology, a number of interesting and counter-intuitive things: that a life-supporting universe, besides being almost empty, must be big and old, dark and cold. These are features that are inevitable if life of any complex sort is to be possible in the universe.

Long ago, before astronomy came on the scene in the twentieth century, these would have been regarded as features of the universe quite antithetical to life, proof that somehow life was a mere accident or trace element in the universe. Modern astronomy turns that perspective, in some sense, on its head. We see that these strange features of the universe that look so discouraging at first, are essential features if life of any sort is to exist within it. So things are often not quite what they seem. These life-averse features of the universe turn out to be essential prerequisites for complexity of any sort to develop.

There is more to the universe than just being big and getting bigger. Different sorts of universe are possible. You can have universes that are rather agoraphobic: they expand and keep on expanding for ever. Or you can have ones that are rather claustrophobic and will one day stop expanding, reverse, and start to contract back towards a big crunch. In between, there is a sort of 'British compromise' universe that just manages to expand fast enough to keep going for ever, and that is interesting to us, because our universe expands tantalizingly close to that critical divide.

In some sense, this is not entirely surprising. Universes that try to deviate too far in one direction or the other from the critical divide end up lifeless and uninteresting. You could expand so fast that material cannot overcome the expansion to condense under gravity to form galaxies and stars and carbon. At the other extreme, you could run into a big crunch before the stellar show even opens. So, in a general way, we understand why it is not surprising that we live fairly close to that divide, but such an argument is not enough to explain why we live so very close to the divide that we are unable really to tell on which side we lie, and have not been able to for a long time.

Another feature of the expanding universe that puzzled people for a long time, particularly until 1980, is that if you look at this expansion in different directions, it proceeds at the same rate in every direction to very high precision: we say the expansion is extremely isotropic. When this was first discovered in 1967, the precision was one part in a thousand, at least; now we know that the precision of the isotropy is to at least two parts in a hundred thousand. So you can think of the universe as expanding spherically to very high precision. This is a puzzle, because it is so much easier to imagine universes that expand very, very differently in different directions. There are many more ways to be irregular than there are to be regular.

Lastly, although there is directional regularity in the universe, there is also a graininess, a variation in density from one place to another over its largest observed dimensions, and that graininess is present at a level of about a few parts in a hundred thousand. It is, again, essential to the whole story that leads to us, because it is this graininess that amplified over time and turned into the galaxies, stars and planets. Without some graininess, those crucial lumps and bumps will never form. Perfect symmetry is lifeless.

The physical process that amplifies small irregularities in density into large ones was first revealed in those letters from Newton that helped Bentley prepare his inaugural Boyle Lectures. Newton pointed out that there is an inevitable tendency for gravity to make things that are a little bit lumpy become a lot lumpy. Where there is more material, it exerts a stronger gravitational pull and enhances its excess density even further at the expense of the sparser regions. In fact, in the last of those first Boyle lectures, Bentley departed in a very interesting way from his general focus upon the regularities and the laws of nature to discuss the problem of the irregularities of nature – mountain ranges, and other things that do not fit the patterns of symmetry and perfection – and discussed how they are important in the make-up of the world, and also appreciated by our aesthetic sense. So in the structure of our universe we are interested both in regularity and irregularity, in the laws of nature and the flaws of nature.

These puzzles – the puzzle of the special expansion rate of the universe, its similarity from one direction to another, its overall smoothness but with a little smidgen of graininess – were features that all suddenly appeared to have a single explanation in a new perspective on the universe that emerged at the beginning of the 1980s. That perspective has become known as the 'inflationary universe'. The word of course derived from economic conditions that existed in the world in the early 1980s, but the idea of this theory is very simple.

Earlier, we considered a universe expanding in a concave sense, the trajectory curved over as time passed, indicating that the universe was decelerating. Inflation is the simple idea that there was a brief interlude in the very early history of the universe when this deceleration switched to acceleration. There was a surge in expansion that resulted in the universe becoming much larger than it otherwise would have become by any given time and, in so doing, the expansion is driven tantalizingly close to that critical divide and makes it extremely isotropic. This provides a natural explanation as to why we find it so today.

This idea was not an arbitrary one. Particle physicists had begun to explore new varieties of theory in which unusual types of matter field were predicted to exist that, if they were in the universe in this early time, would persist for a while and then decay away into ordinary radiation and other particles; but while they are around they produce a surge of expansion. After they decay away, normal service is resumed, and the universe continues to expand and decelerate.

Today from St Mary-le-Bow, with a perfect telescope, we might expect to be able to see only out to a distance of about 14 billion light years (actually nearer to 42 billion light years, after the effects of the expansion are taken into account). There has not been time since the beginning of the expansion for light to reach us from further away. So we call that region within our cosmic horizon the 'visible universe'. There is much more universe no doubt beyond, and tomorrow we would be able to see another light day's worth of universe.

If we run the plot backwards in time, we can ask how small is the region out of which our entire visible universe has expanded? The problem with the old pre-inflationary picture of the universe was that this embryonic patch of space out of which our whole visible part of the universe emerged was always required to be far too large for us to make sense of what resulted. It was so large that there was never time for light signals to travel from one side to the other, for smoothness to be produced, for the expansion rate in different directions to be co-ordinated, and no way for any process to seed little grains and fluctuations that grow into galaxies in a similar way everywhere within it. Inflation solved that problem. Its surge of expansion enabled the whole of our visible universe to be grown out of the image of a region that was small enough for everything to be co-ordinated by light signals, and for there to be enough time for one side of the region to be co-ordinated with another.

This theory gave us at once an explanation as to why our whole visible universe, on average, is so smooth. It carries with it, as it were, the genetic code of a single fluctuation that is co-ordinated by signals, by radiation moving from one side to the other. The acceleration drives it close to that critical divide and, in so doing, it ensures that the expansion proceeds at the same rate in every direction, with very high precision.

But what happened next was really rather fascinating, and brings us to the heart of the topic of this lecture. First of all, it was recognized that the tiny patch that expands to become our whole visible universe will not be perfectly smooth. There must always be some fluctuation across it, some little statistical variations, perhaps of quantum origin, present, and we know what they are. We can apply our mathematical understanding of high-energy physics to predict their form and also then to predict what will happen to them when the expansion stretches them, and they will show up in the radiation in the universe today. They will leave their footprint in the temperature variations of the radiation that comes towards us from every direction in the sky when we point our satellites from above the Earth. In the last few years, NASA, and in coming years, the European Space Agency, has been hunting for those fluctuations, at enormous expense and with great technical expertise.

I have a map of the pattern of temperature variations found by the Wilkinson Microwave Anisotropy Probe (WMAP) telescope on the sky. The variations in colour represent deviations above and below the mean temperature of the radiation in the universe. If you are a statistician, an analysis of this picture will give you a detailed statistical description of the appearance of our sky, and that is what you require to test whether this extraordinary idea about the inflationary phase of the universe is something that ever happened.

It shows the variations in the temperature from place to place, and a measure of their angular size on the sky, or how big they are. You can see that the predictions of this theory lead to a very characteristic ringing like the bells of St Mary-le-Bow we heard beforehand: there is a great peak and then a dying away of the oscillations of the variations in the radiation temperature and energy. There are black dots that show you the state of the data gathered by the satellite. The impressive thing is that there really is a remarkable correlation between the predictions and the theory, so there is surprisingly good observational evidence that, in the past of our observable universe, there was an experience of this surge of rapid expansion that we call inflation. These observations are allowing us to test directly a theoretical prediction about what the universe must have been like, when it was ten to the minus 35 of a second old.

However, this theory that we can test in this way, we hope with ever-greater precision – although we can do other things besides – also leads to much more outrageous and unusual predictions about the structure of our universe and our place within it. The first lesson it teaches us is that geography is a much more complicated subject than when we were at school. You see, we focused just now on one little patch of the universe, the piece that was once the small, contracted image of the whole observable universe that we see today. We know, from what we saw earlier, that we require that patch to have expanded a lot and for a long time in order that it gives rise to a region here that is old enough and large enough for stars to form, explode, die, produce carbon and other life-supporting elements.

But in reality the whole universe may be infinite, certainly a good deal bigger than that one patch, and so we might envisage the situation when inflation occurs as rather like a tiny foam of bubbles that then randomly expand. Some of the bubbles expand a lot, some only a little, some not at all. We have to find ourselves in one of the bubbles that has expanded enough to allow enough time for the stars to make their carbon. This leads us to predict that the geography of the universe is extraordinarily complex, that if we could see beyond our visible horizon, if we could take a God-like view of the whole, and were not limited by the finite speed of light, we would find the universe to be extraordinarily different in structure compared with how we find it within our local horizon.

There have always been sceptical philosophers who would warn you against extrapolating from what we see in the visible universe to what it might be like in the parts that we cannot see. But for the first time we have a positive reason to expect the universe to be quite different in structure beyond our visible horizon than it is within it, and by different we do not only expect things like the density, or the temperature, or the graininess of the universe to be different, but the differences could include far more fundamental things, like the number of forces of nature, even the number of dimensions of space that become large, the values of some constants of nature. Some of these quantities, in more elaborate versions of this theory, are predicted to fall out differently in different regions.

It is bad enough finding out that cosmic geography is more complicated, but we discover also that history has become an extraordinarily more elaborate subject because of cosmology. Soon after the chaotic spatial structure of the inflationary universe was recognized, it was then realized by Alex Vilenkin and Andrei Linde in the United States that inflationary universes possess an instability that renders the whole inflationary process apparently eternal and self-replicating. If we were to focus on one of those little bubbles, one of the patches that has undergone inflation, then it necessarily creates within itself the conditions needed for little sub-regions of itself, to undergo explosive inflationary expansion. The process is self-replicating: those regions inflate, they produce within themselves the conditions for further inflation to occur, and the whole process continues, apparently without end, to the future. Each one of those little bubbles in this process is allowed to take on rather different conditions from the others. How do we see ourselves in this scenario? We inhabit one of those bubbles in this so-called multiverse of possibilities. Our universe is one region in a potentially infinite universe that is very diverse and different from place to place and also from time to time.

The issue of the beginning of the universe is also muddied by this scenario. You see, if we asked, Did the universe have a beginning?, it is quite possible for our piece of the universe to have a beginning. It can be a dramatic Big-Bang-type beginning out of infinity or a more quiescent one out of finite quantum fluctuations, but it would still be possible for the whole multiversal process to have neither a beginning nor an end. So each piece of the multiverse may have a beginning, some parts may have an end, yet the whole self-reproducing process could be past and future eternal.

This is a strange scenario that this inflationary universe impresses upon us. It was not looked for; it is a by-product of the study of what happens to one of those patches. One of the concerns about it is: Can you test such an idea? Well, you might be able to. It could be that a theory that gives rise to this replication process leaves a particular observable stamp upon each member of the multiverse, and if that stamp is not present, then the replication process could not occur. So in that sense, just by looking in our patch, and not finding that stamp, we would falsify such a replication process on all the other parts of it.

On the other hand, perhaps there is no way to test whether we are part of this infinitely more complex scenario. After all, it would be extremely anti-Copernican to regard the universe as having been constructed for our convenience. So we can test and try out every theoretical idea that we might have about it. There is no reason why every true theory of the universe should allow us, at this time and in this place, to be able to critically test it.

One of the things that we see from this developing picture of the multiverse is that it greatly blurs the distinction between the laws of nature and the outcomes of those laws, which that first Boyle Lecture by Bentley sought to distinguish. The laws of nature, we are in the habit of recognizing, are typically surprisingly simple, highly symmetrical and few in number. We think that just four fundamental laws, of electricity and magnetism, radioactivity, nuclear forces and gravity, are enough to explain the rules of cause and effect that dictate what goes on in the universe. Maybe one day there will be only one such law, a so-called 'theory of everything', perhaps of a string-theoretic variety. But the simplicity of the laws of nature is really something that is a little deceptive. You see, the outcomes of the laws of nature are much more complicated, far less symmetrical, and far more difficult to understand than the laws themselves. Sometimes, in science, we find that we can find a theory, we can find the laws, but we cannot find the outcomes, we cannot find the solutions.

You could understand rather easily why this is the case. If I balance a pointer vertically on my hand, then it is very symmetrical in its position. If I let go, it becomes subject to the law of gravity. The law of gravity is symmetrical and highly democratic, and in a perfect vacuum, at zero temperature, there is an equal probability that the pointer will fall in any direction. Pointers do not tend to fall in the direction of Bow Bells or towards the Bank of England; there is an equal probability, in perfect conditions, that it will fall in any direction. But once it falls, the symmetry of the law is broken, and this outcome has picked out a particular direction in the universe. What we see, in this type of multiverse picture, is how so many of the things that were once regarded as irrevocable, unchangeable laws of nature – features like the values of the constants of nature, the number of forces of nature – become outcomes rather than fundamental laws.

Let us turn to some of the symmetry-breakings, some of the outcomes of that inflationary production of different regions of the universe. You might imagine that there is a collection of different resting places, rather like a corrugated iron roof, and when you throw a ball in the air, like the National Lottery selection process, the ball will end up falling into one or other of those resting places. As the universe expands in different places, at different rates, in different parts of the universe, the ball will fall into different resting places, different ground states, as physicists call them, but those ground states are really very different in what they require of the universe where that happens. They will determine how many forces of nature there are. One world may have just gravity and no other forces. One world may have six dimensions. One may have three.

So this process creates a vast diversity of possibility in the outcomes of the chaotic and eternal inflationary process, and we see ourselves as part of a large complex process. We appreciate that the conditions that are needed to allow life to develop in one of these patches, say the one that we reside in, are in some respects very special. So we then recognize that, in this type of modern cosmological scenario, all we can ever hope to predict about our situation in the universe is something that involves probabilities. We might like to know how likely is it that things fall out in a way that allows planets like the Earth to develop, elements like carbon to exist, or consciousness to develop. That creates a big problem for us, because you might have imagined that mathematicians could simply go away and take these theories and compute those probabilities, but the situation is, again, not quite what it seems. So far, nobody has been able to compute such probabilities. We do not know how to do it. Maybe one day we will, but even when we do the answers that we determine are really likely to be somewhat confusing.

Suppose that we make a prediction about some quality of one of those patches in the universes that undergo inflation. What would you be interested in about that prediction? Would you be interested in the sort of bubble that is most likely? You see that if this was the outcome of the calculation, universes in a particular place would be the most probable, but suppose that we graft on to this picture what would be the probability of universes that allow complexity of any sort to develop? So suppose we ask which are the universes where stars as possible, or any elements at all? We might find, indeed, that this is a very, very narrow range indeed, and it may be a highly improbable part of the probability distribution but, no matter how improbable it turned out to be, we would have to find ourselves inhabiting that narrow niche of possibilities, because we could exist in no other.

I have mentioned already, and will ask again in closing: Did the multiverse have a beginning? We do not know. We have got all sorts of different options. Our own universe within the multiverse may have had a beginning; it may not have had a beginning. It could be that the multiverse itself had no beginning, or it could have had a beginning, or neither need have a beginning. We have these three curious options. In all cases, the idea of a beginning is a rather tantalizing one for cosmologists, just as for everybody else. A conventional beginning to our universe always seemed to require some physical infinity in Aristotle's ancient sense, an infinity of a physically measurable quantity, like temperature, or density, or gravitational force.

What is our view of that today? If you are a physicist of a more conventional sort, whenever an infinity pops up in your calculation, you take it rather like the remark on your old school report: 'Must try harder'; that it is a signal that somehow something has gone wrong in the formulation of the theory; that if you had only included some extra detail, the infinity would be exorcised and it would become simply a very, very extreme but entirely finite effect. That would still be the attitude of most people working in fundamental particle physics to the appearance of a beginning to the universe in time.

Cosmologists are more accommodating to infinities. They are generally more willing to admit the possibility of singular events, and what could be more singular than the beginning of the universe? The centres of black holes and the beginning of the expanding universe might be where you would be happy to allow something infinite to occur that would begin the expansion of everything out of nothing. So we have a number of completely different attitudes towards those sorts of beginnings to the universe that you will find on offer among cosmologists today.

What is the relation of all this to the big questions of ultimate concern that these lectures focus upon? That, within the last 20 years or so, there has been a dramatic change in cosmologists' perspective on the universe. I showed you how, by a careful consideration of what is going on in the expanding universe, you discover that the huge distances of space and extents of time are by no means divorced from ourselves here on Earth. We are intimately entwined with the conditions within the universe that gave rise to the building blocks of living complexity, and that insight enables us to understand why the seemingly life-averse features of our universe are actually critical requirements for complexity and life of any sort, including our own. Then we have seen, in a less parochial way, how the inflationary perspective on the universe, underpinned by its careful observational testing within the part of the universe that we can see, leads to quite dramatic reconsiderations of our place within the universe as a whole, and indeed, a vast enlargement of our perspective of the universe as a whole. We see it as more complex in space, more complex in time. Our position within it is likely to be rather particular, somewhat special, and one that we might hope to understand more fully in the future.

I hope Dr Bentley, were he here, would feel that Newton's perspective on the laws of nature has led to a wider vision that is richer and more spectacular in many ways; that the universe remains as complex as we can imagine, even today (Barrow, 2011).

5

Psychologizing and Neurologizing about Religion: Facts, Fallacies and the Future

MALCOLM JEEVES

'Scientific theories of human nature may be discomforting or unsatisfying, but they are not illegitimate', correctly proclaimed a leading article in the 14 June 2007 issue of *Nature*. With equal confidence, the paper also claimed, incorrectly, that, '[w]ith deference to the sensibilities of religious people, the idea that man was created in the image of God can surely be put aside'. The search for well-grounded theories of human nature is to be applauded but the project is not helped by wider unsubstantiated claims that exhibit a lack of awareness of advances in other fields of scholarship, such as biblical and theological, which have much to say about in what sense humans are made 'in the image of God'.

Gaining perspective

Psychologists interested in religion have concentrated on what we might call its roots and its fruits. For example, Hearnshaw identified four significant influences at the end of the nineteenth century that provided the basis for later psychological studies of religion: (1) Francis Galton's studies of the manifestations of religion (such as prayer); (2) studies by anthropologists, such as Sir James Fraser, of comparative religion and the origins of religion; (3) the writings of theologians such as W. R. Inge on mysticism and religious experiences; and (4) the beginnings of the systematic psychology of religion, such as E. G. Starbuck. These in turn culminated in William James's classic *The Varieties of Religious Experience* (1902). In the twentieth century, the picture changed as Sigmund Freud's radical views became more widely known in society at large, leading to a strong resurgence of the warfare metaphor to describe the relationship between science and religion.

Despite Freud's own disclaimers that his accounts of the roots and fruits of religion were neutral as regards the truth value of specific religious beliefs which, he agreed, must be decided on other grounds, nevertheless his own accounts were soon interpreted as 'explaining away' religious beliefs and exposing the practices of religions as 'nothing but' the persistence of an interim social neurosis.

One major problem for the psychoanalytic claim that religion is the product of unconscious wishes is that psychoanalytic theories can be applied equally well to the understanding of the *unbelief* of those who wish to refute religion. This was penetratingly demonstrated by Rumke in his little book *The Psychology of Unbelief* (1952). In it, he looked carefully at the history of Freud's own life, such as his poor relationships with his father, his intense dislike of his Roman Catholic nanny, and he put these together to show how, on the basis of Freud's own theory, a picture emerges from which we would predict that a person with such a background would, on reaching maturity, produce a rationalized set of beliefs, in which he would reject religion, and in particular a religion in which God was seen as a father figure. And Freud did just that.

While Freud and Jung captured the headlines and the public interest in what was happening at the psychology-religion interface in the first half of the twentieth century, there were others, such as R. H. Thouless, who were writing on the same topic and, in many psychologists' judgements, making a much more lasting contribution, as evidenced by the 1971 reprinting of his book *An Introduction to the Psychology of Religion*, first published in 1923. Thouless's approach was primarily constructive and a complete contrast with the warfare metaphor.

Since the Second World War, there has been an exponentially increasing literature on psychology *and* religion and on the psychology *of* religion. Much of this has been in North America where, of the more than 200 varieties of psychotherapy currently in the market place, some are more strongly endorsed than others by religious groups.

In the second half of the twentieth century, one of the most influential psychologists was B. F. Skinner. Having achieved considerable success in the development of techniques for shaping and modifying behaviour, Skinner went on to speculate about how such techniques might be harnessed to shape the future of society. He believed that similar principles, based on rewards and punishments, could explain how the practice of religion functions psychologically. 'The religious agency', he said, 'is a special form of government under which "good" and "bad" become "pious" and "sinful." Contingencies involving positive and negative reinforcement, often of the most extreme sort, are codified – for example, as commandments – and maintained by specialists, usually with the support of ceremonies, rituals and stories' (Skinner, 1972, p. 6). He argued that the good things, personified in a god, are reinforcing, whereas the threat of hell is an aversive stimulus. Both are used to shape behaviour.

Underlying Skinner's whole approach is a reductionist presupposition. Thus, he speaks of concepts of god being 'reduced to' what we find positively reinforcing. There is no doubt that Skinner provided ready ammunition for anyone wishing to perpetuate the warfare metaphor of the relation of psychology and religion. Another distinguished figure in psychology in the second half of the twentieth century took quite a different view from Skinner. Psychologist, neuroscientist and Nobel Laureate Roger Sperry wrote not only of the bankruptcy of some forms of behaviourism but strongly advocated the benefits of a positive relationship between psychology and religion viewed as allies engaged in a common task (Sperry, 1966). Typical of Sperry's views is the following:

The answer to the question, 'Is there convergence between science and religion?' seems from the standpoint of psychology to be a definite emphatic 'yes.' Over the past 15 years, changes in the foundational concepts of psychology instituted by the new cognitive or mentalist paradigm have radically reformed scientific descriptions of human nature, and the conscious self. The resultant views are today less atomistic, less mechanistic, and more mentalistic, contextual, subjectivistic and humanistic. From the standpoint of theology, these new mentalistic tenets, which no longer exclude on principle the entire inner world of subjective phenomena, are much more palatable and compatible than, were those of the behaviourist-materialist era. Where science and religion had formerly stood in direct conflict on this matter to the point even of being mutually exclusive and irreconcilable, one now sees a new compatibility, potentially even harmony with liberal religion – defined as religion that does not rely on dualistic or supernatural beliefs, forms of which have been increasingly evident in contemporary theology (Sperry, 1988, p. 609).

Two other people prominent in the history of psychology in the second half of the twentieth century, Gordon Allport, a leading personality theorist in the USA and Sir Frederic Bartlett, pioneer of memory research in the UK, emphasized the potential for a positive cooperative relationship of psychology and religion, at the same time underlining the limits of psychological inquiry, at least when practised as a science.

Allport wrote that

different as are science and art in their axioms and methods they have learned to cooperate in a thousand ways – in the production of fine dwellings, music, clothing, design. Why should not science and religion, likewise differing in axioms and method, yet cooperate in the production of an improved human character without which all other human gains are tragic loss? From many sides today comes the demand that religion and psychology busy themselves in finding a common ground for uniting their efforts for human welfare (Allport, 1951, p. viii).

Bartlett was described recently as making 'one of the most substantial contributions to psychology of the past century' (Wagoner, Gillespie and Duveen, 2007, p. 680). One of the architects of 'the cognitive revolution' in psychology, he wrote:

It is inevitable that the forms which are taken by feeling, thinking, and action within any religion should be moulded and directed by the character of its own associated culture. The psychologist must accept these forms and attempt to show how they have grown up and what are their principal effects ... So far as any final decision upon the validity or value of such [claims] goes, the psychologist is in exactly the same position as that of any other human being who cares to consider the matter seriously. Being a psychologist gives him neither superior nor inferior authority (Bartlett, 1950, pp. 3–4).

Thus, both Allport and Bartlett held a high view of the potential benefits of a developing science of psychology. They also recognized the distinctive approaches to the gaining of knowledge made possible through the scientific enterprise – a view already well-articulated by leading physical scientists of earlier generations.

Contemporary writers in the psychology of religion, such as Fraser Watts and Mark Williams, echo these views:

We need to make absolutely clear here that we are not, as psychologists, commenting on whether or not religious beliefs are correct, whether they are justified by rational argument and empirical evidence. Our concern is rather with how people arrive at what they take to be religious knowledge (Watts and Williams, 1988, p. 4).

As the domains of religion and science converge, psychology can be an ally of religion in the shared search for truth. In religion, we feel, at times, that we have intuitive insights into another realm of reality, and at times, we are too readily judgemental of those who do not share our views and, if we believe Freud in the early twentieth century and Dawkins today, we are prone to illusory beliefs. Psychology can offer help in curbing such knee-jerk reactions. Myers reminds us that '[t]he story of psychology ... enhances our abilities to restrain intuition with critical thinking, judgmentalism with compassion, and illusion with understanding' (Myers, 2007, p. xix). And in the same spirit, for their part he encourages psychologists to be 'sceptical but not cynical, open but not gullible'.

Mind and brain: body and soul – relationships of irreducible, intrinsic, interdependence?

It is one thing to demonstrate the intimate inter-relationship between what is happening at the conscious mental level and what is happening at the level of the brain and the body. The unanswered question is how can we most accurately characterize this intimate relationship without making claims or assumptions about what we know about the relationship between the two that have not yet been demonstrated?

Clearly, there is a remarkable interdependence between what is occurring at the cognitive level and what is occurring at the physical level. We could perhaps describe this as a relationship of intrinsic interdependence, using intrinsic to mean that, as far as we can see, it describes the way the world is in this regard. Could we perhaps go further than this and say that on our present knowledge it is an irreducible intrinsic interdependence, by this meaning that we cannot reduce the mental to the physical any more than we can reduce the physical to the mental? In this sense, there is an important duality to be recognized, but it is a not a duality that necessarily implies a substance dualism.

It is significant that equally committed Christians hold differing views about how to model this duality. Thus we have emergent dualism (William Hasker, 2005), non-reductive physicalism (Nancey Murphy, 2005), substance dualism (Stewart Goetz, 2005), a constitution view of persons (Kevin Corcoran, 2005) or dual aspect monism (Malcolm Jeeves, 1997; Donald Mackay, 1991). All share the view that eliminative materialism is inadequate in that it fails to give adequate weight to the primary data of conscious experience.

Very recently, Thomas Nagel, a leader among contemporary philosophers, had no doubt that, 'so far as we can tell, our mental lives and those of other creatures, including subjective experiences, are strongly connected with and perhaps strictly dependent on physical events in our brains and on the physical interaction of our bodies with the rest of the physical world' (Nagel, 2007, pp. 96–7). Nagel had no doubts that 'we have to reject conceptual reduction of the mental to the physical' (p. 99). But if that is the case, how are we to think about it? He acknowledges that 'the mind–body problem is difficult enough so that we should be suspicious of attempts to solve it with the concepts and methods developed to account for very different kinds of things. Instead, we should expect theoretical progress in this area to require a major conceptual revolution' (p. 100). He believes this will require a change in our thinking at least as radical as relativity theory was in physics.

Specific challenges to some long-held religious beliefs

Humans made in the image of God?

The notion that humans possess a soul was typical of the thinking of major figures from the past, such as Plato, Aristotle, Origen, Demetrius, Augustine (who held a modified Platonic view) and Descartes. Until relatively recently, in the Western world, the dominant cultural influences have been the religious ones. Robert Boyle, according to Hooykaas, thought, as did his contemporaries, within a dualistic framework, so that he believed that, 'although in physical respects man is a tiny and negligible part of the universe, he alone has a rational soul' (Hooykaas, 1997, p. 72). At the same time, Boyle firmly believed that man is God's image bearer (p. 78).

More recently, there has been a return to a Hebrew–Christian view of the person advocated increasingly over the past century by biblical scholars. They have urged us to remember that within Scripture the question posed is never simply: What is a human being? 'There is always more to the question', writes Old Testament scholar Patrick Miller, 'so that the answer offered in each instance is indirect in that it is in response to the more specific formulation of the question rather than to a generalized and abstracted request for a definition of human existence, of human being' (Miller, 2004, p. 65). Miller illustrates how, in Scripture, the question: What is a human being? is 'never asked in the abstract nor posed as a theoretical question. It is always asked in dialogue with God, and its formulation is a basic clue to the fact that the Psalms are not going to answer the anthropological question about who and what we are as human beings except in relation to God' (p. 65).

Today, the accumulating evidence from neuropsychology makes it extremely difficult to maintain a view that there are two different substances interacting in the human person. All the emphasis rather is on the unity of the person, two aspects of which must be studied and taken seriously if a full account is to be given of the mystery of the human person (Berry and Jeeves, 2008).

Among theologians, there seems to be now a general agreement that the *imago dei* is not anatomical, genetic, neurological or behavioural, and that it combines functional and structural elements, for example, J. R. Middleton (Middleton, 2005). Chris Wright puts it well:

We should not think of the image of God as an independent 'thing' that we somehow possess. God did not give to human beings the image of God. Rather it is a dimension of our very creation. The expression 'in our image' is adverbial (that is, it describes the way God made us), not adjectival (that is, as if it simply described a quality we possess). The image of God is not so much something we possess, as what we are. To be human is to be the image of God (Wright, 2004, p. 119).

Morality without a soul?

If you hold a body–soul dualism view of the person, processes of moral decision-making are presumed to happen primarily in the domain of the soul, not the body. In contrast, a non-dualist view of the person would presume that it is the brain/body doing the deciding. It is as yet not entirely clear what one might expect regarding the engagement of brain systems in such behaviours. So we pause to ask: What is known and being learnt about brain systems and processes that contribute to the moral regulation of behaviour?

Study of patients with damage to the frontal lobes of the brain frequently show that they typically have difficulty regulating their behaviour in order to abide by norms of socially acceptable or moral behaviour. Such individuals may, capriciously and without malicious intent, violate social conventions, laws, ethical standards, or the rules of courtesy, civility, and regard for the benefit of others.

Today, there is a rapidly developing field in neuroscience that involves the mapping of the brain areas involved in different forms of interpersonal, economic and moral decision-making. The general approach in this form of research is to have persons engage in decision-making tasks while their brains are being scanned using functional magnetic resonance imaging (fMRI). For example, a number of studies have demonstrated the activation of the limbic (emotional) areas of the brain during what one would presume to be tasks requiring merely the 'cold' calculation of the likelihood of financial gains and losses. Limbic involvement is particularly intense when the financial decision also involves interpersonal variables such as trust.

The general finding from this kind of research is that moral regulation of behaviour is an embodied process, and that different forms of moral decision-making involve different patterns of brain activity. The somatic marker theory suggests that important elements contributing to moral behaviour are the feelings elicited during interpersonal encounters – both feelings towards others (such as empathy and compassion) or feelings about the interpersonal nature of a situation (such as unfairness or social isolation). Like moral reasoning and religious experiences, various aspects of the experiences of human relatedness have been the subject of neuroscience research over the last two decades. This rapidly growing field of research is referred to as social neuroscience.

Chemically and neurologically induced religious experiences and vice versa?

Ancient religious rituals used plants to facilitate ecstatic and mystical states – for example, mushrooms (by the Aztecs), peyote cactus (by the Huicol of Mexico) and ayahuasca (by the natives of north-western South America), as well as substances from water lilies, mandrake, opium poppies, morning glories and marijuana plants. Since these drugs act on the brain to bring about their effects, study of these effects on various brain systems can reveal brain mechanisms relevant to understanding more about experiences that people often describe as religious (Nichols and Chemel, 2006).

The relationship between the alteration of the brain serotonin systems by hallucinogenic drugs and the subjective qualities of either psychedelic or religious experiences remains speculative. However, based on what is known of the systems affected and the nature of the changes created by the drugs, it has been suggested that such drugs 'perturb the key brain structures that inform us about our world, tell us when to pay attention, and interpret what is real. Psychedelics activate ancient brain systems that project to all of the forebrain structures that are involved in memory and feeling; they sensitize systems that tell us when something is novel and when to remember it' (Nichols and Chemel, 2006, p. 26). The common subjective experiences elicited by these drug-related changes in brain systems include: 'altered perception of reality and self; intensification of mood; visual and auditory hallucinations, including vivid eidetic imagery and synesthesia; distorted sense of time and space; enhanced profundity and meaningfulness; and a ubiquitous sense of novelty' (p. 3). Whether these experiences are interpreted as a psychedelic 'trip' or as spiritual and transcendent, is hypothesized to be due primarily to one's experience-based expectations, the setting in which the drugs are taken, and the cognitive/theological network out of which one provides a post hoc interpretation of the experience.

There is a significant literature in clinical neurology that suggests that in some cases, individuals with temporal lobe epileptic seizures experience intense religious states as a part of the aura leading up to a seizure. In these persons, experiences of intense religious awe, ecstasy or ominous presence appear to be a product of the abnormal electrical activity of the brain that constitutes their seizures. Although such cases are rare, they happen often enough to suggest something about the physical processes that may be associated with normal religious experiences.

Fyodor Dostoyevsky (who himself had a seizure disorder) gives a particularly graphic literary description of subjective feelings during some seizures in his account of the experiences of Prince Miskin in *The Idiot* (Dostoyevsky, 1969). The following is a passage from this book in which Dostoyevsky describes (in the thoughts of Miskin) the sort of religious experiences that are sometimes associated with temporal lobe seizures:

> he fell to thinking that in his attacks of epilepsy there was a pause just before the fit itself ... when it seemed his brain was on fire, and in an extraordinary surge all his vital forces would be intensified. The sense of life, the consciousness of self, were multiplied tenfold in these moments ... His mind and heart were flooded with extraordinary light; all torment, all doubt, all anxieties were relieved at once, resolved in a kind of lofty calm, full of serene, harmonious joy and hope, full of understanding and the knowledge of the ultimate cause of things (p. 236).

A recent literary reference to this phenomenon can be found in Mark Salzman's modern novel *Lying Awake* (2000). Salzman writes about a nun with religious visions associated with temporal lobe seizures.

Accounts of religious-like experiences associated with a temporal lobe seizure can be found in the modern neurological literature. Naito and Matsui present the following self-description (similar to Dostoyevsky's) from one of their patients of the experience of the aura preceding a seizure: 'Triple halos appeared around the sun. Suddenly the sunlight became intense. I experienced a revelation of God and of all creation glittering under the sun. The sun became bigger and engulfed me. My mind, my whole being was pervaded by a feeling of delight' (Naito and Matsui, 1988, pp. 123–4).

It is clear that certain patterns of electrical activity involving the temporal lobes (sometimes occurring during a seizure) can cause intense, personally significant experiences that some persons describe as religious.

Abnormal activity of the temporal lobes can be induced artificially in non-epileptic individuals using a non-invasive procedure called Transcranial Magnetic Stimulation. Michael Persinger reports experiments where electromagnetic stimulation of the right temporal lobe results in the person reporting a 'sense of presence'. This 'sense of presence' is sometimes experienced by the person as the presence of God or angels or other supernatural persons. This has led Persinger to suggest that all persons who have religious experiences are having micro-seizures of the right temporal lobe (Persinger and Makarec, 1987; 1987). A similar explanation is given by Persinger for other paranormal experiences, such as reports of encounters with aliens (Persinger, 1983). These findings of Persinger's should, however, be treated with caution, since a recent report at an attempted replication of Persinger's studies, but using better controlled experiments including double-blind techniques, failed to replicate Persinger's results.

Andrew Newberg and his collaborators have studied brain activity during various religious states (Newberg et al., 2001). In these studies, they observed changes in regional cerebral blood flow using Single Proton Emission Computed Tomography (SPECT scans). They first studied religious meditation in both Buddhist monks and Catholic nuns. In both groups, the results showed increased bilateral frontal lobe activation and decreased right parietal lobe activity, when the meditator reported reaching a state of total absorption and 'oneness'. Decreased activity of the right parietal lobe was interpreted as a neural correlate of the absence of a sense of self that is experienced in such meditative states.

Newberg et al. have recently extended this research to include another religious state that is very different from meditation – that is, the ecstatic religious state involving glossolalia (speaking in tongues). Their studies suggest both that religious states are associated with identifiable changes in the distribution of brain activity, and that different religious states are associated with different patterns of brain activity – in some cases quite opposite changes in brain activity.

Brain function and religious experiences: how to interpret the data?

Whether drug-induced, seizure-related, caused by magnetic stimulation or simply brain changes associated with normal religious states, it is clear that the functioning of the brain is intimately involved in our religious states and experiences. The question is: what is to be made of such relationships?

Ramachandran believes there exists within the temporal lobe a 'God module' in the form of a neural area dedicated to religious experiences (Ramachandran et al., 1997). Religious experiences are, in the view of Ramachandran, a unique and intrinsic class of experiences served by a unique brain structure. A different interpretation of the same clinical data has been offered by Rubin and Saver (Saver and Rubin, 1997). They argue that certain temporal lobe seizures activate a brain system that marks mental processes with a quality of deep significance, harmoniousness, joy, etc. Whether or not the experience is described in religious terms is a product of the prior experiences and interpretive networks of the person having the seizure. This interpretation is consistent with the theory of religious experiences offered by William James, according to whom differences in the religious (or non-religious) interpretations given by persons to mundane or unusual experiences are related to culturally inherited 'over-beliefs'. Religious meaning is not intrinsic to the experience, but applied by the interpretive network of the experiencer.

Newberg's original understanding of the results of his studies of meditators indicated to him that the brain is wired for religious experiences and, as expressed in the title of his book, that is *Why God Won't go Away*. However, his studies of glossolalia do not support the idea of a particular and unique brain module or system for religious experiences. Rather, the brain activity associated with different religious experiences is different. There is no single brain area where greater or lesser activity is necessary and sufficient for one to have an experience that is understood as religious. It is not necessary to interpret any of the changes in brain activity found in these imaging studies as unique to the religiousness of the experience, but as manifestations of the operation of more general systems commandeered as a part of the neural realization of a particular religious state and interpreted as religious by the context of the experience and the personal history of the experiencer.

Embodied spirituality

The view that brain function, brain damage, brain stimulation or even genetics can in various ways affect, or give some account for, our moral, religious and interpersonal experiences and behaviours sits uneasily with the beliefs of many people that such experiences are manifestations of non-material human minds, souls or spirits. It raises the further question: Is our spirituality embodied?

Sarah Coakley helpfully reminds us that since 'spirituality' has become so much of a buzzword in the hand-waving category, it is doubly important that anyone using it must be clear about their meaning (Coakley, 2013). She points out that for some, 'spirituality' is a sort of controlled religious 'high' frequently devoid of almost all the precise content that it would entail if one were talking about the 'spirituality' of institutionalized Christian churchgoers holding clear doctrinal beliefs.

Spirituality involves experience, belief and action, the study of which, as we saw at the beginning, is the bread and butter and staple diet of psychologists: experience in terms of our awareness of the transcendent, beliefs in terms of what we believe about God, about ourselves and about the world in which we live, and action in terms of how we live our lives. The evidence reviewed repeatedly highlighted the intimate interdependence between brain processes, cognitive processes and behaviour, and this is relevant to understanding how those aspects of spirituality that mobilize and depend upon cognitive processes are not free floating but firmly embodied. Such embodied beliefs and expectations are major factors in understanding some of the spiritual dimensions of life. At the same time cognitive processes such as beliefs and expectations are frequently held within social contexts, and that reminds us that spirituality is also firmly embedded (Murphy and Brown, 2007).

Religion embodied and embedded

Can the fruits of psychologizing and neurologizing about religion offer any hints to help us to a deeper understanding of religion itself? Let me offer some suggestions.

It is simplistic to believe that religion can be reduced to a primary form of cognitive activity such as language or speech and then linked with identifiable neural systems and structures. Within the Christian tradition, it is 'together with all the Lord's people' that we are able 'to grasp how wide and long and high and deep is the love of Christ' (Ephesians 3.18). I should like to recapture this emphasis by borrowing from and adapting a metaphor suggested by Warren Brown, that 'religion' is like 'football' (for Warren Brown it was baseball) – a cultural and sociological concept that summarizes a wide variety of group and individual activities, events and experiences (Brown, 2006).

Brown suggests that games such as baseball, or in the British context football, encompass group participation as either spectators or players. For participants, there is a form of group activity involving particular sets of motor skills. For the spectator and fan, it is a topic of continual interest, conversation and occasional attendance at games. It is evident from watching the crowds that football can involve moments of intense emotional experience (for some, for example, when a decisive goal is scored, it seems not unlike a moment of religious ecstasy) and certain ritual-like participations (such as pre-game warm-up for players, singing songs well known to the supporters, 'You'll never walk alone' and such like). Clearly, football involves many complex layers of interpersonal and social organization. By analogy, we should consider the possibility that religion is not itself a basic cognitive process like language or speech, but rather is a more broadly inclusive social phenomenon like football.

Such a view has several implications. As Brown asserts, we would not expect to find a specific 'neurology of football' – that is, no unique neurological systems that would contribute specifically to football and not to other forms of life. Football is neither sufficiently unitary as an experience or event, nor sufficiently temporally bound for study at the level of neurology. Second, we would not expect a neuropathology specific to football, although many forms of neurological disorder might have an impact on different forms of participation in, or appreciation of, football. Third, it would be somewhat far-fetched to imagine an evolution of the specific capacity for football, or to argue for the survival advantages of football to individuals or social groups, or to argue that the specific capacity for football is 'hard wired'. Rather, football is a complex social emergent of many more basic sociocultural systems involving a wide variety of activities and experiences that, in turn, piggy-back cognitively, neurologically and evolutionarily on a large number of more general cognitive capacities and skills.

There would, therefore, not exist a unique neurology of religion, per se, nor would there be a distinctive neurology of particular forms of religious behavior or experience, but rather a neurology of contributory neuropsychological systems which interact with the individual and between the individual and the socio-cultural environment, such as to allow for the emergence of religious behaviors and experiences (Brown, 2006, p. 234).

Facts, fallacies and the future

Facts

Psychologizing and neurologizing about religion has moved from being parasitic to a field in its own right. It will, however, most likely continue to reflect major developments within the fields of psychology and neuroscience. Psychology can continue to help us to check and to validate some of our deepest intuitions. It should inculcate within us a greater compassion for those whose embodiment is compromised through disease and aging. It will serve as a constant reminder against jumping to simplistic conclusions about profound issues about our mysterious nature, such as the dualism–monism debates.

There are many beneficial outcomes of psychologizing and neurologizing about religion, in addition to the way it prompts us to greater compassion, such as the need to recognize that our spirituality is both embodied and embedded. It will afford us new insights into the nature of religious knowing, as has already been demonstrated by Fraser Watts and Mark Williams. It may help us to come to fresh insights into understanding the words of Christ himself, as Fraser Watts has recently suggested.

It may also, as one of today's leading international New Testament scholars has shown, be able to shed new light on enduring issues about the interpretation of the ancient texts, about the extent to which they are, as was claimed last century, inevitably encrusted with traditions and the extent to which they are still properly to be regarded as eyewitness accounts. Richard Bauckham, in his most recent book, *Jesus and the Eyewitnesses*, has a most insightful chapter in which he draws upon the very latest evidence from psychological studies of memory to give profound new insights into the way in which the evidence points to the text as giving eyewitness testimony to the person of Jesus (Bauckham, 2006).

Such an approach would surely have been warmly endorsed by Robert Boyle, who wrote, 'We know a revelation through testimony, not through ratiocination' (Hooykaas, 1997, p. 122).

Fallacies

Whenever we are offered a new psychological or neurological account of some facet of religious experience, cognition or behaviour, we shall do well to remember the ever present temptation to slip into 'nothing buttery', a term used by Donald Mackay in his debate with B. F. Skinner, who from his underlying reductionist presuppositions, said that when listening to someone talking about God, he 'ran a translation inside'. The translation was from 'God talk' to what he regarded as the original version, namely statements in terms of schedules of reinforcement. At the time, Mackay pointed out to Skinner that what he was saying was tantamount to asserting that a 'No Smoking' sign is nothing but ink on cardboard and therefore it is perfectly alright to go on smoking. It is like saying that what is going on in a computer when it is solving a mathematical equation is nothing but electronics.

We shall find the answer to questions about the existence of God by considering the relevant evidence with a critical and open mind, with a readiness to be confronted with the truth when it, or as we would prefer to say He, is presented to us. Our task, as one high profile Christian reminds us, is to continue our 'personal search for the face of the Lord', so as to 'help foster the growth of a living relationship with him' (Ratzinger, 2007, pp. xxiii; xxiv).

The future

What about the future? Recently it was reported that the UK's largest medical research charity was going to 'plough £1 million into the search for the nerve mechanisms that explain beauty – and with it love, truth and happiness'. The leader of the project is to be Professor Semir Zeki, already with a distinguished reputation as a neuroscientist with experience 'in using functional MRI brain scanning to study the "neural correlates of subjective mental states" – in layman's terms what happens in the brain when we experience strong feelings'. Zeki was asked, 'What if this is all, to use the words of Keats, unweaving a rainbow – a momentous endeavour that in the end removes the mystery and awe from the things that make life worth living?' He responded that '... he had pondered this possibility at length'. He went on, 'I don't see it like that, my sense of awe of Michelangelo's pieta isn't diminished by knowing that there is a part of my brain that responds to the human body and another part that responds to the face. There is still a feeling of wonder. What we gain is the knowledge of the characteristics of the human brain that give us our common humanity' (*The Times*, 10 November 2007).

Zeki is here underlining yet again the point that at times more than one level of explanation is necessary to do full justice to a phenomenon – a view, I suspect, that would have been endorsed by Robert Boyle who, we are told, '... viewed his theological interests and his work in natural philosophy as forming a seamless whole and constantly used results from the one area to enlighten matters in the other' (MacIntosh and Anstey, 2006).

However successful we are in identifying the psychological and neurological roots of various aspects of religion, we must resist the temptation thereby to claim that we have now shown that religion is nothing but this or that facet of our neuropsychological make-up. Perhaps this message will come home most clearly in the future when brain imaging techniques have become so miniaturized and so mobile that you will all be able to sit in a lecture and be told afterwards which parts of your brains were most active (and when you went to sleep!). You will also have available at the end a readout of what was happening in the brain of the lecturer. What I think no one will believe is that their judgement of the truth or falsehood of what was said can be read off from any of this information about your own or the lecturer's brain activity. That must be judged against the relevant evidence (Jeeves and Brown, 2009).

6

Misusing Darwin
The Materialist Conspiracy in
Evolutionary Biology

KEITH WARD

Science and materialism

> We take the side of science ... because we have a prior com-
> mitment, a commitment to materialism ... moreover, that
> materialism is absolute, for we cannot allow a Divine Foot in
> the door.

Sometimes people can be more embarrassed by their friends
than by their enemies. It is surely embarrassing for science to be
defended on the grounds that it is founded on an absolute prior
commitment to a highly disputed and deeply problematic philosophical view. If ever there were a dogmatic, unquestioning faith
that zooms well beyond the evidence, this is it. Who could say
such a thing? It was Richard Lewontin, a highly respected Harvard professor and evolutionary naturalist. Admittedly, he said it
in the *New York Review of Books* in 1997, but even so he presumably meant it. He is not alone. Francis Crick said that it was
his distaste for religion that largely motivated his search for a
purely chemical basis for life. Once again, the dislike of divine feet
drives the search for mechanical causes, and nothing but mechanical causes, of all events in the cosmos. A lead article in the science
journal *Nature* (June 2007) reported: 'The idea that man was created in the image of God can surely be put aside.' It went on to
suggest that 'scientific theories of human nature' are necessarily

in conflict with outdated religious views. If the scientific account is accepted, it would no longer be possible to hold that there is something special about humans that gives them a particular function or form of conscious relationship to a God.

The same journal (July 1984) declared that all supernatural causes were absolutely ruled out by science. Why is the possibility of divine causality so disliked and even dogmatically denied? One reason can be found in a major article, 'Evolution: The Ultimate Guide' (*New Scientist*, April 2008). Michael le Page says: 'The genomes of complex creatures reveal a lack of any intelligence or foresight ... the inescapable conclusion is that if life was designed, the designer was lazy, stupid and cruel' and that humans are 'a crude early prototype thrown up by a desperately cruel process'. In a book about Darwin, philosopher A. C. Grayling writes, 'Biological "design" is manifestly not the outcome of previous planning and execution by an intelligent purposive agency, unless that agency is markedly incompetent or markedly malevolent' (Kelly and Kelly, 2009, p. 232).

One leading evolutionary biologist assured me that the word 'purpose' is a red rag to a biologist, to be avoided if you hope to be published in a peer-reviewed journal. Another told me that he would not publicly discuss his belief in God lest it compromise his biological reputation and make people suspect that he was prejudiced. The admission of atheism, of course, is not prejudiced, and it enables biologists to be purely and relentlessly scientific, without any bias whatsoever. So there is not even a door into which a divine foot could be wedged. Evolution is a long series of accidents and mistakes, and it is not going anywhere. The suggestion is that evolutionary biology shows the development of life on Earth to be the result of innumerable copying errors in the replication of DNA and RNA, chances of cosmic collisions and meteorite impacts and of basic laws of thermodynamics. Humans exist by chance, and we will probably not be here for long. There is no place for God or purpose in such a universe.

KEITH WARD

Different kinds of explanation

The argument seems strong, especially when it is backed by the authority of leading biologists. But we must ask whether explanation in terms of pure chance is good evidence for materialism, or whether it is rather forced and one-sided.

There is clearly a strong anti-religious bias to much evolutionary biology. And yet a number of highly competent biologists have been religious believers – Theodosius Dobzhansky, Carolus Linnaeus, Gregor Mendel and Alfred Russell Wallace among them. Ronald Fisher, Sewall Wright, Simon Conway Morris, Francis Collins, Alister Hardy, Warren Weaver, Francisco Ayala and Kenneth Miller are modern evolutionary biologists who have espoused various forms of belief in God. So it cannot be quite obvious that evolutionary biology is committed to materialism. The materialist presupposition often extends beyond biology, even beyond science, to the humanities in general.

E. O. Wilson, in his book *Consilience* (1998), explicitly proposes a programme of reducing all the humanities to rigorous science, expunging the remaining references to consciousness, value and purpose, and replacing them by physical explanations as evolutionarily successful strategies. All real facts are scientific facts, and all values are subjective expressions of taste. Many of the best-known evolutionary scientific leaders are committed to propagating a reductionist, materialist worldview as 'proper science' even though materialism and reductionism are philosophical theories that are not entailed by the practice of evolutionary biology. A. C. Grayling expresses a widespread scientific consensus that Darwinism is a theory of explanation competing with theism and that as theism, is obsolete it has thus been replaced by Darwinism.

This shows a refusal properly to differentiate between philosophy, religion and science. There are many sorts of scientific explanation, but a paradigmatic one seeks to explain the behaviour of physical objects in terms of general mathematical laws that generate predictions confirmed or falsified by experimentally controllable observations. Philosophy is not about predictions, experiments or conclusive confirmations but about the meaning

96

of the terms we use and the different sorts of things we talk about and refer to. Thus, a philosopher might ask whether scientific explanation is the only sort of explanation. Historical 'explanations' refer to general behaviour patterns, common human desires and intentions. But they must always remain disputable, imprecise and about events that are unrepeatable in principle.

Just as there is historical explanation, so there is religious explanation. Religious believers do not seek to experiment on God or observe God under controlled conditions, but worship God in a quasi-personal relation, where non-physical reality is expressed in some way in the physical universe. Does God explain the universe or anything in it? Theists think that God explains the existence of the universe by generating intelligent agents as companions of the Creator. This is an explanation, but one without laws, and it makes no predictions about what precisely God might do. It is an axiological explanation, in terms of values for the sake of which the universe exists.

Typically, religious believers do not believe because they have a better scientific explanation of the world than atheists, rather because they feel a sense of awe and gratitude at the wonder of nature, or of personal inadequacy or ineffectiveness, and are searching for a meaning and a sense to their lives. Religious belief often begins with a sense of personal inadequacy, a dream of a moral ideal and a desire for personal liberation from hatred, greed and ignorance; it does not attempt to explain the world's physical structure. Modern materialism does not accept the possibility of axiological explanation but sees existential self-understanding as mere subjective narcissism; all true understanding must lie in a dispassionate experimental attitude to the world. It is not surprising, then, that materialists systematically misunderstand religion.

Understanding religion

When Grayling gives the explanation of thunder as a god walking on the clouds as an example of religion as proto-science, he has completely missed the point. In fact, nothing is certain about early religion, as anthropologist Evans-Pritchard highlights in his

Theories of Primitive Religion (1965). What sort of magic insight do people like Grayling have that enables them to know, without any evidence, that early humans thought gods walked on the clouds? No doubt there were early attempts to explain the occurrence of thunder; but why should anyone think that such attempts formed part of 'religion'? Anthropologists are wary of attempts to separate out religion as a distinct identifiable aspect of early cultural life. In the first written accounts of so-called proto-religion in Babylonia, we find cultic rituals of sacrifice and prayers to gods in which we may see the first historically ascertainable beginnings of religion.

It is only by heroic special pleading that we would call sacrifice and prayer 'proto-scientific'. Such activities, after all, still exist, and it seems fairly evident that singing hymns, genuflecting before holy objects and fasting or meditating are not done by scientists in their professional capacities. Religious activities seem not to be concerned with what Peter Strawson called 'objective attitudes' (Strawson, 1974). Religious acts are more concerned with 'reactive attitudes', involving some sort of self-discipline intended to establish a positive relation to quasi-personal and non-physical (spiritual) entities or their material symbols. Why hold, without evidence, that early humans sacrificed to encourage a god not to walk on the clouds, when contemporary religious believers would not describe their cultic activities like that? The sacrifice of the Mass, for example, expresses worship of a spiritual entity of supreme beauty, confession of one's own moral failures, prayer for forgiveness and reconciliation with God and for the well-being of others. To see it as a bribe to get a god to do what you want is to pervert what believers think. And why could that not be what religious believers have always thought?

The crucial question, therefore, is whether there is a spiritual reality of supreme value to which humans might consciously relate. This is not the place to answer that question. What is relevant is that this is not a question of whether a god is needed to explain various puzzling events like thunder. But if religious activity is distinct from scientific activity today, why could it not have been so in proto-human times? And why, anyway, should what proto-humans did and thought help to explain what religion is today, any more than a study of Babylonian astrology can help to explain what astronomy is today?

Basic ontological commitments

This determination not to understand the nature of a religious explanation is deeply puzzling. Suppose I said that Plato's idea of the Good was an attempt to explain why thunder occurred. I hope you would say that I had made a category mistake. I would have mistaken an ultimate ontological postulate for a specific scientific explanation. Plato said that moral truths are objective, and that this world of appearances is founded on a deeper spiritual and intelligible reality. If he is wrong, his mistake is not in physics or chemistry but in his commitment to the ontological priority of intelligible and moral truth. Such is the basic commitment of most major religions. They add to it specific ways of consciously relating to that ultimate truth partly in terms of symbols taken from the physical world. But the relation of such a postulate and commitment to the basic postulates and methods of scientific explanations is very indirect.

Idealism and materialism

One of the great philosophical disputes is that of idealism versus materialism. Materialist biologists do not usually consider the arguments that most philosophers have brought against materialism. It is difficult to give a rigorous and comprehensive definition of materialism, but typically materialists believe that everything that exists has a place in space and time, that existent realities are made of material elements, and that there is nothing else that really exists.

Hard materialists think that this is a necessary truth. Nothing *could* exist that is not locatable in space–time. It is impossible, however, to think of any reason why this should be a necessary truth. It is certainly not self-contradictory to say that some reality exists beyond space–time. Indeed, most modern cosmologists talk about this space–time originating from quantum fluctuations

KEITH WARD

in a vacuum. For that reason some materialists prefer the term 'naturalism'. But it still seems unjustifiable to deny that there are or could be any entities or realities that do not fall under the definition of naturalism, whatever naturalism is.

It is more reasonable to espouse contingent or soft materialism, which concedes that there *might* be non-material realities but says that as a matter of fact there are none. Such universal negatives are virtually impossible to establish. We might therefore say that at least we have no positive evidence that there are non-material objects.

What could such evidence be? If by definition we confine evidence to that of the senses, and if we define the senses as giving nothing but immediate apprehension of spatio-temporal particulars, then there could be no possible evidence for the existence of non-material objects. The irony of this position is that there could be no possible evidence for the existence of objectively existing material objects either. Modern science knows that material objects when unperceived by us are nothing like the objects of our immediate experience.

John Locke pointed out that our phenomenal awareness of colours is not of objects that possess those properties but is caused by a set of electromagnetic waves to which the cones of human eyes are sensitive. The lesson is clear: what we are immediately conscious of is not the world as it actually is apart from human consciousness but as it appears to us with our organs of perception and our form of consciousness. The world in its appearance to human consciousness is not the world as it is in itself. Materialism, therefore, is not based on direct evidence of the senses but on argument, not immediate and unreflective experience.

There is no question that physical theories have to be testable by experiment, though in some cases it may be very difficult even to think of experiments that would be conclusive. Without a sophisticated theory to guide our observations we would have no hope of understanding modern physics. Evidence, in fundamental physics, is not a matter of just looking, seeing and recording but of devising a mathematical model that will produce predictable observations under closely controlled conditions that have been artificially constructed with the aid of the model itself. This presupposes that the cosmos is intelligible, mathematically structured, and that the human mind can comprehend such structures by intellectual effort, coupled with carefully devised experimental observation. Ironically, therefore, scientifically informed materialism is committed to a strict form of supernaturalism. If the 'natural' is all that exists in space–time, then whatever exists beyond space–time is supernatural. Yet scientific materialism postulates a supremely elegant and intelligible mathematically structured realm from which many space–times may and possibly do arise and which is knowable by the creative activity of the intellect, not directly, much less solely, through the senses.

Materialism, then, is much more akin to supernaturalist theism than it is to common-sense empiricism. The evidence for a supernatural reality is that the natural realm apprehended by our human senses is revealed by scientific investigation and by the nature of scientific method as only an appearance of a mathematically describable reality – a supernatural reality – beyond it.

The supernatural

I would expect many scientists to be shocked by this statement, as they systematically confuse the 'supernatural' with the 'superstitious'. They think that religious people postulate the existence of things like fairies and ghosts, whimsical and unreasonable causes of events and violations of physical laws. But any half-competent theologian knows that God is not material at all and has no location in space–time. Moreover, if there is a God, God is wise or reasonable, not whimsical and subject to arbitrary impulses, and is thus more likely to create a universe of intelligible law than of unpredictable surprises. If there are miracles, they are events not wholly explicable by laws of physics, but disclosive of a deeper non-physical reality. It is not at all absurd to think there may be such events. Indeed, it seems sheer dogmatic presumption to think that all events whatsoever and everywhere must fall under some regular law of physics. My own view is that this dogma is almost certainly false and no less extreme or weird than the postulate that there is an ultimate cosmic mind, which has created the laws of nature and is capable of acting in ways that the laws of nature alone do not fully explain.

Materialist biologists do not usually pay close attention to theological tradition. If they did, they would see that the supernatural of which Christians speak is a wholly intelligible realm accessible, to some extent, by the human intellect and which underlies and somehow accounts for the natural realm that we observe with our senses. So God belongs to the same type of being as the quantum vacuum. It is therefore wholly mistaken to say, as Nigel Franks does in his article 'Convergent Evolution, Serendipity, and Intelligence for the Simple-Minded', that 'science has nothing to say directly about worldviews that postulate the supernatural' (Franks, 2008, p. 124). It is precisely science at its most materialist that postulates a supernatural basis of the natural world. Yes, but this scientific supernatural has no purpose, intelligence or consciousness. This, of course, points to the central distinction between materialism and idealism as I call it, and means that consciousness is a basic and irreducible element of reality and source of the physical cosmos. Consciousness does not emerge from the physical as an unexpected and unpredictable new sort of reality; the physical emerges from consciousness as an expression or appearance of its nature and purpose.

Contemporary science generally is not about consciousness but deals with the purely physical nature of things. If we suppose that the supernatural origin of our space–time has the nature of consciousness, we might then postulate that a logical space of all possible states of affairs exists as an eternal (supra-temporal) object of knowledge, within a unitary consciousness. However, we may prefer to think that a supra-temporal consciousness would contain, not every possible state but a set of generic archetypes, so that these states could be evaluated as desirable or undesirable and the cosmic mind could intend to realize some set of desirable states. Our space–time could originate through an intention to actualize a set of values that could only come to exist within our space–time. For this scenario, there would be foresight, value and purpose involved in the origin of space–time. The postulate is elegant and simple, since there is just one basic reality from which all things originate, and they do so for one basic reason.

So the cosmic mind has the sort of necessity that many physicists desire in any final theory of the cosmos containing all possible states where there is no change, succession, or pain or happiness. But the contemplation of them is itself blissful, comprising one unrestricted act of complete understanding. If goodness lies in the perfect comprehension of that which is intrinsically worthwhile, then God is supremely good, surveying all possibilities with passionless attention. There is no evil when there is no actual pain, frustration or destruction. So God is wholly good, without pain, frustration or destruction. Such a God would have the sort of value that provides the best possible reason for its own existence. There is also good reason for the actual existence of entities in time, which realize the possibility of creative change, action and relationship. New and distinctive sorts of goodness arise. For such a view, there is no ultimate chance or accident about the existence of the cosmos. It is founded on necessity and goodness.

But there could be an important place in such a rational cosmos for chance that may be a condition of the development of genuine creative and moral agency in created entities, as John Polkinghorne suggests in his *Science and Providence* (2005b, pp. 77–8). But this would be a restricted sort of chance existing within a general process directed to the existence of conscious intelligent beings.

The elegant efficiency of evolution

If this were true, what could we expect of the cosmos? We would expect to see in it an intelligible and efficient process that realizes many sorts of distinctive values. Is that what we do see? Materialists sometimes concede that is how it seems. First, as to the efficiency of the process: 'The complexity of living organisms is matched by the elegant efficiency of their apparent design', says Richard Dawkins (1986, p. xiii). Or again, 'We animals are the most complicated and perfectly designed pieces of machinery in the known universe' (1976, p. xi). Elegant efficiency is hardly a matter of luck but an elegant, efficient, and well organized design – though Professor Dawkins argues that this is only apparent, not real. This is a very long way from the *New Scientist* claim above that any designer of evolution would be lazy and stupid.

Proponents of blind chance rarely follow through on just how blind chance would be. David Hume was clearer: if chance rules the world, anything at all is possible. There is no reason why the laws of nature should still operate and be mathematically elegant and comprehensible by human minds. There is no reason why there should be any laws of nature at all. But there are laws: elegant and reliable laws that have generated complex organized forms of intelligent life. Out of the logical space of possible states of affairs, the laws of physics generate 'a process that is capable of picking its way through the tree of all conceivable animals, and finding just that minority of pathways that are viable' (Dawkins, 1986, p. 315). However improbable the process, Dawkins has tended to the view that sooner or later intelligent life is inevitable or at least that the constraints of the evolutionary landscape lay down a preferred evolutionary pathway towards intelligent life.

On the one hand, the trend towards intelligent life seems to be inherent in the basic structure of the natural world. On the other hand, there is a long chain of extremely improbable events that are needed for this trend to be actualized. Any hypothesis that reduces the improbability of the process must be a good one. An obvious hypothesis is that there is a direction in evolution – towards increasing consciousness and intelligence, understanding and creative freedom – and that events that would otherwise be extremely improbable are in fact made highly probable by the influence of the guiding intelligence that has set the general direction of the process. Dawkins is opposed to any such guiding intelligent influence. But it is clear that the hypothesis is not as superfluous as he claims. It vastly increases the probability that finite intelligence will come to exist in the universe. And it raises the probability that there can be veridical experience of the cosmic intelligence, in ways that that intelligence makes possible.

Dawkins protests that there is no scientific evidence for it. But the evidence is precisely that an efficient and elegant process does result in states of great value, enjoyed by intelligent agents. It is true, however, that this is not scientific evidence. It is not subject to experimental confirmation, and it does not issue in precise and quantifiable predictions, because it is evidence for something non-physical and not within the scope of physics. However, it is evidence that suggests the hypothesis of an intelligent creator, and that partially confirms this hypothesis.

How absolute are the laws of nature?

But it does not follow from the hypothesis either that the cosmic creator will intermittently intervene in the natural process or that its purposive influence will be detectible by observation. The language of 'intervention' belongs to a post-Newtonian philosophical worldview (which Newton did not share) that nature forms a closed and deterministic causal network; every event is determined to be what it is by a finite set of universal laws and a preceding physical state that entail only one possible outcome. Philosophers continue to debate this theory, but it is certainly not established by modern science. There are many contrary suggestions, including the Heisenberg Uncertainty Principle, which suggests that strict determinism is not a presupposition of good science, and quantum non-locality and entanglement, which imply that the laws of physics are not well-enough understood to enable us to claim that we can be certain of what all the laws of nature are. Determinism is a very dogmatic view, going well beyond the available evidence, and existing in some tension with many leading views of the nature of the laws of science.

If we take physical laws as prima facie principles of regularity that operate in relatively isolated conditions, then they are more like mathematical models for idealized situations, which do not fit the complex interfused patterns of the real world with perfect accuracy. As John Polkinghorne has put it, 'We have no compelling grounds for regarding current theories as being more than a form of approximation to actual physical reality as it is encountered in the limit of effective isolatability' (2005, p. 34). The laws of nature give us approximations to reality, not precise depictions of it. They model real situations in isolation from the many complex conditions that obtain in most of the actual world. And they model reality as we encounter it, rather than as it may be in itself.

Thus, there may be many sorts of influence at work in the cosmos of which we are unaware, or that cannot be captured by our equations in precise form, or that do not operate in complete general, predictable, law-like ways.

If there are any personal influences in the universe, they are unlikely to be completely general or law-like, since they will express unique intentions in complex and unrepeatable situations. If there is a personal ground of the cosmos, its influence on the cosmos will be personal, not nomological (that is law-like). Such influence will not be capturable by any set of quantifiable regularities. But this does not mean that such influence could not exist. If there is a cosmic mind that intends the cosmos to produce intelligent agents, then physical processes will be shaped so that they realize that intention. But the shaping need not consist in discrete and occasional violations of causal laws. It may be a more continuous and not precisely measurable influence on a physical system as a whole.

From this it follows that there will not be unambiguous evidence of particular divine actions but evidence of general purposive influence. Even though such evidence will always be ambiguous and susceptible of diverse interpretations, that does not mean it is not real. But where a cosmic mind and its intentions are not, even in principle, observable, it is rather unlikely that anyone could unambiguously identify precise and discrete events that could prove the existence of such a mind.

Creationism, intelligent design and creation

Many scientists unfortunately fail to distinguish between general purposive influence and discrete and unambiguously identifiable events or objects that require reference to an intelligent designer. Confusion is further compounded when critics talk about 'intelligent design creationism'. The term creationism is better reserved for literal readings of Genesis 1. There are two forms of creationism. The young-Earth theory is that the six days were short periods of time, so that the Earth is less than ten thousand years old. The old-Earth theory is that the 'days' could be long periods of time, even millions of years. But what makes these views 'creationist' is that in both cases God created each species *de novo*, and humans did not evolve from some other species.

Intelligent design theorists are not creationists, and most of them accept the descent of all organic life, including humans, from some original simple life forms. ID theorists like Michael Behe accept evolution, but hold that some organisms cannot be explained in terms just of random mutation and natural selection; there are specific evidences of an intelligent designer in nature (Behe, 2007). Debate in the USA has raged around whether intelligent design is a properly scientific theory. ID criticizes the neo-Darwinian synthesis by pointing to evidence that, its proponents say, Darwinians cannot explain. This part of the ID case is, in principle, scientific. But it has not found much favour with biologists, who point out that 'irreducibly complex' systems may emerge by the opportunistic combination of parts developed for different purposes, rather than being assembled all at once in isolation.

The real problem is that ID theory does not propose a scientific hypothesis in its place. God is not a scientific hypothesis. God is not a physical entity that can be measured or experimented upon or that operates according to regular physical laws. So God seems to lie outside of present, and probably of any future, science. If a scientific explanation is one that accounts for the occurrence of specific events by pointing to general regularities and prior physical conditions, and that can give rise to confirmable predictions, then there cannot be a scientific explanation of any acts of God, who is not a prior physical condition, who does not act in accordance with general and impersonal laws, and whose actions cannot be predicted. Any explanation of an act of God would have to be in terms of purpose that exists in an evaluating consciousness not accessible to humans. Physical science does not deal with private consciousness and purposes. Such purposes are extremely difficult to identify even in the case of ordinary human actions. Where the agent is not identifiable, it will be even more difficult to be sure whether there is a purpose in a specific set of events, and what it is.

Probably, the best we can do is to identify events that look as if they could be purposive and attempt to place them within a general pattern of purposive activity that looks as if it is directed to some overall goal. The history of religion is littered with failed attempts to make such identifications, just as the history of science is littered with failed attempts to explain occurrences in terms of basic physical elements and laws. Does this mean that there cannot be a God, or that a God could not have a causal influence on physical events? No, not unless the only sorts of entities that can exist are physical entities, and science can give a complete account, in principle, of all causal influences by referring only to physical entities and the laws of their relationship. Neither of these premises belongs to science, for the simple reason that the premises do not account for occurrences in terms of general regularities and prior physical conditions.

Philosophical statements about reality do refer to observations and to empirical knowledge. But they are not observational or empirical statements; they are meta-statements about the nature, the proper interpretation, the implications and presuppositions of the statements people make in the sciences, as well as in morality, art, religion and politics. Thus, a philosopher might ask whether there are any non-physical causes. No experiments will be carried out, or precise measurements recorded, or specific predictions made. There are no philosophy laboratories. Instead, there are philosophical armchairs, in which philosophers sit and think.

So ID seems to be a combination of a scientific claim – that Darwinian explanations are insufficient – and a non-scientific claim – that specific empirical occurrences require reference to an intelligent designer. There are thus two interesting questions at stake. Are Darwinian explanations of evolution sufficient? And is there, or could there be, scientific and convincing evidence for specific and identifiable acts of an intelligent designer?

Most biologists would affirm that Darwinian explanations are quite sufficient. But the issue is not closed. Proposals like Stuart Kaufmann's hypothesis of a principle of complex self-organization are not absurd, and there may be other possibilities yet to emerge (Kaufmann, 1995). But it is not good enough to say that since the Darwinian synthesis has not yet fully explained every biological fact, it never will; equally, it is not good enough to say that we absolutely know that purely Darwinian explanations are comprehensive and complete. Evolution is a fact. Random mutation and natural selection are major driving forces of evolution, and most biologists think they are all we will ever need. But whether they are in fact the only ones, we are not yet in a position to say.

The trouble with the ID view is that it will only appeal to those who think there is an unembodied mind, a God, or that such a thing is possible. A cautious ID theorist would not say that the bacterial flagellum proves a designer. But it is so complex and amazing, so improbable and composed of such highly co-ordinated parts, that it *could* be designed, even if indirectly. If there is a designer, at this point the divine hand, if not the divine foot, could be discerned by believers. This would be beyond scientific proof, but it could be evidence, for a believer, of the hand of God at work. And would believers not be rational to expect some such evidence, somewhere?

Materialists often show a complete inability to empathize with idealists, or to try to see how they would expect to see the world, however hypothetically. 'We do not need that hypothesis', materialists might say. Well, the ID theorist might not *need* it either. But a theist might have it already, for instance on the basis of personal experience or of revelation. And in that case some evidence could help to confirm the hypothesis, by showing signs of organized complexity that look very like design. In the same way, of course, some evidence could help to disconfirm it. It would show a remarkable prejudice to accept evidence against design, while disallowing any evidence in favour of it. It is fairly clear that suffering and inefficiency in evolution is evidence against design, and that efficiency and highly improbable organized complexity is evidence in favour of it. If so, the issue is not absolutely convincing, either way.

Acts of God

Could there be better empirical evidence for God? Some materialists seem to assume that if there is a God, it would have to be one that performs physical acts. But why? An alternative hypothesis is that God does not wish to make the divine existence unmistakably clear and does not wish to perform many public and unambiguous physically inexplicable acts. Most religions promulgate reports of physically inexplicable acts – miracles – that confirm belief. But miracles are very rare, almost never unambiguous, and are not powerful enough to convince everyone. The resurrection of Jesus, for example, was not seen by everyone in Jerusalem, was very ambiguous, only happened once in the whole of human history and was only reported by a small group of close disciples, in accounts that vary in detail.

If the standards of scientific evidence are applied – repeatability, testability, observation under controlled conditions – the resurrection does not do very well. But if one thinks that life after death is possible, that Jesus may have been the Messiah, that some visions are veridical and that the disciples were trustworthy and reliable, then one may take the resurrection to be a set of veridical visionary appearances of Jesus to a group of those who were partly prepared for and open to such visions. This is confirmation. But it is not public (open to all), for the sake of proving something beyond reasonable doubt and testable by dispassionate and detached observation. Thus the root question is: are there personal experiences, only open to some people, which provide visionary apprehensions of a non-physical reality?

The nature of God

This opens the way to a different view of God – one that is the inner nature of the universe itself, as universal mind. Mind is the nature of reality, but that nature is hidden from finite beings who turn away from it towards the material world of desire, self-interest and attachment. The laws of the universe are the laws of the self-expression of universal mind. God, it would be held on such a view, has no need to prove the divine existence. God may desire that humans become aware of the true nature of reality as the result of a disciplined ascent from illusion and attachment towards an ego-transcending and all-pervasive Spirit. Dispassionate knowledge of God (of the true nature of reality) is not possible by any science that limits itself to the physical. It comes from a development of personal vision and insight.

Knowledge of the spiritual nature of reality is not knowledge of an additional entity beyond the universe. It is insight into the true nature of the universe itself and the result of a journey of self-discovery. God does not need to be proved. That is why it cannot be scientifically demonstrated that there is a God, that reality is spiritual in nature. We can ask if there are signs of purpose, value and awareness in the universe; but in doing so we will be going beyond the self-erected boundaries of natural science. That is why the ID proposal offends many scientists – it challenges their ultimate worldview, and tries to import into science all that has been specifically excluded from it since the sixteenth century.

I have argued that the general process of evolution can be seen as evidence for an intelligent creator, though I concede that many, perhaps most, biologists do not agree, largely because they hold a materialist worldview that does not allow the possibility of a conscious supernatural reality. I have also shown that many biologists argue that Darwinian evolution eliminates the possibility of an intelligent designer, holding that any such designer would be lazy, stupid and cruel. But that is only true if we think of a designer directly designing every organism as perfect. As I have stressed, the ID view is not creationist, and sees evolution in terms of mutation, trial and error, and natural selection. The designer of such a process would be extremely intelligent, since the process is both efficient and guaranteed to reach goals of great value.

The basic laws and processes of nature are remarkably, indeed perhaps uniquely, well-formed for the arising of conscious intelligent agency by a process of cumulative and progressive development from a primal and relatively simple material origin. That is one vital element of a design-explanation.

Values

But what of the values it produces? Are they really worthwhile? In Richard Dawkins' words, 'Evolution is an amazing, sublime, reverence-inspiring process, of great beauty and elegance' (Dawkins: 2005). This seems to be supremely worthwhile. And the particular values of this world could not exist at all in a world without risk, pain, conflict or frustration.

There could, after all, be an intelligence who wanted to create the kinds of value that could only exist in a universe that contained some suffering and the ineliminable possibility of much more suffering under specific conditions. Perhaps the creator necessarily expresses itself by creating such a world. We need to escape the naïve picture of a supernatural person who could create a perfect world but chooses not to, and consider instead of a cosmic mind that by its own innermost nature expresses itself in relation to a community of personal beings, who are morally free, capable of self-development through disciplined action, uniquely creative, cumulatively complex, socially related and oriented towards the ideals of beauty, goodness and truth. The existence of such beings could reasonably be considered to be intrinsically worthwhile. But they can only exist in a universe the structure of which permits creative and cooperative action. That entails that the physical laws are flexible and open enough to allow alternative possibilities of action, and forms of holistic causality that enable complex organized physical structures (like brains) to exercise causal influence on their less complex constituent physical elements.

In such a universe, chance would play an important part, as the necessary basis for emergent creativity and personal agency. Such a world would contain the possibility of conflict, evil and frustration of the divine intention. But in such a world, God could also work patiently to attract persons by love towards the goal of a creative and harmonious community, devoted to goodness and beauty and friendship. God creates such a cosmos and seeks to move it towards conscious communion with that perfect Beauty beyond all finite worlds. In this process, values are realized that could exist in no other world. The nutshell response to the very real problem of suffering and evil is that we humans could only exist as the sort of emergent, creative, social and self-shaping beings we are, in a universe like this in its general features. If we are to exist, this universe, in its general structure, is necessarily the way it is.

Evolution teaches us that we are integral parts of a developing cosmos, and that we could have been born in no other universe.

So it certainly looks purposive. But it contains much suffering, conflict and destruction, and that certainly leads one to question whether a good and intelligent creator could be responsible for such a process. I think the only possible response is to say that these things are necessary to the sort of universe in which alone we could exist. That would enable us to affirm that all things work together for good and that the creation is indeed very good. I would not expect evolutionary biologists to accept that on the evidence of biology alone. But I would expect them to allow that there might be other sorts of evidence and argument about the ultimate nature of reality, about the objectivity of consciousness and value, and about the possibility of revelation.

If evolutionary biology does indeed rest on a presupposition of materialism, and if it encourages ill-considered and prejudicial remarks about religious beliefs, then it should not be taught in schools. What that shows is the urgent necessity for some clear distinctions to be made and for some hard thinking to be done about the way in which ideological presuppositions can be built into what is called pure science in a most misleading way. And the culprits in this case are not ID theorists. The time for a more serious and penetrating discussion has come.

7

The Legacy of Robert Boyle Then and Now

JOHN HEDLEY BROOKE

Late in the seventeenth century, in the church of St Mary-le-Bow, a sermon was preached on the folly of atheism. It was an unusual lecture, because the congregation heard how the denial of a God was at odds with the latest science. The orator was a fine scholar and sure of his facts. The design of the universe had to be ascribed to divine wisdom. Who was this confident apologist? His initials were RB. His name: Richard Bentley.

A classics scholar, Bentley gave the first of a long and distinguished series of what came to be known as the Boyle Lectures. They owe their name to the fact that one of England's greatest scientists provided the legacy that made them possible. In his will, Robert Boyle bequeathed the sum of £50 per annum 'for ever, or at least for a considerable number of years'. The lecturers would have as their brief: to prove the Christian religion 'against notorious Infidels, viz. Atheists, Theists, Pagans, Jews, and Mahometans'. And as a rider, to which we shall return, he added that they were not to descend to 'any controversies ... among Christians themselves'. Boyle's philanthropy was not just a post-mortem gesture. In a life dedicated to conciliation between science and Christianity, he had financed translations of the New Testament into exotic languages and funded numerous foreign missions. So who was this figure, without whom we would not be gathered here?

Who was Boyle?

Young Robert had been born into one of the most elevated aristo-
cratic families in England. He was the youngest son of Richard
Boyle, Earl of Cork and Lord High Treasurer of Ireland before
the English Civil War. Robert may have been surprised to find
that he had been born at all. He was the fourteenth of 15 children.
His education included three years at Eton and was extended by
foreign travel in the company of a private tutor. He would learn
Italian in order to read the works of Galileo, and it was while
abroad that he read meaning into a violent thunderstorm. He saw,
as it were in a flash, that he was ill-prepared for the Day of Judgement. His religious conversion did not kill his curiosity, and it has
been said of his time in Italy and France that he was repelled, but
also fascinated, by Roman Catholic religious practices that he had
been taught to see as superstitious. He never lost interest in stories
relayed to him about the paranormal and the supernatural.

A reversal in the family fortune as a consequence of the Civil
War and Irish Rebellion was itself gradually reversed. From 1645
to 1655, Boyle lived on the family estate at Stalbridge in Dorset.
As Michael Hunter has pointed out, there were features of aris-
tocratic society that, to the studious, were less than congenial. In
Boyle's own words, how easy it was to 'squander away a whole
afternoone in tatling of this Ladys Face & tother Lady's Clothes;
of this Lords being Drunke & that Lord's Clap; in telling how
this Gentleman's horse outrun that other's Mare' (Hunter, 1999,
p. 261). If Boyle had already had his religious conversion, his conversion to science came during his Stalbridge years. By 1649, he
had set up a chemical laboratory where he subjected chemical
substances to analysis by fire. A fume-filled chemistry lab is not
everyone's vision of heaven, but for Boyle it almost was. To his
sister he wrote: '*Vulcan* has so transported and bewitched me,
that I fancy my laboratory a kind of *Elysium*' (Hunter, 1999,
p. 262). In 1655, he moved to Oxford, where he was welcomed
in the scientific circle that gathered around John Wilkins, Warden
of Wadham College.

Wilkins played a leading role in the establishment of the
Royal Society, which was founded in 1660 after a lecture by Sir

Christopher Wren at Gresham College. Boyle played his part, attending its meetings, serving on the Council, proposing new members and occasionally donating apparatus. This was necessary because, in its early years, it was a Society with a Royal Charter but without royal cash. In 1668, he moved from Oxford to London, where he lived with his sister Katherine for the rest of his life, never marrying.

Those who have studied Boyle in depth invariably refer to the strength of his religious convictions. Why, despite encouragement, did he decline the Anglican priesthood? He had a thoughtful answer to that question. His defence of Christianity and of its harmony with science would be more effective if he remained a layman. To write as a clergyman would have risked the cynical retort that 'He would say that wouldn't he?' Boyle was content, in his own words, to be a 'priest in the temple of nature'.

In the world of science, Boyle enjoys the reputation of a progressive, as the proponent of a mechanical philosophy of nature that challenged Aristotelian accounts of why substances have the properties they do. The title of his book *The Sceptical Chymist* has suggested to the unwary that he must have cleansed chemistry of its alchemical pretensions. But he is best known for the discovery of a law with his name on it – the inverse relationship between the pressure and volume of an ideal gas at constant temperature.

There are, however, problems with each of these pictures. Boyle's Law was never formulated as a law by Boyle. He simply tabulated pressure readings and the volume readings with which they were correlated. He was much less interested in *ideal* gases than in real ones. He did explain chemical reactions mechanically by supposing that hierarchies of particles or 'corpuscles' of matter were broken down and reassembled in different ways. Why is an acid an acid? The Aristotelian might say: 'because it has the form of acidity'. Boyle was not alone among seventeenth-century chemists in wanting more than this. It might rather be that the constituent particles of an acid were in particular states of motion or had sharp edges that would account for their potency. Swill an acid around your mouth and you can feel the little daggers in your tongue – not an experiment I particularly recommend! But it is easy to exaggerate the scope Boyle gave to his mechanical explanations. His universe contained many non-material items, of which the human mind was a primary example. He tells us that he *was* long distrustful of stories about the philosopher's stone; but increasingly he became what Larry Principe describes as an 'aspiring adept' (Principe, 1998). His scepticism in *The Sceptical Chymist* was not directed against the possibility of metallic trans-mutations but against prevailing methods of fire analysis that purported to reveal the true elements of bodies.

There *were* chemical adepts who abandoned their alchemical dreams. Boyle kept a more open mind. He even believed that if the philosopher's stone could be found it might have the property of attracting spirits, hopefully angelic rather than demonic. And that would meet another of his lifelong concerns: the refutation of atheism. He worried about the probity of experiments that might compromise his piety; but as he once wrote, it required only one properly authenticated relation of a supernatural phenomenon to defeat the atheist. When one of the characters in a dialogue composed by Boyle suggests that '[t]is not likely that air and fluid parts of the world should be destitute of spirits', adding that '[t]is not likely that there should be so few spirits or so few orders of them as is commonly presumed', we are taken back to a world we have lost (Principe, 1998, p. 310). And if the past to which Boyle belonged is such a foreign country, is there any point in resurrecting him? Is it even meaningful to ask whether he left an intellectual legacy that might be of any relevance today?

Deterrents to the resurrection of Boyle

Discontinuities between Boyle's time and ours are of course legion. The world we have lost was one in which scientific truths might still be authenticated in Scripture. Boyle's contemporary Henry More declared Moses to have been the first atomist. There are echoes of such an outlook today in some Muslim attempts to authenticate the Qur'an from its supposedly scientific presci-ence. But this is not a strategy approved by discerning Muslim scientists.

Boyle's world was a world only just dislodged from the centre

of the universe, John Wilkins having championed the Coperni-
can system in England. It was a world that by our standards was
still young, no more than a few thousand years old. Humans had
been on the Earth from the beginning and references to a created
world were to one in which God's creatures had been preserved
in their original form. The spectre of mass extinctions was far in
the future and public debates over Darwinian evolution still some
200 years hence. And because Darwin's science was to threaten
the design argument in its seventeenth-century formulations, we
cannot ignore Richard Dawkins' well-known objection that any
philosophy of nature constructed before Darwin will be worth-
less.

Boyle was a creature of his time, and we saw this in the chau-
vinism inscribed in his will. You will have noticed that Muslims
and Jews are aligned with atheists, and even plain theists, as
opponents. It is not my aim to abstract a sanitized Boyle from
the scientific and religious worlds he occupied. His assumption,
for example, that matter is entirely passive and amenable to
immaterial influences contrasts with modern images of active,
self-organizing matter. His clockwork universe, elaborated in its
more familiar Newtonian form, has not survived the revolutions
in twentieth-century physics. But there are certain parallels with
our own time that bear investigation.

We often hear today about a 'new atheism', for which Dawkins
is the best-known proselyte. There was a new atheism in Boyle's
day, typified by a renaissance of the atomic philosophy of Epi-
curus and Lucretius. We face a threat from the zeal of religious
fundamentalists. Boyle had to contend with their equivalents in
mid-seventeenth-century England – Protestant zealots with their
hot lines to God. To Boyle's annoyance, they were giving the
false impression that Christianity and philosophy were incompatible. Despite the far higher profile that a culture of science and
technology enjoys today, we often hear of a public suspicion of
scientific authority. It is a suspicion not so dissimilar to that faced
by Boyle and his contemporaries, who had to make the foundational case for the utility of science.

There are other parallels. Standard neo-Darwinian mechanisms
for evolution do constitute a difficulty for those seeking a provi-

dential God having recognizable purposes in the world. But ends, goals, final causes, purposes in nature were already under threat when Boyle took up his pen. And this from two different directions: from the Epicurean vision that the world is the chance product of atomic collisions; but also from the philosophy of Descartes. I am always reminded here of the student who revealed in his essay that Descartes was a Cartesian! The challenge came from Descartes's insistence, ostensibly on theological grounds, that it is presumptuous to imagine we can discern God's purposes in nature. We shall see later how Boyle rose to this dual challenge. He deserves a hearing because he illustrates a point that the modern world sometimes forgets – that it was possible to find in Christian theology resources to promote, to legitimate and in some instances motivate an intensive study of nature. If Boyle contributed to an *enduring* scientific movement, then there is a sense in which his legacy has been enduring. Michael Hunter, who has written so authoritatively on Boyle, declares that it is 'not an exaggeration to describe Boyle as the founder of experimental science in the modern sense' (1999, p. 263). And if Hunter is right, as I believe he is, in seeing 'great profundity' in Boyle's reflections on the relationship of science to religion, then we should not be stalled by deterrents.

Boyle and the promotion of experimental science

It is sometimes said that without Christianity there would have been no modern science. A doctrine of Creation provided the grounds for believing that nature was ordered and intelligible and that the human mind had a God-given capacity to understand it. The more we have learnt of scientific practices in other cultures, especially the achievements of the medieval Islamic world, the more difficult it is to argue for an exclusively Christian impetus. But there remains a question, recently addressed by Peter Harrison and Stephen Gaukroger: Why was it only in the West that an enduring scientific culture was established? Other cultures had their science but the pattern was 'boom and bust' (Gaukroger, 2006). By contrast, the scientific movement in seventeenth-century

Europe gained a momentum that proved unstoppable. The reasons are many and complex, but they include the fact that within the Judeo-Christian tradition there were resources for legitimating a humble, experimental science. Francis Bacon had tapped some of these earlier in the seventeenth century. In Boyle, we have a window on how Christianity and scientific virtuosity were fused together.

Like Bacon before him, Boyle spoke of God as the author of two books: the Bible and the book of his works. As there was a duty to study the Scriptures, so there was a duty to study the Book of Nature. Since the two books had the same author, they could not conflict. Knowledge gleaned from nature might assist the interpretation of Scripture, as Galileo had argued. Boyle underlined the same point: 'God has made some knowledge of his created book, both conducive to belief, and necessary to the understanding of his written one' (Harrison, 1998, p. 136).

Today we take experimental methods in science for granted. In Boyle's day, they were problematic. One could argue that it was less arrogant to investigate the world empirically than to take one's authority from Aristotle or to philosophize in an armchair. But there were at least three problems. If someone came along claiming they had performed an experiment that exploded a prevailing view, why should you believe him, why should you believe his experiment had been well designed and properly conducted, and why should you believe his interpretation of the data? It helped, of course, if the experimenter were a trustworthy gentleman, an advantage that a refined Robert Boyle certainly had. This means that there was a moral and social dimension to the corroboration of scientific knowledge. Credible witnesses to an experiment were not always available, but when they were they were a godsend. It was a complicated matter, because automatically to reject reports of strange natural phenomena ran the risk of encouraging a mindset in which witnesses to the biblical miracles might be impugned.

When Boyle commended an experimental philosophy, it was not a philosophy based simply on observation. As Bacon had recognized, one had to intervene in nature to extract her secrets. Boyle's experiments in chemistry show how he helped to consolidate the Baconian programme. For example, through an elaborate sequence of operations, he not only decomposed saltpetre but also managed to recompose it. So what? – you might think. In fact, his experiment was a significant moment in the long history of differentiating nature from art. It was conventionally supposed that a product found in nature owed its integrity to a homogeneous 'form' that could not be replicated artificially. In Boyle's mechanical chemistry, it could be. And I use the word 'mechanical' deliberately, because there was a far wider sense in which the distinction between nature and art was breaking down in seventeenth-century science. When the universe was compared to a machine, there was a sense in which nature became an artefact, the work of a divine craftsman. All things are artificial, wrote one contemporary, because 'nature itself is nothing but the art of God' (Brooke and Cantor, 1998, p. 323).

Now we can perhaps begin to see how Boyle could present himself as a Christian virtuoso. One of his favourite moves was to compare the universe with the cathedral clock in Strasbourg. The analogy might have its problems. How could God act in a universe that ran like clockwork? But for Boyle the analogy played a powerful heuristic role. It created the space for both science and religion. The task of the scientist was to investigate the machinery of nature, the cogs, the wheels and the springs. He would speak of the 'spring' of the air and even suggested it might be made of microscopic springs that accounted for its greater pressure when compressed. But the clockwork analogies also left room for religious belief because clocks, after all, are made for a purpose. Machines do not spring into existence by themselves. And it was not merely that room was left for religious belief. The exquisite machinery to be found in creation positively required it. The construction of the human eye, for example, was a work of such delicate craftsmanship that it testified to divine wisdom.

The connections that Boyle made between his Christianity and his science are manifold and intimate. As he set the parameters for a science-based natural theology, he argued that it was the accomplished natural philosopher who was in the best position to appreciate God's workmanship. One had to pry into the recesses of nature to fully appreciate divine wisdom, and that in turn required a competence in anatomy, optics, mechanics and chemistry

(Goodman, 1973, p. 126). Chemistry in particular helped to realize the Baconian dream. It offered the prospect of improving the world and of restoring a dominion over nature lost at the Fall. There was the seductive promise of a better world if scientific knowledge were applied to the relief of man's estate. There is a sense in which Boyle personifies the application of chemistry to medicine. He had his own chemical cordials, which he trusted more than any physician. Indeed, it was reported that when he woke each morning, he would consult his ceiling compass to see from which direction the wind was coming and then take the appropriate antidote. So, observed Roger North, if the wind were often to change direction, Mr Boyle was wont to become drunk (Hall, 1958, pp. 18–19).

Boyle and the revival of natural theology

Claims are sometimes made today for a revival of natural theology. By revisiting Boyle, we can see some of the reasons why arguments from nature to God have had a recurring appeal. Boyle never believed that a rational theology could be free-standing. Scripture had a crucial role in revealing a God with intentions for humanity, one of which was that we *should* have responsibility for and dominion over nature (Goodman, 1973, pp. 116–17). In Boyle, there was an interweaving of natural and revealed theology. But as we have just seen, one of his objectives was to sanctify the sciences against religious suspicion.

There were clearly other pressures to which Boyle responded and which have their modern equivalents. One was the threat to Christianity from internal divisions. In the late 1640s, the proliferation of Puritan sects was such that Boyle counted 'no less than 200 several opinions on points of religion' (Rattansi, 1972, p. 21). The problem was that dispute brought disrepute. To come to London, Boyle warned, was to come nigh to losing one's faith. I am told this may still be the case. Boyle developed a double strategy to meet the threat. He stressed that in Christian doctrines, such as the Trinity, there were elements that were 'above reason'. To dogmatize about so incomprehensible a matter as the nature of

God was therefore inappropriate. But it also helped if one could restore a fundamental belief in the existence and wisdom of God. This might be accomplished through appeals to design in nature.

A quite different threat to Christianity came from the scoffers, immortalized in Restoration comedies. Let me remind you of a few titles: *The Merry Milkmaid of Islington, Love Lost in the Dark, The Politic Whore or the Conceited Cuckold*. These were encounters one might have when visiting what Boyle called this 'libertine city'. In 1675, a wonderful description was given of *The Character of a Town-Gallant*. Frequenting the coffee houses and pretending to know something of Thomas Hobbes, he would laugh at spirits and maintain that there are 'no Angels but those in petticoats' (Principe, 1998, p. 203). A practical as well as a cerebral atheism had to be addressed. Boyle resolutely wrote that only someone who had not studied nature could be an atheist. Even those of the meanest intellect, according to the great naturalist John Ray, could appreciate nature's marvels and their testimony to divine wisdom.

In his discerning work on the history of natural theology, Geoffrey Cantor, has stressed one of the key rhetorical functions of arguments grounded in nature: to reassure those whose faith might be wavering (Brooke and Cantor, 1998, pp. 196–7). Boyle again provides a perfect illustration. He wished to provide firmer grounds for belief, to prevent the faithful from falling by the wayside and to startle the irreligious out of their stupor.

If Boyle raised the profile of natural theology, it was for yet another reason. He was genuinely overawed by what science was revealing about the world. The revival of natural theology today has been inspired in part by the discovery of the anthropic coincidences and the claim that the universe appears to have been finely tuned for life (McGrath, 2009). The revelation in Boyle's day was of an entirely new world, visible only under the microscope. With a genuine sense of wonder, Boyle marvelled that God had been able to pack life into the minutest mite. The eye of a fly, famously depicted by Robert Hooke in his *Micrographia*, was for Boyle a 'more curious piece of workmanship than the body of the sun' (Goodman, 1973, p. 111). The gargantuan flea to be found in the *Micrographia* might evoke other feelings, but there were those who found a place for its bite in the economy of nature. For the poor, it provided a cheaper mode of bloodletting than an expensive visit to the doctor!

When responding to Descartes's censure of final causes, Boyle conceded that there were inanimate objects that did not testify to divine wisdom. He also conceded that many of God's purposes were likely to be beyond human grasp. But surely no reasonable person could deny that eyes had been made for the purpose of seeing? Other features of human anatomy, the valves in the veins for example, might once have appeared useless, but with William Harvey's discovery of the circulation of the blood, their purpose had become clear. Immediate objections are likely to occur to us. What of the diseases of the eye? For Boyle they served to demonstrate just how delicately the healthy eye had been crafted. This was no facile response. Boyle's own vision was impaired, and for much of his life he needed the help of an amanuensis. What about inherently imperfect eyes, of the mole for example? Not a problem: nature had designed moles to live underground. Boyle recognized many gradations of perfection in the eyes of other animals; but this only confirmed that his God favoured biodiversity.

The real problem of course is that in a post-Darwinian universe eyes are the product of evolution, not of contrivance. Surely we cannot pull Boyle through the Dawkins barrier? No – and yet. There is a partial resemblance between Darwin and Boyle. When Darwin defined what he meant by 'nature' it was this: 'the laws ordained by God to govern the universe' (Richards, 2009, p. 61). For Boyle, too, it was a more elevated understanding of God to suppose that the material world God had created and organized was now running according to 'laws' of motion. For Boyle, and most of his successors in the discourse of natural theology, you could not *have* 'laws' of nature without the existence of a Lawmaker. Boyle's God, Newton's too for that matter, could change the laws if he wished. Boyle was astute enough to realize that to speak of 'laws' at all was to use a figurative expression. Matter, after all, is not intelligent enough to know what a law is or how to obey one (Stewart, 1979, p. 181). Nevertheless, for both Boyle and the Darwin of the 1850s, the order of nature had been ordained by a deity. Science was possible for Boyle because the laws were upheld by God's sustaining power; for Darwin, because they were fixtures in an evolving universe. But even for Darwin the laws were not bereft of purpose: they had enabled the production of the higher animals, which he once described as the greatest good we can conceive (Richards, 2009).

I come now to the final section of this lecture, where I want to show that there *were* insights in Boyle's philosophy that bear scrutiny today – that there is a legacy.

Boyle's insights: then and now

As restorers of purpose and design to the universe, Boyle and his successors had their detractors. The eighteenth-century deist Anthony Collins famously observed that no one had doubted the existence of God until the Boyle Lecturers undertook to prove it. Collins had a point (Brooke and Cantor, 1998, p. 198). But it hardly applies to Boyle himself. His take on the issue of proof was more subtle. In a lengthy, unpublished manuscript on atheism, he devoted many pages to explaining why a demonstration of God's existence should not be expected (MacIntosh, 2005, pp. 70–170). For those with an open mind, a Creator God gave the best explanation of why there is a world at all and why it is ordered rather than chaotic. But inference to the best explanation was not the same as proof. Boyle's use of language is interesting here. Knowledge of nature could illustrate divine attributes, it might 'induce one to conclude' or 'persuade' one of God's existence, or to 'settle' such a belief in one's mind. But none of this amounted to a proof that would compel an atheist to believe.

Boyle was as interested in the psychology of religious belief as in its logic, and that is arguably another of his legacies. In observing the wisdom of God in nature, Boyle wished his readers to be 'affectively' convinced of it (Davis, 1994, p. 162), in as much an emotional as a rational response. 'Most atheists' (he did not say all) had other 'affections', even a 'depraved frame of mind' that predisposed them against the proofs. And there was another blockage. Boyle wrote: 'the difficulty of such speculations as belong to the contemplations of God's attributes keeps the generality

JOHN HEDLEY BROOKE

of atheists and libertines from being *qualified* for such enquiries' (MacIntosh, 2005, p. 49).

Boyle had few doubts about his own qualifications, and he remained deeply interested in what made some persons believers and others not. In one manuscript, he jotted down at least nine 'causes of infidelity' (MacIntosh, 2005, pp. 162–3). You do not want to hear them all, but they included a 'love of independency' and a 'vain affectation of applause'. So you will know what not to do after this lecture! They also included what Boyle called the 'obviousness' and 'intelligibility' of objections, meaning, I think, that the devil, even then, had the best sound bites. Another cause of infidelity was what Boyle described as 'corrupt principles of philosophy'. And here we might begin to recognize another of his insights – that how one responds to reasoned arguments depends on where you are coming from.

In a recent study of the relations between religion and the physical sciences in the nineteenth and twentieth centuries, the American historian Frederick Gregory has come to a conclusion that has profound implications. He writes: 'throughout the last two centuries in virtually all cases of interaction between physical science and religion, the diversity of opinion displayed has stemmed from the variety of assumptions ... *brought to* the issues by the participants' (Gregory, 2003, p. 53). There can be a universal consensus on what the scientific data are, but their cultural meaning is a different matter. Scientific theories rarely, if ever, entail metaphysical or theological conclusions. I think Boyle deserves some credit for appreciating this. In our post-Enlightenment world, we recoil at his tendency to regard immorality as a primary cause of irreligion, but he was well aware that in reactions to natural theology, everything depended on what one brought to the issues (Goodman, 1973, pp. 125–6).

In the first volume of his trilogy, *A Scientific Theology*, Alister McGrath reflected on the critical word 'natural' when contemplating the possibility of a natural theology. McGrath made the shrewd observation that the word 'nature' is itself imbued with so many meanings and carries so much cultural baggage, that there is scarcely a stable platform on which a 'natural' theology can be erected. In certain respects, Boyle would be sympathetic to that diagnosis. From 'then' to 'now', the concept of the 'natural' has been rendered increasingly problematic by human interference. In this, the sciences have played a crucial role. Think of our biotechnologies and visions of genetic engineering to transform, enhance, even immortalize what it is to be human. Ironically, ambitions to prolong human life were part and parcel of the alchemical traditions in which Boyle took so keen an interest. More to the point, Boyle was acutely aware of ambiguity in the very word 'nature'. In fact, he was so bothered about it that he wanted to banish the word altogether. This meant finding substitutions for all its common uses. Just to give you a taste: instead of speaking of the 'nature' of a body, Boyle wanted to substitute the word 'essence'. When 'nature' was used to refer to the 'world' or entire 'universe', it was no hardship to substitute those words instead. If by 'nature' one meant an established order of things, why not simply say that? One use above all others was dissonant with his Christianity. The vulgar often spoke of nature doing this or that. In Aristotelian natural philosophy, it was said that 'nature abhors a vacuum'. But, Boyle protested, 'nature' was not an agent as if it were a person with intentions. It was in precisely this context where the word 'God' should be substituted, in order to highlight the difference between the Creator and his creation. The wonderful word 'de-deification' has sometimes been used to express this dismissal of pseudo-gods from the world – sanitizing the creation in a way that helped to make a mechanistic science possible.

The word 'nature' has, of course, survived Boyle's onslaught; but at least he perceived the problem and sounded the alarm.

Conclusion

I have not been arguing that we need to revert to Boyle for a better understanding of the world. Those who invoke intelligent design today to pick holes in neo-Darwinian accounts of evolution are, in my view, seriously misguided. To modern ears there is much in Boyle's moralizing that will sound sanctimonious. Much of his science was eclipsed by that of Newton. But his legacy was far more substantial than the £50 per annum with which he endowed the eponymous lectures. His pursuit of experimental methods had enduring consequences. And there is something in Boyle that many would say we *have* lost to our detriment – a profound sense of the wonder of nature and how to communicate that to a younger generation. Contrary to the stereotypes of modernity, Boyle bequeathed a view of the world in which there was space for both empirical science and religious faith – space for both a mechanical universe and belief in providence. He had a special gift for finding positions that transcended opposing views, in both matter theory and theology (Davis, 1994; Wojcik, 1997). He saw himself as a peacemaker, which is why the Boyle Lecturers were not to descend to controversies among Christians themselves. The wish to mediate wherever possible was a personality trait of which he was deeply self-conscious. 'I love to speak of persons with civility', he wrote, 'though of things with freedom'; for 'a quarrelsome and injurious way of writing does very much unbecome a philosopher and a Christian' (Davis, 1994, p. 166).

These are no mean legacies, and the example of an honourable peacemaker has never been more necessary than it is today.

8

Is the World Unfinished?
On Interactions between Science and
Theology in the Concepts of Nature,
Time and the Future

JÜRGEN MOLTMANN

For me, science is a 'Paradise Lost'. I wanted to study mathematics and physics. But in 1943, just while I was reading Louis de Broglie's book *Matière et Lumière*, I was called up and conscripted into the German army (Broglie, 1943). At the end of five years of war and captivity, I came back as a theologian. The question about God had become more important to me, but the question about scientific truth has remained with me ever since.

I have felt the invitation to this Robert Boyle Lecture to be a reminder of the lost dream of my youth. Robert Boyle founded the lecture 'for the defence of faith'. According to my own experiences in the border zone between theology and science, when faith encounters serious science, it requires no defence but only interest and curiosity.

The question about God and the question of 'what holds nature together in its innermost being' (as Goethe put it) are not wholly divergent questions. They are not controversial. According to Plato, wonder is the beginning of all knowledge. According to the Jewish–Christian tradition, the fear of God is the beginning of all wisdom. Don't these two things belong together? If wonder over the phenomena of nature converges with reverence before the great mystery of the whole, the outcome is the humble search for truth, and joy in its discoveries (Moltmann, 2003, pp. 141–57).

Theologians and scientists encounter each other with respect and consideration. So I can understand the annoyed reaction of exactly thinking scientists towards pseudo-scientific creationism, and you will understand the critical reactions of theologians who take up cudgels against the new naturalistic atheism. Ideologies spring up as a result of the reduction of complex forms of life or because of totalizations of individual aspects. Scientists and theologians dislike ideologies of this kind, because they distort the view of truth and serve irrelevant interests.

And yet how many theologians read scientific books in order to understand God's activity in nature? And how many scientists turn to theological books, except, maybe, in order to understand their personal faith, but hardly for scientific reasons?

The logical systems of theology and the sciences can be compared as a way of stimulating each other mutually to new ways of thinking, for example the inter-relationality in the Christian doctrine of the Trinity and in nuclear physics, or the wave–particle complementarity and the person–energy complementarity of God's Spirit in human experience (Polkinghorne, 2010).

But it is also possible to work on common topics in the reality in which we live and think. In this lecture, I should like to try to do this with regard to the concept of nature, the concept of time and the idea of a world open to the future. Theology does not call in question the results of scientific research, but it does set these results in the context of wider horizons of interpretation, because it has different questions.

In the ancient world, physics according to Aristotle required a metaphysics in order to explain the presuppositions, which it had not itself created but continually applied. Similarly, the modern sciences too must open themselves for new metaphysical questions if they do not want merely to register facts but to interpret signs as well. We know more from year to year about natural processes, but do we also understand what we perceive? Science is a hermeneutics of nature as well if it does not merely aim to know nature but also wants to understand what it perceives. In the sphere of hermeneutics, scientists and theologians meet (Moltmann, 2010, pp. 189–208).

In this Boyle lecture, I should like to consider the interactions between theology and the sciences. I am interested here in the influence of the Jewish–Christian doctrine of creation on the modern concept of nature and time and in the influence of the modern sciences on the new theological concept of a creation open to the future.

The readability of the world

The initial premise of all science is the knowability of nature (Blumenberg, 1983). However initial and fragmentary our knowledge may be, there is a correspondence between our reason and the reasonableness of the world.

In describing modern genetic researches, a metaphor often used is 'the book of life' (Reiter, 2006). In its genetic structures, life becomes 'readable'. In the gene sequences, we learn 'the spelling of life', the human genome is a 'dictionary of the human being', the base pairs are like the 'letters' and the genes are like 'the words' of life. President Clinton called the sequences of the decoded human genome 'the language in which God created life'. The other metaphor about the 'genetic code' makes the genetic structures understandable as signals or signs of an encoded message. Both metaphors present nature as a sign cosmos of meanings that have to be understood.

The idea of the readability of the world is derived from the theological tradition of the 'two books'. There is 'the Book of Books' and there is 'the book of nature', said the Cappadocians (Tanzella-Nitti, 2004). Basil the Great believed that our reason has been so perfectly created by God that 'we can read the wisdom of God through the beauties of created things as if they were letters and words of God's wisdom'. For Augustine, only the person who has learnt to read can read the Bible, but even someone who is illiterate can understand the book of nature. John Scotus Erigena thought that the two books were two theophanies, the one given through letters, the other through forms. According to Nicholas of Cusa, 'things are the books of the senses. In them the will of the divine reason is described in sensory images.' However, from Kepler and Galileo onwards, the view came to prevail that 'the book of nature' is written not with letters but in numbers. The cosmic wisdom speaks to the human intelligence through mathematics. That was the famous *reductio scientiae ad mathematicam*, with which the scientific revolution of modern times began.

But how does human reason relate to the reasonableness of the world? With the beginning of modern times, this was described as the relation between subject and object. Through science and technology human beings become what Descartes called 'the lords and possessors of nature'. Kant maintained that human reason has insight only into what it produces according to a design of its own; it constrains nature to give an answer to its own questions. And it is in this sense that applied science is pursued even today: knowledge is power (Moltmann, 2003, pp. 10–15).

But it is possible to see the relationship in reverse as well: the human being does not merely confront nature; in the first place he is part of it. So through the human being's perception, nature arrives at the perception of itself (Scheler, 2009). That does not mean that the modern relationship between nature and human being is restricted, but it is set in the wider association of the nature–human relationship. Human knowledge of nature is also a natural process. Seen in this light, the sciences enter into their ecological age, for it cannot be in the interest of nature to destroy itself through human knowledge and through whatever human beings make of this knowledge. Knowledge is wisdom.

The creation of nature

In the ancient world, when people talked about the *natura rerum*, they meant the essence of things. Like the Greek word *physis*, the Latin *natura* can mean both the nature of things and their coming into being, although the essentialist concept predominates. According to Plato's *Timaios*, the Ideas reveal the eternal nature of temporal things; according to Aristotle, 'all nature' is the essence of reality as a whole and is itself divine; that is to say, it is always identical with itself and is everywhere the same.

How do we perceive the nature of things? By contemplating them – what we today call meditation. We must look through the changeable, sensory appearances of a flower in order to grasp the flower's typical nature. We see the blossom and grasp the timeless idea of blossoming. 'The nature of anything' means its *noumenon*, the thing as it is in itself, not its *phainomenon*, as it is seen by the senses.

The modern empirical concept of nature has no longer anything to do with the metaphysical concept of essence. In order to know something, one must observe it exactly, measure it, weigh it, and calculate it according to its inherent laws. Once we know the laws of nature, we can grasp things, and control them.

How did this transformation in the concept of nature come about? It has been convincingly shown that historically the transformation took place through the influence of the Jewish–Christian concept of nature as God's creation (Howe, 1953). Let me describe this briefly:

First, in the ancient Greek concept of *physis* and in the Latin concept of *natura* there was no distinction between the divine and the worldly. *Physis*, as the power to bring forth, is itself divine, just as the nature of the universe is divine. Our common image of the globe or sphere is derived from these metaphysics, for the sphere is the image of spatial perfection. As a sphere, the universe is founded in itself, is self-sufficing, perfect, displays all divine attributes, and is a self-enclosed system.

Second, if on the other hand creation is interpreted as God's creation, then it cannot itself be divine; it must therefore be understood as worldly. Belief in creation introduces into the experience of reality the fundamental distinction between God and world. Nature is not divine but of this world; it is finite not infinite; temporal not eternal; contingent not necessary; eccentrically based in something other, not concentrically in itself. Figuratively speaking, its form is not that of the sphere. It is an open system of signs, which point beyond themselves. It holds within itself the principle of beginning, and is open for the emergence of the new.

As creation, nature is derived not from God's essential being but from his will. God did not have to create the world. It was created by his free will. Yet it is not a product of God's caprice. God does not throw dice. The world comes into being out of God's love. It is the self-communication of the Good. To put it simply:

God in his freedom brings into being a creation that corresponds to him, to his goodness and beauty. Difference and community characterize the relationship between God and the world.

Community in the fundamental difference is experienced as the presence of the divine Spirit in all things. It is understood as God's indwelling (*Shekinah*) in a world that corresponds to him, and as incarnation of the eternal Logos. In their essential difference, God and creation are seen to be so intertwined that we can talk about God in creation, and creation in God (*perichoresis*) (Moltmann, 1985).

The difference in the community is determined by the divine self-limitation (*kenosis*): the relative can co-exist with the Absolute to the extent to which the Absolute withdraws itself. Creation acquires its space, its time and its potentialities for free development from God's self-limitation (Polkinghorne, 2001). Only God can limit God. God is not 'the all-determining reality', but in himself his power is so great that he concedes to those he has created space, time and liberty in order that he may have an independent counterpart. In his book *Concepts of Space* (1954), to which Albert Einstein wrote the foreword, Max Jammer also discovered the insight into this divine mystery of creation in the Jewish-kabbalistic doctrine of *zimzum*.

To sum up: if the reality of the world is contingent, it cannot be deduced from eternal principles, but has to be perceived from precise observation. The theological reason for the modern empirical concept of nature is to be found in the distinction between God's essential nature and his will. The empirical concept of nature corresponds to the theological concept of creation and does not contradict it, although this is what some fundamentalists and some scientists seem to assume, when they consider the modern sciences to be in principle 'atheistic'.

In classical physics, the natural laws were thought to be timeless, unalterable, always and everywhere the same, like the Platonic Ideas. Does this then mean that they are eternal orders for temporal happening, or are they themselves part of temporal happening? In the theological perspectives described, they belong to creation and, as the theologian Thomas Torrance emphatically put it, are 'contingent orders for contingent happening' (Torrance,

1981). Like time, they are created together with creation. It is not just that the processes in nature proceed according to natural laws; natural laws themselves are part of nature too. Consequently it is justifiable to ask whether natural laws are alterable (Paul Dirac), or whether they have developed in the more complex forms of life as 'habits of nature' (Sheldrake, 1988). This of course also raises the question about the constancy of 'natural constants'. Are they only constant for the time, or were they always constant, and will they always be so? The theologian is concerned with the contingency of the orders of nature not just because of his belief in the Creator, but also as a way of being able to conceive of the new creation of the world.

The discovery of time

Very early concepts of time are derived from the recognition of 'the eternal return of the same thing' (M. Eliade): summer and winter, seedtime and harvest, the return of the sun in the morning, and the 'circular motion' of the stars. In many early civilizations, the circle was taken as an image for time. This is the image of reversible time. Circularity is a reflection of eternity. Its quantitative endlessness corresponds to the qualitative infinity of the eternal. In 'the eternal return of the same thing', the symmetries are dominant.

In the so-called Abrahamic religions, time is experienced differently. The root experience of these religions of history is the experience of God in the Exodus out of a known present into an unknown future. The person who sets out with the divine promise given to Abraham and Sarah leaves behind a past that will never return and seeks a future that does not yet exist. This future is greater than the past: at the beginning there is only Abraham and Sarah, at the end all generations on Earth. This experience of God divides the times into a past that cannot be brought back and a future that has not yet been reached. That is the discovery of irreversible time. The arrow of time pierces and breaks through the circle of time.

In irreversible time, we distinguish between two modes of time, for in every moment that divides past from future there is a before and an after. If we enter past and future along a temporal line, then the present is the point that distinguishes and joins the times. Consequently, time always begins and ends in the present. But 'present' is not a temporal concept; it is a spatial one. The person who experiences time is present, not absent (Thomsen and Holländer, 1984).

If we enter these modes of time on an undirected parameter, then the measurable movements are symmetrical and reversible, as the equations of movement in classical physics show. Newtonian physics presents the picture of a stable world order, with a world clock that can run forwards and backwards.

But the Second Law of thermodynamics introduced into physics in principle the concept of irreversible time. Entropy is not merely a measure for the irretrievable dissemination of energy; it is also a measure for the irreversibility of processes.

The result for Ilya Prigogine is 'the time paradox' (Prigogine and Stenger, 1997). Do we have to reckon with both forms of time, the reversible and the irreversible, or can it be shown that the simple ideas about a reversible time are abstractions of the more complex processes that take their course according to irreversible time? If ever since the Big Bang the universe has been involved in a history of expansion, then the 'paradox of time' is resolved in favour of irreversible time. The concept of a 'history of nature' (C. F. von Weizsäcker) corresponds to the experience of history in the Abrahamic religions (Weizsäcker, 1953).

The new metaphysics no longer takes its starting point, like mediaeval metaphysics, from a Supreme Being, so as to distinguish between being and non-being. It proceeds from the fundamental potentiality for being that distinguishes the actual from the possible. If we relate the temporal modes 'past' and 'future' to the modalities of being 'actuality' and 'potentiality', then the potential corresponds to the future and the actual to the past (Picht, 1980). Inherent in the present is the creative force for realizing the potential. All actuality is realized potentiality, just as every past is a 'past future'. The driving force is the potentiality. Here too irreversibility rules. Potentiality becomes reality, but reality never again becomes possibility. 'Higher than actuality stands *possibility*' in Heidegger's ontology in *Being and Time* (Heidegger, 1962, p. 63).

If 'the future is the time for the potential', then the times 'past' and 'future' are not equal, for potential and actual being are different (Kierkegaard, 1944, p. 108). Consequently the way we deal with them differs. Remembered past is something different from expected future, for what is past is fixed and cannot be changed, while future is open. So our expectations are less certain than our remembrances. But in saying this I have of course already introduced the subject who experiences the times (Koselleck, 1979; Cramer, 1993; Heidegger, 1962, p. 378). Remembrances and expectations are constituted by subjects who are present. That is pre-eminently true for the creative dealings of human beings with the times, both time's realities and its potentialities. But in principle all self-referential forms of life perceive the times in this way, and can distinguish between past and future.

Is the world unfinished?

Right down to the present day, theology assumed that in the beginning God created a finished and perfect world, and that history is merely a story of Paradise Lost and Paradise Regained. Sin distorts the goodly creation, grace restores it (Bultmann, 1960). The original creation is the timeless *status integritatis*. This view makes the Jewish–Christian belief in creation captive to the religious myth of origin and remembrance. This is shown, for example, by the German word for creation, *Schöpfung*, for its final syllable, *ung*, means the concluded process of creating and its result (Moltmann, 1979, p. 116).

The notion of the finished and perfected world also dominated classical physics at the time of Robert Boyle and Sir Isaac Newton. Boyle even proposed talking about 'mechanism' instead of nature. Once produced, a mechanism functions by itself. Out of this idea, the mechanistic worldview of deism developed. God is the architect of a perfect world structure, or the Creator whose genius has brought about a perfect world machine. This world mechanism is so perfect that it requires no further divine interventions. God would contradict his own perfection if he were obliged to correct his perfect work.

This theological idea is called 'deism' and it is generally rejected as being the beginning of atheism, for – as Laplace already said – one no longer needs a God in order to explain the mechanism of the world. But this is not entirely true: isn't deism the world-picture we also find on the seventh day of creation, when, according to Genesis 2.2, God 'rested' from all the works he had made? Seen in this light, seventeenth-century deism would in fact be sabbath theology. This fits that baroque era, which in its church architecture and its music was able to extol Jehovah's glory in contemplation of 'the best of all possible worlds'. God was seen not as the subject of a continuing creative process, but as the resting object of worship, so that the goal of created being is 'to glorify God and enjoy him forever', as the Westminster Confession says. Natural theology, which perceives in the inherent laws of nature the wisdom and beauty of God, serves the glorification and enjoyment of the divine that is present, resting in itself.

The modern sciences have broken down this picture of a perfect and finished world. If we look at the overall history of the cosmos, we recognize today that ever since the Big Bang the universe has expanded and is involved in a singular history open to the future. 'The cosmos is an unfinished process which does not know its own future' (Cramer, 1998, p. 24). The time of the cosmos is irreversible. Its reality proceeds from a potentiality, which we can term a field of expectation, in which the cosmic events emerge. The overall history of life in the creative living space of the Earth is no different. As far as we know, the evolution of life is also singular and open to the future. Its time too is irreversible. New forms of life emerge from a potentiality for life that can be understood as its field of expectation. Evolution too is an unfinished process that does not know its own future. Life in its creativity is an unfinished process.

In the light of these recognitions of an unfinished nature, theologians read their Scriptures with new eyes. If, for once, we read the Bible not from the beginning but from the end, it at once becomes clear that what is meant by the creation stories 'in the beginning' is not a finished, perfect, primal state but only the first act of a creation process that reaches far into the future (Polkinghorne, 1998, p. 74). Creation 'in the beginning' opens up the prospect of history that arrives at its goal only in the new creation of all things. The perfected creation does not lie behind us in a primal state, but ahead of us in a final one. We await the consummated creation and, together with the cosmos, are now existing in its pre-history.

'In the beginning God created the heavens and the earth.' Where is the consummating goal of this beginning? We find the final vision in the prophets: 'Behold, I will create a new heaven and a new earth', we read in Isaiah (65.17), and the visionary John writes: 'And I saw a new heaven and a new earth' (Rev. 21.1). What is to be new in the new creation of all things? 'Behold, the tabernacle of God is among men.' God will 'indwell' his creation on earth as in heaven, and in the presence of the eternally living God, death will be no more; all things will participate in the eternal livingness and righteousness of God.

In this eschatological perspective, nature presents itself as being within a history open to the future. The phenomena of continuity and discontinuity, stability and the emergence of the new, are interpreted theologically as signs of God's faithfulness and his anticipating creation. I may just briefly mention elements in this continuous creation process:

First, preservation. This does not consist of the sovereign rule of the Creator and his direct interventions in his creation, as Jonathan Edwards maintained, in opposition to the mechanists of his time. It means that the Creator 'sustains' his creation, just as in Greek philosophy the *hypokeimenon* sustains all things. God does not rule from above, but sustains from below. That is the way Israel's Exodus story describes it: 'You have seen how I bore you on eagles' wings' (Exod. 19.4). There is a feminine image for this patient and purposeful sustaining: 'as a mother carries her child at her breast' (Num. 11.12) and a masculine one too: 'as a man bears his son on his shoulders' (Deut. 1.31). According to the New Testament, God 'upholds all things through his word of power (*Logos*)' (Heb. 1.3). It is God's patient sustaining that provides the scope for the self-creations and self-organizations of all the living, but for their self-destructions as well. For these too, Israel's wanderings through the wilderness offer vivid pictures.

Second, the creating of the new: 'Remember not the former things nor consider the things of old. Behold, I am doing a new thing; now it springs forth, do you not perceive it?' (Isa. 43.18–19). The singular Hebrew word for create (*bara*) is used more frequently for the process of creation in the present than for creation in the beginning. This process is not a creation out of nothing; it is a renewing creation out of the old one, a renewal, a heightening, and a giving of new form to what is already there: 'And thou renewest the face of the earth' (Ps. 104.30) (Moltmann, 1968). We perceive signs of this innovative creating in the opening up of new possibilities and in the self-transcendence of living things. We perceive them too in the emergence of new wholes that cannot be explained by the characteristics of their parts and by the sum of them.

In closing, I come back to the concept of the two books: the book of the divine promises and the book of nature. Fortunate is the person who delights in reading them both. His world is richer than the world of people who want to know only one of the two books and ignore the other. But how do the two books relate to each other?

In Robert Boyle's time, religion still counted as the interpreter of the world's phenomena. 'The Book of Scripture is the interpreter of the book of nature', claimed Jonathan Edwards, 'because it is illuminating of those spiritual mysteries that are signified in the constitution of the natural world' (Zakai, 2010, p. 255). At that time, scientists freed themselves from the domination of this religious interpretation through the *reductio scientiae ad mathematicam*.

Today, we recognize the limitations of this reduction, and are trying to find new perspectives for the richer realities and the always mysterious potentialities in the world process. 'The book of divine promises' offers only one of these new perspectives on the enigmatic book of nature. That book was not written in order to save its readers from making their own investigations into the book of nature: on the contrary, it stimulates them to scientific researches because it awakens their curiosity about God's presence in all things. The unambiguity of science doesn't put an end to the immensely rich ambiguity of the world.

Perhaps there is still more to be read in the library of this world than in these two books alone.

9

Christ and Evolution
A Drama of Wisdom?

CELIA DEANE-DRUMMOND

In this chapter, I intend to make three main points. The first is that the classic tradition about who Christ is as divine and human is often thought difficult to understand in a scientific era, so the tendency has been to respond to this difficulty by stressing Christ's humanness. Evolutionary biology presents a particular and specific challenge to theology, and this is more often worked out through relating God and evolution. But if we do this, then the main tenet of what Christianity is all about – Christ – is missed out. The second point I want to make is that rather than succumb to this difficulty, theology needs to be more confident about naming Christ as being integral to a theological drama where wisdom helps to express what this drama means. The third main point is that the long history of evolution should be thought of as woven into the drama of human history with God in Christ, rather than excluded from it, and we can do this in the light of modern evolutionary biology and its current debates.

One of the reasons there is a question mark after the title of this article is that I am intending the discussion to be deliberately exploratory. I am offering this account, therefore, as an exercise in constructive theology that is open, rather than closed to further debate. A focus on God in theology and science discussions has the advantage of being inclusive towards other religious traditions, at least theistic ones. But I suggest that the mark of faith that most distinguishes Christian belief from other religious traditions is belief in the incarnation of Christ; the Word made *flesh*, belief that God in Christ becomes one with the human, material world. But ever since Darwin that flesh is also *evolved* flesh. In what sense, therefore, can it make sense that God is present in Christ, but Christ as fully human is also part of the evolutionary world, along with the other billions of creatures on Earth? It is hardly surprising that many theologians wanting to match up a scientific account with God's activity in the world prefer to envisage God's action as virtually synonymous with evolutionary means. But if we follow this route, where does this leave the significance of the incarnation?

One of the reasons that Robert Boyle inaugurated the Boyle Lectures was for the defence of Christianity in the wake of pressures from natural science. By this he was not wanting to undermine science, but develop a 'natural theology' that could be more in tune with it, while holding to theological premises. He was also defending the possibility of a genuine conversation between science and theology. Historian John Hedley Brooke suggests that Boyle wanted to work against the premise of libertines, who thought a scientific virtuoso ought not to be a Christian. Other observers thought that if a scientist did happen to be a person of faith, then they could not be a true one. Brooke aptly comments that the endowment of Robert Boyle was such that '[t]he lecturers would have as their brief: to prove the Christian religion "against notorious Infidels, viz. Atheists, Theists, Pagans, Jews, and Mahometans." And as a rider, he added that they were not to descend to "any controversies … among Christians themselves"' (Brooke, 2010). Further, and significantly in my view, in Boyle we find an interweaving of natural and revealed theology, with the natural world expressive of divine wisdom. He recognized, above all, the need for a genuine and open dialogue, and it is his particular wisdom that is vitally needed today in the wake of pressures from creationism, hostile responses of the new atheists and public confusion more generally about the compatibility of science and Christian faith.

What I hope to do in this lecture, therefore, is to map out a possible ground for a more constructive conversation between how to think about Christ and evolutionary science in the spirit that Robert Boyle originally intended. Of course, inevitably there will be areas where some tension remains, and I suggest that this is more or less unavoidable. If all tensions go completely, then one of the following options comes to the surface. First, theology could collapse *into* science while still asserting its position of faith, but now religious faith is joined with science, rather than faith in conversation with that science. Theological shifts to understand God as somehow simply synonymous with evolutionary processes fall into this category. Second, theology could be perceived as no longer viable in a scientific age, so religious belief or theology founded on that belief are explained away by that science. This encourages what might be termed a post-Christian stance in relation to science where traditions of faith have virtually disappeared. A third possibility, somewhat in between the first and second alternatives, is to reshape theological analysis. Theology denies the importance of faith and gives priority to reason. Theology takes shape primarily through rational analysis mapped out by scientific forms of reasoning, rather than as a commentary on a way of life lived through faith. There are also, fourth, what might be termed withdrawal movements possible in theology that have a similar end result, where theology turns its back on science and ignores its claims or imagines theology and science in parallel but non-competing realms, none of which are very helpful or constructive. I will deal with only some of these difficulties. But at least, or as a bare minimum, I hope to show that it is possible to think in a creative way that is both theologically articulate and scientifically meaningful.

In the light of the above, the basic argument that I will develop in this chapter is fairly simple. First, the classic accounts of who Christ is are, in their theoretical elaboration, too detached from accounts of the natural world to be meaningfully related to it. They fall into what might be termed the withdrawal tendency in theology. Second, if we are to hold to a traditional account of Christ as both human and divine, and so retain a traditional view of theology as faith seeking understanding, one way to do this in a way that still makes sense from an evolutionary perspective is through envisaging Christ as a key player in a dynamic theo-drama. Third, it is possible to envisage evolutionary theory and current debates in evolution as woven into that drama while still retaining their credibility as science.

Classic tradition and modern responses

A brief look at the way theologians in the early Church came to express belief in Christ is important as a first step in showing both the difficulties of any conversation, and what parameters might be important theologically. Classical debates on Christ's humanity and personhood raged around the meaning of Christ's human and divine nature. The framework eventually adopted was the Chalcedonian definition (AD 451) affirming that Christ is one person, but having a divine and human nature. Even then it was difficult to understand how divinity could become en-fleshed in humanity without either destroying that humanity or weakening that divinity. Two compromises emerged, with the Alexandrian view stressing Christ's divinity and the Antiochene tradition Christ's humanity. Further theoretical discussion followed about how one might consider human nature assumed by Christ – is it an abstract universal that is somehow in God, or does it only make sense in the particular human person of Jesus Christ? – along with related technical discussion about *an-hypostasia*, human nature as an abstract universal, and *en-hypostasia*, the particular human nature in Christ's person (Crisp, 2007, pp. 72–89). All these technical discussions are essentially closed insofar as they represent internal theological debates about what might be logically possible, given certain premises. They seem to bear little or no relationship to evolutionary biology, except inasmuch as the concept of two natures and one person becomes incredible or difficult to understand. If I talk to biologists about such theories, the most likely reaction is a blank stare of incomprehension or even incredulity at such beliefs rather than furthering any fruitful discussion.

It is hardly surprising, given such difficulties associated with classical ontological definitions of Christ's two natures, that there are prominent writers in the contemporary dialogue who, if they tackle the topic at all, lean more towards a liberal Christology. The point is that the first paradigm is the evolutionary story of humanity's emergence, and Christology then becomes compatible with this. In Arthur Peacocke's account, for example, Jesus seems to *become* a fully God-informed subject, rather than being endowed with divine subjectivity from the beginning (Peacocke, 2007). Traditional belief in the divine Word of God incarnate in human flesh seems compromised. Put more bluntly, would I really be inclined to worship *as God* and name as *Kyrios*, Lord, a man who merely expresses that divinity by being or becoming perfectly obedient to God?

Christ and theo-drama as divine wisdom

Part of the problem in such accounts of Christ is that an evolution-ary, emergent view of history has taken over a more theological future-orientated view of history. This is sometimes exasperated further by a stress on cosmological evolution, so that the whole sweep of human history becomes aligned with a grand story of an unfolding emergent cosmology. But what if a theology of history becomes much more vivid, and perhaps truer to itself as theology, through a different reading of history, one that draws specifically on drama?

Beneath the surface there is another problem here that is worth identifying. Evolutionary history, with its tremendously long time-scale and habitually reaching back to an account of cosmic history of the Earth, almost always becomes a grand narrative or *epic*. Theology may of course also suffer from this tendency as well. What do I mean by epic? In the second volume of his great trilogy *Theo-Drama*, Roman Catholic theologian Hans Urs von Balthasar considers whether there is ever a standpoint from which we can be merely observers to a sequence of events, including the events of Christ's death and resurrection (Balthasar, 1990b, p. 54). He suggests that we can never be so detached, and if we assume as much, we are deluding ourselves. Evolution as incorporating some sort of *necessity* is also a typical reading of evolutionary history.

Rather than using the language of epic, the language of theo-drama encourages viewing ourselves as participants in a story, one where we have a deeper sense of agency, rather than being mere observers to an inevitable process. The difference between drama and grand narrative is that drama puts much more em-phasis on *agents*, on particular activities of particular players and contingent events, while grand narrative stresses the inevitable chain of events in a way that I suggest is ultimately disempowering, rather than empowering. Therefore, theo-drama, like drama generally, stresses contingency, freedom of agents and unexpected twists and turns to the plot.

Crucially, theo-drama, as I envisage it, takes as its starting point *theological* categories prior to turning to evolution (Quash, 2005, p. 2). Theo-dramatics is therefore a way of thinking about eschatology and history together in their relationship with each other. Drama, as commonly understood, is about human actions and particular events in particular contexts, but theo-drama is how those actions are specifically connected to God's purpose. Theo-dramatic consideration will therefore include *subjects*, the acting area or the *stage* and the movement of the play or *action*, but when considering the incarnation, God in Christ *becomes* one of the subjects and is not simply having oversight of the play. Another key issue that arises here is that of freedom and what this means in the Christian life. If we perceive God as one who is in possession of divine freedom, this means that history is not just an inevitable chain of events. The advantage of theo-drama is that it envisages an encounter between the freedom of God and that of God's creatures, but the two freedoms are not in competition.

In the sweep of history, some moments are crucial, what the biblical tradition has named as *kyrios*, and in theo-dramatic perspective the particular coming of Christ and his passion, death and resurrection are pivotal. One could even say that the particular theo-drama of Christ's coming shows up a pattern of divine Wisdom that then provides clues to understanding the dramatic relationship between God and God's creatures. The difference between the emergent divine Christ and the one I am suggesting is that now the divinity of Christ is present from the beginning. It is, therefore, a profoundly Trinitarian drama that involves the cooperation of all three persons of the Trinity, but only the Logos/Wisdom is fully incarnate *in the flesh* as a subject in human history. While in one sense wisdom remains an ontological category, it also implies activity, *agency* or, in theo-dramatic language, *performance* compared with rather more static classical concepts of divine and human natures in Christ.

The reception of divine Wisdom/Logos by the Virgin Mary is an expression of the mysterious drama of the economic Trinity, understood not just as the action of God in history, but now God becoming part of that history. But as drama this also means that Mary had creaturely freedom to turn away from or align with divine intent, so that Mary's *Yes* could also have been *No*. Such a drama at the heart of the story of the incarnation unfolds to reveal that the very human son born to her is also the Son of God. But at this stage the divinity of Christ is almost completely veiled from human view, God appears in the form of a very vulnerable, very human baby. Jesus' divinity only becomes obvious to outside observers in his obedience to the Father through the power of the Holy Spirit, but that does not mean that he was not sharing in the divine from the beginning of his existence.

Christology in this conception is a *kenotic* Christology, where the eternal God freely and out of love for the world through the Son chooses to become one with human flesh, to become fully human, but without loss of divinity. This is not so much about God 'giving up' divine characteristics in order to become human, but showing up divine Wisdom precisely *through* becoming human, the divine incarnate in the flesh witnessed as a vulnerable baby just like every other human person (Evans, 2006). Further, the power of that divinity is also in a paradoxical way found in the powerlessness of the man hanging from the cross; this is what Paul envisaged in 1 Corinthians 1.18–26, when he spoke of the divine Wisdom of the cross. But for bystanders Christ's divinity only becomes visible in the next scene, in the light of the dramatic event of the resurrection (Deane-Drummond, 2009).

We can envisage, therefore, God as the playwright, where the plot and the script are known in a very general way, but the details are yet to be worked out, improvised according to the particular circumstances. Christ's death was the result of the specific free action of human players in the theo-drama. Once the drama becomes too controlled, too subject to a fixed or even necessary account of God's action in history, or Christ's coming perhaps the result of an inevitable evolutionary emergence of natural cooperative tendencies in human beings or his death the result of inevitable selfish tendencies, then drama gives way to epic narrative.

The theo-drama of creaturely, human and religious origins

But what if we allow theo-drama to include not just human history but evolutionary history as well? Such an expansion has the advantage of viewing other evolved creatures as more than simply the stage for human action. The ability to read evolution not just as science, but also as history means that through evolutionary accounts, nature as such becomes historical, a perspective that is arguably one of the most significant discoveries of science (Haught, 1996, p. 57; 2010).

This evolutionary drama will be judged in the light of what happens in the main act, namely, the act of Christ's coming, but that does not mean that earlier or later players are insignificant. Balthasar made the mistake of assuming that because different evolutionary accounts were philosophically materialistic, they could not be taken seriously. While he had a wider cosmic vision of creation, he did not give creatures other than humans any significant role in his theology.

Evolutionary biologist Jeffrey Schloss, following Evelyn Hutchinson, has described evolution in terms of a play on an 'ecological stage'. He suggests that '[t]he lines, the players and even the plot may change over evolutionary time, though they are ever constrained by the props and setting and choreographic syntax of the ecological moment' (Schloss, 2002, p. 58). While I agree with the analogy, I suggest that we can go even further than this, in that ecology is rather more dynamic than this view might imply. Of course, the degree of awareness of divine action will be different according to different levels of consciousness and cognitive capacity, but by placing creatures in kinship with humanity the evolution of life is perceived as integral to the theo-drama.

The difficulty of course, when it comes to the millions of years of evolutionary history, is that human imagination finds it hard to appreciate the dynamics of the particular in any 'scene'. Also, given that evolution takes place over a long period of time, the 'play', if it is to do justice to the individual characters concerned, will find itself dealing with long epochs of history where some characters disappear. Sometimes it may prove preferable, therefore, to use a close examination of those creatures that we know, in order to provide an analogy of earlier epochs.

A good example of this is the study of primates in order to give clues as to the life of early hominids (Zilhao, 2011, pp. 111–31). Yet such study also helps open up the realization of human ignorance, by focusing on the rapid shifts in evolutionary change where improbable events came together in a way that meant only one lineage survived and not others. Such events, such as the increasing aridity in Africa in the early history of the hominin line, *Homo erectus*, which may have triggered an increase in brain size, but at a cost of the loss of other species or variants (Conway Morris, 2003, p. 249), means that what might be termed the tragic nature of the evolutionary drama comes into view. Rather more complex and fascinating is the specific complexity associated with symbolic thinking in different archaic hominids that could be related to brain size and what is known as Robin Dunbar's levels of intention (Pettitt, 2011, pp. 141–61).

The scientific account, for example, of the emergence of *Homo sapiens* and its evolutionary relationship with hominid species makes for fascinating reading. Unravelling this particular act in the particular drama of human history could be the subject of another chapter; but all I want to point to here is the contested manner in which evolutionary biologists are engaged in heated debates about when and why religion has appeared in human societies. For example, different possibilities include (a) religion is not biologically adaptive, so human nature is like a 'blank slate' on which religion develops *de novo* in different cultures, or (b) religion is an adaptation that has evolved under the selective pressure of the need to cooperate, either as an (b1) adaptation, that implies a link to genetic characteristics, or (perhaps rather more convincing in my view) (b2) as an adaptive phenomenon, so that religious belief enhances cooperation and so religious communities survive better, or some combination of b1 and b2. In the former, b1, adaptation scenario, debates exist as to the timing of the appearance of this particular trait(s). Was this prior to the emergence of the hominid line, or coincident with what has been termed 'modern humans' or some time in between (Barrett, 2011, pp. 205–24; Wilson, 2012, pp. 133–9)? While the biological basis for religious belief is still a matter of intense research, even if evidence proves eventually that there are biological characteristics that make human beings more likely to be religious, that does not undermine theological discussion, any more than knowing that there are biological aspects of attachment to my child undermines genuinely felt commitment to that child and its articulation in poetic or theological language. The point is that religion is about an intense *relationship* and our perception of how to live in that relationship; in the Christian case, an understanding of a relationship with God in Christ.

In theological terms, theo-drama forces us to acknowledge humanity's role as *subjects*, a pattern of thinking that scientific methodology deliberately tries to resist.

One of the key differences, therefore, between a theological and scientific approach to evolutionary history is that in the former human beings deliberately and self-consciously enter into that history. On the other hand, while evolutionary science attempts to be objective, there are subjective elements in the myths that shape the way that evolutionary science is presented. This is part of the fascination with evolutionary science; different elements provide competing narratives that try to capture our attention, imagination and perhaps even our commitment. The crucial difference in epic accounts is that we are not necessarily aware of any subjective elements. This may also be the power of the new evolutionary atheism in that it wears a mask of objectivity in rejecting religion but moves its subjects so that they feel part of a grand, or even noble, scientific enterprise.

Theo-dramatics and contemporary evolutionary debates

We can now ask more specifically if this theo-dramatic account of God is ever going to be compatible with contemporary debates in evolutionary science. Just to recap, I am arguing here for a theological starting point, then making sense of evolution, rather than the other way round. I am not expecting those who have no experience of religion to find such a metaphysical starting point acceptable or even convincing. Rather, given certain premises, belief in God and the incarnation, in what way can we understand that belief and still make sense of evolution? Is religious belief still possible in such a scenario? This is surely the spirit behind the inauguration of Boyle's lectures: a defence of the reasonableness of religious belief and yet acknowledgement of what might be termed natural wisdom along with the pressures towards disbelief stemming from modern science.

If I restrict discussion to microevolution, where biologists are more in agreement, there are still heated debates about the way in which natural selection works. Although Stephen Jay Gould is often known best for his stress on evolutionary contingency, he also argued for constraints in evolution, both as a consequence of particular histories, and as result of physical properties (Gould, 2002, p. 49). The evolutionary consequence of a particular history in effect locks organisms to particular specialist modes in a way that reduces the capability of those organisms to evolve. But the manner in which such species end up arriving at such a constrained position is, for Gould, fortuitous and as a result of the random walk of evolution through natural selection.

Simon Conway-Morris, on the other hand, is much bolder in his interpretation of constraints in evolution, pointing to the numerous examples of evolutionary convergence, understood broadly as similarities in form and function, from molecular biology through to physical characteristics, when faced with similar environmental conditions. Conway-Morris goes further than Gould in arguing for a *directional signal* in evolution (Conway Morris, 2003). He therefore believes that human beings are inevitable, so that if the tape of history were to be played again and again, human beings would turn up *again and again*. Gould, on the other hand, while he recognizes constraint, resists the idea that there is an inbuilt evolutionary flow towards human beings; rather, for him constraints flow from random narrowing of evolutionary flexibility concurrent with specialization to a specific ecological niche. Would either view make sense in theo-dramatic terms? My answer is yes, for whereas Gould's position would amount to pure divinely dramatic improvisation, Conway Morris's view allows for a specific divinely directed plot, even if details are flexible. Of course, I should stress once again that neither needs a theological explanation, but both are entirely compatible with such an account.

Other aspects of evolutionary research are still unfolding. Recent research on evolution and development by David Stern on fruit flies tends to support the idea of restraint at the level of molecular genetics. He has found that evolutionarily significant mutations accumulate at certain 'hotspot' genes and even specific portions within those genes (Stern and Orgogozo, 2009, pp. 746–51; Stern, 2010, pp. 149–74). This goes some way to explaining examples of parallel evolution between different populations of the same species. The remarkable fact is that even though other genes are also involved in the regulation of specific characteristics, only some of them are active in evolutionary terms. For example, hundreds of genes regulate the pattern of fine epidermal projections or trichomes on *Drosophila melanogaster* larvae, but only one of these genes, *shavenbaby*, has evolved variants that alter that pattern of trichomes. The reason for this seems to be that this particular gene plays an integral role in the development of trichomes, so that patterning genes marking out spatio-temporal information regulate the expression of the gene *shavenbaby*, which then in turn regulates the development of trichomes.

These discoveries show not only the incredible complexity of gene regulation in a relatively simple organism, a fruit fly larva, but also the crucial evolutionary importance of flexibility combined with constraints. Further, and significantly, these constraints seem to have a molecular basis. How far this might work as an explanation of other hotspot genes remains to be seen. Michael Shapiro, for example, who works with sticklebacks, has found other hotspot genes that do not have the same crucial regulatory function as *shavenbaby* (Kiefer, 2010, p. 3502). Gene expression is also known to vary depending on genetic background, a phenomenon known as *epistasis*. This can impact on the rate of evolution in the short term as more variability shows up with the presence of a given gene mutation. Contingency is therefore present along with constraints, and this contingency is not simply mapped directly on to variations of single gene expressions, but it is far more complicated. Precisely how constraints operate at a molecular level to produce *convergent* phenotypic characteristics between species for given environments is much harder to explain in molecular terms compared with the parallelism case, though some conservation of crucial gene-regulating factors exists across species, such as the Pax 6 found to regulate vertebrate eyes in mice and compound eyes in fruit flies.

The above demonstrates the interplay of contingency and constraint in evolutionary theory in a way that is at least compatible with a theo-dramatic interpretation of events. In the dramatic emergence of species, the contingency of external conditions are in dynamic interaction with historically evolved constraints. The pattern of contingency and constraint is not yet properly understood, but provisionally can be thought of as integral to a *drama of life*, but where full awareness of that drama only finally becomes explicit and self-conscious in the human species, *Homo sapiens*, or perhaps in some other earlier hominid lines. Neanderthals have, for example, habitually received a bad press, but the most recent research suggests that Neanderthals were assimilated into *Homo sapiens* populations through interbreeding, rather than simply killed by the rival *H. sapiens* 'species' (Zilhao, 2011, pp. 111–31). The possibility of Neanderthals or other creaturely agents sharing in a *performance*, it seems to me, makes for a more readily accommodated perception of inclusiveness with other finite creatures, compared with, for example, a simple portrayal of evolution in terms of a rational system of truth claims.

Also highly relevant is the work on development by ethologist Sir Patrick Bateson and his colleagues (Bateson and Gluckman, 2011). He presents a fascinating alternative to the understanding of development through genetic mapping characteristic of Stern's work. Bateson has consistently argued against viewing evolution as simply acting through a passive process, where natural selection acts rather like a winnowing process where only the fittest survive and reproduce. Rather, Bateson argues that mobility is significant, so that creatures also play an active role in evolution in the way that they seek out new environments, choose particular mates, show evidence of immense creativity and innovation, and in some cases actually actively construct their environment. Finally he has suggested that learnt behaviour may eventually become 'fixed' genetically, not through Lamarckian processes of acquired

characteristics, but by genetic variation picking up a spontaneous expression of characteristics that were originally learnt. This
fascinating research shows that creatures, including humans, can
be authors of their own destiny. Theologically creatures can now
be understood as part of a theo-drama, but only humans have
the possibility of a conscious sense of their own agency. In many
cases, of course, humans will not be aware of how their actions
will impact on that of future generations, and so their own role in
the drama will be disguised or hidden from view.

It is also worth dwelling for a moment on what might be termed
contemporary *cooperative* theories of evolution. Martin Nowak
is an evolutionary biologist from Harvard University, well known
for mathematical modelling of human behaviour based on what
might be broadly termed the prisoner's dilemma. This states, in
simple terms, that it is more effective for social groups to cooperate, but it is always tempting for individuals to seek the benefits of
the social group, without contributing to the cost of such cooperation. In other words, to cheat or defect. Nowak goes further in his
claim that cooperation is *built into* the process of evolution from
the beginning, from the first fragile life forms through to the most
neurologically advanced species (Nowak, 2006a, 2006b). Nowak
identifies five different mathematically consistent 'rules' for the
evolution and maintenance of cooperation, operating in different
ways to enhance the likelihood of cooperation conferring a fit-
ness advantage. These are, briefly, Hamilton's rule, related to 'kin
selection'; Trivers' direct reciprocity rule based on expectation of
later reward; third an increase in 'reputation', fourth, network
reciprocity where the cooperators form alliances or clusters, and,
more controversially, group cooperative selection, rather than
group defection. In the long term, defection or refusal to cooperate does not seem to be favoured in evolutionary terms.

At this juncture, it is important to distinguish between the evolution of biological cooperation, that can be found in, for example,
social insects, and what might be termed deliberative moral capacities. While the two are certainly not the same, they are not likely
to be completely disconnected either. There is a strong tendency
for biologists to elide both types of behaviour, which is clearly
mistaken, or for philosophers to assume that *only* sophisticated

linguistic humans can exhibit genuinely moral behaviour. Precisely how the human cognitive power of moral abstraction is related to more innate tendencies to cooperate is unclear, but the former does depend on what might be termed higher cognitive and symbolic capabilities. But that does not mean that other socially advanced animals have no symbolic capabilities either. Further, claims that human societies operate just through absolute abstraction either in the moral sphere or the scientific one should be met with a certain amount of scepticism. The dynamic drama of contingency and constraint expressed eventually either as cooperation or selfishness is also likely to be operative at different levels, but that drama becomes self-conscious only in human beings.

Evidence for genuine cooperative tendencies also comes from a close study of the behaviour of captive primates by Frans de Waal (2009). While his discussion of the experimental basis for cooperative (pro-social) behaviour in primates is fascinating here, there are some philosophical gaffs, such as the implication that human morality can be shaped by primate behaviour. Also, a naturalistic view of ethics is understandable but his case is not adequately presented. 'Morality' here, like cooperation, is a biological term and means that judgement has taken place within group standard norms. It also serves to distinguish between more sophisticated cooperative social action and innate automated cooperative behaviour as in insects. What may be selected for in evolutionary terms is a *general* capacity to be cooperative and learn in social groups. Some evolutionary psychologists want to go further than this and claim that *specific* human relational skills reflect evolved discrete modular components of brain function (Tooby and Cosmides, 2009, pp. 114–37). While I agree that the social skills set of the primate mind may well be distinct from the skill set for tool making, claims that individual human behaviours are tied to specific and evolved modular elements in the brain operating rather like an advanced computer seem to me to go beyond the available evidence.

From the account so far, we can say, perhaps, in a qualified way that cooperation has appeared in evolutionary history on a number of occasions, that it is *convergent* – and it is this cooperation perhaps that leads eventually to the emergence of wisdom.

I would also concede that there could be specific forms of natural wisdom in other social species, just as 'wild justice' is identified in social animals (Bekoff and Pierce, 2009). How far and to what extent any traits representing wisdom shows convergence, that is, similar phenotype or behaviour due to similar external pressures, or parallelism, that is, having a similar genetic lineage, is impossible to discern, as this is largely speculative.

A theo-dramatic approach also takes proper account of the tragic, one that is intensely vivid in terms of the evolutionary history of the Earth, but now brings this into juxtaposition with an understanding of how God works in human history. It therefore will resist any generalization of evil or attempt to wash over the contingency of events. In theo-drama, in as much as it takes its cues from the death of Christ, the tragic comes to the surface, rather than being absorbed or neutralized. The tragic has been the pattern for the drama of evolutionary history for millennia, as witnessed in the palaeontological record, but it might be more appropriate to suggest that a theo-drama is characterized as a comedy in that its ultimate vision is a hopeful one.

Cooperative theories show up the propensity to 'cheat', but in theological terms when humans are self-conscious agents this is judged as 'sin'. There are of course rather too many occasions where human beings are free to conduct what society judges as evil acts according to their own selfish desires. Aquinas long ago recognized that a person commits what they see as a good for themselves, even if others will recognize this as an evil act (Aquinas, [1963] 2006, 1a 48.3). Even Hitler thought (wrongly of course) that what he planned was a good for that society. Sin could be thought of as an inability to see the good for all, understood in its most extensive sense, balanced in relation to the good for each. Sin at its most pervasive and deceptive is evil wrought in the name of a supposed good. According to the theo-dramatic metaphor that I have been postulating, this makes sense, for in any good drama there will be scenes where cooperation allows breakthroughs in the unfolding drama towards God-given ends, but where the possibility of what might be termed tragic cooperation working for horrendously evil ends, perhaps even disguised as a good, also hovers in the background.

Christ as the theo-dramatic way, truth and life

As well as expressing the dramatic ontological act of God in history, the coming of Christ can be thought of as one who came to show in his person the manner in which human beings are to live out their human and social life. His own human capacity for self-sacrifice and obedience to God was partly shaped by naturally defined characteristics that he inherited from his mother, Mary. But he also learnt to express his religious belief through an educative process at home and in the social and political life of his generation. These capacities were, of course, imbibed with God's graceful action working through his dedication to prayer and communion with God, so that according to the early Church's tradition his own humanity was gradually divinized (or deified) during his lifetime (Deane-Drummond, 2009, p. 98). Such a process is outside the bounds of what can be explicable by modern science, apart from very general notions of psychological change in response to religious commitment, a view that is an impoverished thin version of the rich, thick theological notion of grace.

If other human beings choose to follow this pattern, then they would try and perceive goodness through the crystal lens of truth set forth by the purity of Christ's manner of living and dying and rising again. The specific possibility of what might be termed *absolute cooperation* in relation to goodness and truth is only possible for human beings. This may be one reason for the affirmation of Romans 8, that all creation waits in expectant and eager longing, waiting like an audience, or perhaps we should say other players, at the edge of a stage for human beings to act. When we reflect on the tremendous practical ecological and social problems facing our own generation, many of these have tragically been of our own human making. However, the hope that Christian faith in Christ can inspire is one that affirms that self-destruction and that of our world need not be the final act in the theo-drama that interweaves both human and creaturely life. The hoped for future is one where creaturely wisdom and divine Wisdom engage once more, but after the pattern set in that crucial act in the theo-drama, namely, the coming of Christ.

10

Science and Religion in Dialogue

JOHN POLKINGHORNE

The key to understanding the relationship between science and religion lies in the recognition that both are, in their own specific ways, concerned with the search for truth, a truth that is attainable through commitment to well-motivated beliefs. The 'new atheists' fail to acknowledge this fact, polemically alleging that religious people believe without evidence, or even against the evidence. This false caricature results in the new atheists paying no honest attention to serious theological discussion. Their writings are full of assertion but lacking in engaged rational argument.

Of course, in their search for truth science and religion are exploring different dimensions of the human encounter with reality. Science is concerned with impersonal encounter – reality treatable as an 'It', you might say. This is a realm in which experience can be manipulated and repeated as often as is desired. This ability gives science its great secret weapon of experimental testing. If you do not believe that the pressure and volume of a given quantity of gas at constant temperature are inversely proportional, just investigate for yourself, and you will find that Robert Boyle was right.

Yet, we all know that there is a different dimension of reality, the personal and transpersonal, where reality is encountered not as an 'It' but as a 'Thou', and in that realm testing has to give way to trusting. If I am always setting little traps to see if you are my friend, I shall soon destroy the possibility of friendship between us. The attempt to manipulate God and put God to the test is the sinful error of magic. It is in this rich and profound realm of personal and transpersonal experience that religion pursues its quest for truth. In consequence, its questions are different from those of science. The latter is concerned with the processes by which things happen and it has achieved its great success by the modesty of its ambition, bracketing out from its consideration issues of meaning, value and purpose. These latter questions – whether there is something going on in what is happening – are central to the concerns of religion. We know, in fact, that we have to ask both sorts of question if we are to understand the world adequately. The kettle is boiling, because burning gas heats the water; the kettle is boiling, because I want to make a cup of tea. Both statements are true and are necessary to a full understanding of the event of the boiling kettle.

The difference between the How questions of science and the Why questions of religion might at first sight seem to suggest that the two are so distinct that they have no real connection with each other. Stephen J. Gould took this view and called them Non-Overlapping Magisteria. However, this is not true, because though the questions are different, their answers have to be consonant with each other. Putting the kettle in the refrigerator is not compatible with wanting to make a cup of tea! Consequently science and religion interact and complement each other, and John Hedley Brooke's Boyle Lecture reminded us that the conversation between them has in fact had a long history. Science and religion are friends and not foes in the great quest for truthful understanding. They have things to tell each other. In actual fact, a fruitful dialogue is currently taking place between the two.

The tenth anniversary of the revived Boyle Lectures offers an opportunity to review the present state of this conversation. I want to take us on an excursion along the busy frontier between science and religion, starting in my home territory, the end where the physicists dwell. They are deeply impressed by the wonderful order of the universe, revealed to us through its remarkable rational transparency to our enquiry. Of course, it is not surprising that we can understand the everyday world in which we have to be able to survive. Evolution will surely have shaped our brains to that end. But why are we able also to understand the hidden subatomic world of quantum physics, remote from direct impact upon us? That world is quite different in its character from the Newtonian world of everyday. The latter is clear and regular in its character, but the quantum world is cloudy and fitful. In it, if you know where an electron is, you cannot know what it is doing; if you know what it is doing, you cannot know where it is. That is Heisenberg's uncertainty principle in a nutshell. Yet we can understand that world on its own terms and, it turns out, the key to this understanding is the seemingly abstract subject of mathematics.

It is an actual technique of discovery in fundamental physics to seek theories that are expressed in equations that the mathematicians can recognize as being beautiful. Not all of you may know about mathematical beauty – it is a rather rarefied form of aesthetic experience, concerned with qualities such as elegance and economy – but it is something that the mathematically minded can agree about. Time and again in the history of physics, it has turned out that it is only such theories that have the power of long-term explanation that persuades us of their validity. The greatest physicist whom I have known personally was Paul Dirac, one of the founders of modern quantum theory. Asked once about his fundamental beliefs, he strode to a blackboard and wrote 'The laws of physics are expressed in beautiful equations.' He made his great discoveries by a lifelong devotion to that belief.

The rational transparency and rational beauty of the universe are facts that scientists are happy to exploit, but that science itself does not explain. Yet these are surely remarkable facts that it would be intellectually lazy just to treat as fortunate accidents. Theology can make the deep intelligibility of the universe itself intelligible when it sees cosmic order as a reflection of the Mind of its Creator. I believe that science is possible in the deep way that it has proved to be, just because the world is a divine creation and we are, to use an ancient and powerful phrase, made in the image of our Creator.

This insight is an illustration of the right relationship between science and theology. Religion should not pretend to be able answer science's questions for it, for we have every reason to believe that scientifically stateable questions will receive scientifically stateable answers, but religion's role is to address questions that arise out of scientific experience but that go beyond science's self-limited power to address. The learned call these metaquestions. Such questions are deep, and it cannot be claimed that the answers proposed are logically certain beyond demur. Rather, the claim must be that they are insightful and intellectually satis-fying. It is not being asserted that atheists are stupid, for many are in fact highly intelligent and truth-seeking people, but that theism explains more than atheism can. This kind of reasoning is called natural theology, appealing to aspects of general experi-ence, such as the character of the world that science explores, that are claimed to be best understood as offering hints of the veiled presence of God. Belief in the possibility of a natural theology of this kind has been a key theme in the Boyle Lectures.

A second meta-question relevant to natural theology asks 'Why is the universe so special?' On the whole, scientists prefer the gen-eral to the particular, and their natural expectation was that our world is just a common or garden specimen of what a universe might be like. However, as we have come to understand many of the processes that over 13.7 billion years have turned the almost uniform ball of energy that sprang from the Big Bang into the pre-sent world that is the home of saints and scientists, we have come to realize that it is only a very particular – one might say 'finely tuned' – universe that is capable of the astonishingly fruitful pro-cess of generating carbon-based life.

This surprising and unexpected conclusion is often called 'The Anthropic Principle', and many considerations have lead to it. John Barrow's Boyle Lecture summarized many of them. Here, one example will have to suffice. The very early universe is so simple that it only makes the two simplest chemical elements, hydrogen and helium. There is only one place in the universe where the vital element carbon, essential for life, can be made, and that is in the interior nuclear furnaces of the stars. Every atom of carbon in our bodies was once inside a star. We are people of stardust. One of the triumphs of astrophysics in the twentieth century was the unravelling of the processes by which the heavier elements were made. It turns out that the generation of carbon depends very delicately on the details of the nuclear forces involved. If these had been only a little bit different from what they are, there would have been no carbon and we would not be here. Again, it would surely be intellectually lazy to treat this fine-tuning of the laws of nature, which science accepts but does not explain, as just a happy accident. The theist will see it as an expression of the Creator's will in bringing into being a creation endowed with great potentiality. Those who resist the threat of theism are driven to the somewhat desperate expedient of the hypothesis of the multiverse, the supposition that there exists a vast, possibly infinite, array of different universes, each with different laws of nature and all of them, apart from our own, inaccessible to us. In this vast collection, ours is just by chance the one capable of being anthropically fertile.

Because of the lack of the possibility of direct observation, the prodigal assumption of the existence of a multiverse is as metaphysical as the assumption of the existence of a divine Creator, and it does not have the kind of collateral support that considerations such as cosmic intelligibility afford to the concept of creation. Moreover, without further argument, it is by no means clear that even an infinite multiverse must include an anthropic member. An infinite array does not necessarily include every possibility. After all, there are an infinite number of even integers, but none of them has the property of oddness.

Physicists are deeply impressed by the wonderful order of the cosmos and by the profound potentiality, which was already present in the fabric of the laws of nature immediately following the Big Bang that has enabled the universe, after ten billion years of unfolding development, to generate life. Many physicists, even if they are not conventional religious believers, feel a kind of cosmic religiosity such as Einstein expressed, when he said that in making his great discoveries, he felt like a child in the presence of the Elders.

However, when we move to the biological sector of the frontier, the scene changes and there is a great deal of border warfare. Partly, this is due to the unwise way in which some religious believers have mistakenly refused to accept the insights of evolutionary biology, but it is also due to the fact that the biologists see a much more complex and ambiguous scene than the physicists' view of deep cosmic order. Biological evolution is certainly fertile, but at the cost of predation, parasitism and extinctions. The Boyle Lectures of Celia Deane-Drummond, John Haught, Simon Conway Morris and Keith Ward addressed these issues from a variety of perspectives.

The basic theological way to think about evolution was neatly formulated by Charles Darwin's clergyman friend, Charles Kingsley, soon after the publication of *The Origin of Species*. He said that Darwin had made it clear that God had not created a ready-made world but had done something cleverer than that in bringing into being a world so endowed with fruitful potentiality that creatures could be allowed to 'make themselves' by their unfolding exploration of divinely given fertility. From the theological understanding that the Creator is the God of love, such a creation, in which creatures are given the freedom to be themselves and to make themselves, is truly fitting, since the gift of love is always the gift of some appropriate measure of freedom afforded to the objects of love.

An evolving creation is, therefore, a great good, but it has a necessary shadow side. It is a fundamental scientific insight that regimes that are capable of generating true novelty always exist 'at the edge of chaos'. That is to say, they are regimes in which order and disorder, regularity and contingency, necessity and chance, interlace. If things are too orderly, they are too rigid for anything really new to emerge. If there were no genetic mutations, no new forms of life could appear. Yet if things are too disorderly, nothing of novelty that emerged could persist. If there was too much genetic mutation, no species could become established on which the sifting and preserving process of natural selection could act. The fruitfulness of the 3.5-billion-year history of life on Earth, which has turned what was originally a world of bacteria into a world with elephants and human beings in it, has depended on there being just the right amount of genetic mutation to be the engine of fertility.

Yet if germ cells are to mutate and produce new forms of life, it is inevitable that somatic (body) cells will also be able to mutate, and sometimes this will result in malignancy. The anguishing fact of cancer is not something gratuitous, which a Creator, who was a bit more competent or a bit less callous, could easily have eliminated. It is the necessary cost of a creation, in which creatures are allowed to make themselves. Ironically, biological evolution is not the point of irreconcilable confrontation between science and religion, but it is where theology receives some help from science as it wrestles with what is surely its most challenging perplexity: the existence of natural evil and suffering in a world claimed to be the creation of a good and powerful God.

We all tend to feel that if we had been in charge of creation, frankly we would have done it better. We would have kept all the nice things (flowers and sunsets) and got rid of the nasty things (disease and disaster). However, as science has shown us how the world actually has to work, we have come to see that it is a kind of package deal, in which 'good' and 'bad' are inextricably intertwined as fruitfulness comes to birth at the edge of chaos. I do not suggest for a moment that this removes all the perplexity and anguish that we feel about evil and suffering, but I think these insights are of some help as theologians continue to struggle with these issues.

Evolutionary process is not restricted to biology alone. Its general character is the interplay of regularity and contingency. For an example from physics, consider the history of the generation of cosmic structure. The very early universe following the Big Bang was not completely uniform but there were small random fluctuations in its energy density (contingency). Through the contractive influence of gravity (regularity) these inhomogeneities were progressively enhanced, resulting in a snowballing effect, which over about a billion years led to the vital emergence of stars and galaxies. The universe itself is fundamentally an evolving world.

In relation to biology, the question naturally arises of whether the role of contingency implies that the eventual emergence of self-conscious beings in the history of life is no more than a fortunate but ultimately meaningless accident. Stephen J. Gould notoriously claimed that if the tape of life were to be rerun a second time, so to speak, nothing remotely like ourselves could be expected to result. Certainly homo sapiens in all our five-fingered specificity would not be expected a second time, but Simon Conway Morris has argued that self-conscious beings of some kind would be a natural expectation. He points to the phenomenon of convergence in biological evolution, suggesting that the history of life is not some kind of random drunkard's walk through an infinite possibility space, never likely to be in anything like the same direction twice, but something much more constrained.

The number of systems that are both biologically accessible and functionally effective seems to be quite limited. In consequence, there is a notable degree of repetition in evolutionary process. For example, the eye has evolved independently several times in the course of terrestrial history. The symphony of life is neither like the performance of a fixed score predetermined in eternity, nor like random noise, but like a grand improvisation with the strikingly fruitful harmony in its contingent variations taking place within the laws of biological counterpoint. This view of unfolding fertility has encouraged theologians to add to the venerable concept of creation out of nothing (that is, the timeless holding of the world in being by an eternal Creator) the further concept of continuous creation, the unfolding within time of the Creator's will realized within the divinely ordained processes of nature. The balance between creaturely action and divine providential action is one to which I shall return shortly.

We now move to the final sector of the frontier, the place where theology's neighbours are the human sciences, such as psychology and anthropology. The Boyle Lectures of Philip Clayton and Malcolm Jeeves surveyed this territory. It is clearly one of great significance for theology, but I think that a great deal of exploration still remains to be done. Our attention will be directed briefly to what can be learnt about the nature of the human person. Neuroscience is currently making great progress in identifying the neural pathways by which our brains process the information coming to us from our external environment. This work is surely significant, but I believe it is also necessary to be aware of its limited scope.

It is clear that we are intrinsically embodied beings and our conscious experience is closely linked to the physical state of our brains. A smart tap on the head with a hammer would be a crude way of making the same point. Yet there is a great gap yawning between talk of neural firings and the simplest mental experiences, such as seeing red or feeling toothache. This is a gap that no one currently knows how to bridge. The problem of qualia (feels) is a very hard problem indeed, which we are far from being able to solve. Bombastic talk of consciousness being 'the last frontier' that the heroic armies of reductionist science just are about to cross is extremely ill-judged. In fact, it is just possible that the nature of consciousness is one that will never be amenable to full understanding in scientific terms alone. Everything else that science studies, whether matter or life, can be treated as external to us, but consciousness is internal and private. We have no direct access to the consciousness of another person. We know that we can agree about attaching the label 'red' to the same object, but I do not know whether your experience of seeing red is exactly the same as mine. Science has certainly not established that mental experience is nothing but the firing of hordes of neurons, though it is certainly related to physical activity in the brain.

Human beings are psychosomatic unities in which the mental and the material exist in some kind of profound complementarity. Such a view of human nature would not have surprised the writers of the Bible, for in Hebrew thought persons were seen, in a celebrated phrase, as 'animated bodies rather than incarnated souls'. Although Christian thinking has often tended to be platonic in character, regarding the soul as a kind of detachable spiritual component temporarily housed in a fleshy body and awaiting release at death, this devaluation of our embodied status was a bad mistake. Human beings are not apprentice angels and our ultimate hope is not spiritual survival but the resurrection of the body.

Must we then give up the idea of the soul? I do not think so, but we shall have to reconceive it. The soul is presumably 'the real me', the carrier of my personal identity. At first sight, it is almost as perplexing to know what this is in this present life as it might be beyond death. What makes me, a bald elderly academic, the same person as the schoolboy with the shock of black hair in the photograph of long ago? It might seem that the answer is material continuity, but that is an illusion. The atoms that make up our bodies are changing all the time, through wear and tear, eating and drinking. I am atomically distinct from that schoolboy. What is the real me – and here the problem is so deep that I admittedly have to wave my hands, but I believe in the right direction – is something like the almost infinitely complex information-bearing 'pattern' (memories, character and so on) carried at one time by the atoms of my body. That pattern is the soul. In a very crude analogy, it is software rather than the hardware. I shall return to this point later.

So far in our perambulation of the frontier, most of what I have said would be as consistent with the spectator God of deism, who simply decreed the order of the world and then stood back to see what happened as a result, as with the God of Christian theism, who is providentially active within the history of creation. But doesn't science portray a world so deterministic in its character that there is no scope for such specific divine action? Certainly, after Newton many people believed the universe to be purely mechanical, a clockwork world, whose God could be no more than a celestial Clockmaker.

In consequence, the eighteenth century saw the rise of deism. Yet the twentieth century has seen the death of a merely mechanical picture of the physical universe. This was due to the discovery of intrinsic unpredictabilities present in nature, first at the subatomic level of quantum theory, and later at the macroscopic level of chaos theory. The word 'intrinsic' is important here, for these are not unpredictabilities that could be removed by more precise calculation or more exact measurement. They are properties of nature. Unpredictability is an epistemological property, concerned with what can or cannot be known. How epistemology relates to ontology (what is the case) requires further metaphysical decision. For example, it has been found that the uncertainty in quantum physics can be interpreted either as due to an intrinsic indeterminacy present in nature or it could be due simply to a necessary ignorance of some of the factors that actually fully determine what happens. It has turned out that there are theories of either kind that give exactly the same empirical results, despite their very different characters. The choice between them cannot therefore be made on purely scientific grounds, but it is a matter for metaphysical decision, which has to be defended by metaphysical arguments.

Those of a realist turn of mind, who think that what we know is a reliable guide to what is the case, will closely align epistemology and ontology and so interpret unpredictabilities as signs of an actual causal openness. To do so does not imply that the future is some sort of random lottery, but that there is space for the operation of other causal factors beyond science's reduction-ist account of the exchange of energy between constituents. An obvious candidate for such causes would be the willed acts of agents, either the whole human person or God's providential action within the open grain of creation. In any case, it is clear that science has not established the causal closure of the world on its reductionist terms alone.

If something like this is right, it has three significant impli-cations for theology. The first is that events cannot be exhaustively analysed and itemized, as if nature did this, human agency did that, and divine providence did a third thing. Details of causes are inevitably partially hidden behind a veil of unpredictability. The eye of faith may discern God's providence at work, but this cannot be demonstrated explicitly. The second point to emphasize is that, while there are these unpredictabilities in nature (clouds) there are also reliable predictabilities (clocks). The Sun will rise tomorrow at the expected time. In consequence, there are some things that it is not appropriate to pray for. The great early Christian thinker, Origen, who lived in Alexandria, said that one should not pray for the cool of spring in the heat of summer, tempting though that must have been to him at times. The third point is to emphasize that this picture of providence portrays God as acting within the unfolding open grain of nature and not fitfully interfering with it from the outside. Christian theology has to steer a course between two unacceptably extreme pictures of divine action: the one the Cosmic Tyrant in tight control of absolutely everything, giving no freedom at all to creatures; the other, the indifferent deistic Spectator. How the balance is actually struck between divine and creaturely action is the classic problem of grace and freewill, now written cosmically large.

A final issue has now to be faced. It is the significance of the future, an issue that Jürgen Moltmann addressed theologically in his Boyle Lecture. Every story that science has to tell ends ultimately in decay and futility. This is due to the second law of thermodynamics, which says that without external intervention the disorder of a system can only increase and never decrease. This is because there are so many more ways of being disorderly than there are of being orderly, so that statistically the waters of chaos continue to rise. We know that we are going to die on a timescale of tens of years and the cosmologists reliably tell us that the universe itself will die on a timescale of many billions of years, most probably by becoming ever colder and more dilute till all life must vanish everywhere within it. Does not this fact put in question theology's claim that the universe is now and always a meaningful divine creation?

There is certainly no natural expectation that science could offer of the hope of a destiny beyond death. Yet the 'horizontal' story that science tells of the unfolding of present process is not the only tale to tell. There is theology's 'vertical' story of the faithfulness of God, who will not allow anything of good to be lost. This is just the point that Jesus made in his controversy with the Sadducees about whether there is a human destiny beyond death (Mark 12.18–27). He pointed them to the fact that at the burning bush God was declared to be the God of Abraham, Isaac and Jacob, commenting 'the God not of the dead, but of the living'. If the Patriarchs mattered to God once, as they certainly did, they must matter to the faithful God for ever. They were not cast aside at death, like broken pots thrown on to a rubbish heap. While there is no natural hope of a destiny beyond death, theologically there is every hope arising from the faithfulness of our Creator. Christians, of course, believe that this hope has been exemplified and guaranteed by the resurrection of Jesus Christ.

Science, of itself, can speak neither for nor against this theological conviction, but the question remains of the credibility of such a hope. Can we make sense of the claim that human beings shall live again after the decay of their bodies? Because I believe that we are intrinsically embodied beings, I believe that this hope must take the form of the resurrection of the body and not some form of merely spiritual survival. If such an idea is to be credible, two basic criteria must be satisfied, one of continuity and one of discontinuity.

It must really be Abraham, Isaac and Jacob, who live again in the Kingdom of God, and not just new characters given the old names for old times' sake. This is the criterion of continuity. It requires a carrier of that continuity between this world and the next, which traditionally has been understood as the human soul. I have suggested that the soul is something like an almost infinitely complex information-bearing pattern. This pattern will dissolve with the decay of my body, but it is a coherent hope that God will not allow it to be lost but will preserve it in the divine memory. That in itself would not be a fully human destiny beyond death, for that would require the re-embodiment of that pattern in some form of environment of God's choosing – in other words, the resurrection of the body.

However, there would be no point is making the Patriarchs live again simply so that they could die again, so this re-embodiment will have to be in some form of 'matter', which is different from the matter of this world. This is the criterion of discontinuity. It seems a wholly coherent possibility that God could create a form of 'matter' so endowed with strong self-organizing principles that it would not be subject to the thermodynamic drift to decay that characterizes the matter of this world. But two further questions then immediately arise. One is: What will be the relation of this 'matter' to present matter? I believe that the one is the redemptive transform of the other, just as Christ's risen and glorified body was the transform of his dead body (hence the empty tomb). Human destiny and cosmic destiny lie together in the Creator's purposes (see the Cosmic Christ of Colossians 1.15–20).

More critical is the second question: If the new creation is going to be free from death and futility, why did the Creator bother with the old creation subject to decay and transience? I believe the answer to lie in a recognition that the Creator's purpose is intrinsically two-step: first the old creation existing at some distance from the veiled presence of its Creator so that creatures can be allowed the freedom to be themselves and to make themselves, and then the new creation, drawn freely into ever closer encounter with the unveiled riches of the divine nature.

These ideas that I have been trying to sketch are inevitably to a degree speculative – in many ways 'wait and see' is the best strategy for eschatological thinking – but I believe they help us not to waver in our trust in a destiny beyond death, whose guarantee lies ultimately in the faithfulness of God and the resurrection of Christ.

Our exploration of the frontier between science and religion has been rather a lightening tour, but I hope it has served to show something of the fruitfulness of the dialogue that is taking place. Both scientists and theologians tend to be critical realists, recognizing that there is a truth to be found but one that is subtle beyond Enlightenment expectations of unproblematic objectivity, for the quest for truth is guided by taking seriously experience, which only becomes meaningful when it is interpreted according to a chosen but potentially corrigible point of view. The claim is not to the attainment of final and absolute truth, either in science or theology, but of conclusions that are sufficiently well motivated to justify commitment to belief, without giving up the hope of attaining further understanding in due course. Both science and theology know that truth often seems surprising, leading us to conceptions that we would not have been able to form without the nudge of reality. In 1899, no one would have supposed that the wave/particle duality of light was a rational possibility, but it proved to be the case. Early Christianity had to struggle with the deeper duality of the human and divine in Jesus Christ.

I see a cousinly relation between my scientific experience and my theological experience. I like to say that I am two-eyed, viewing reality with both the eye of science and the eye of religion. I believe that with this binocular vision I can see further and deeper than I could with either eye on its own.

Bibliography of Works Cited

Adler, Stephen, 2004, *Quantum Theory as an Emergent Phenomenon: The Statistical Dynamics of Global Unitary Invariant Matrix Models as the Precursor of Quantum Field Theory*, Cambridge: Cambridge University Press.

Alexander, Samuel, 1920, *Space, Time, and Deity*, The Gifford Lectures for 1916–18, 2 vols, London: Macmillan.

Allport, G. W., 1951, *The Individual and His Religion: A Psychological Interpretation*, London: Constable.

Anderson, Philip, 2005, 'Emerging Physics: A Fresh Approach to Viewing the Complexity of the Universe', *Nature* 434, pp. 701–2.

Aquinas, Thomas, 2006, *Summa Theologiae*, Vol. 8: *Creation, Variety and Evil*, trans. Thomas Gilby, Cambridge: Cambridge University Press.

Balthasar, Hans Urs von, 1990a, *Mysterium Paschale*, trans. Aidan Nichols, O. P., Edinburgh: T & T Clark.

Balthasar, Hans Urs von, 1990b, *Theo-Drama, Volume 11, Dramatis Personae: Man in God*, trans. Graham Harrison, San Francisco: Ignatius Press.

Barbour, Ian, 1966, *Issues in Science and Religion*, London: SCM Press.

Barfield, O., 1952, *Poetic Diction: A Study in Meaning*, London: Faber & Faber.

Barham, J., 2004, 'The Emergence of Biological Value', in W. A. Dembski and M. Ruse (eds), *Debating Design: From Darwin to DNA*, Cambridge: Cambridge University Press, pp. 210–26.

Barrett, Justin L., 2004, *Why Would Anyone Believe in God?*, Lanham, MA: AltaMira.

Barrett, Justin L., 2010, 'The Relative Unnaturalness of Atheism: On Why Geertz and Markusson are both Right and Wrong', *Religion* 40, pp. 169–72.

Barrett, Justin L., 2011, 'Metarepresentation, *Homo religiosus*, and *Homo symbolicus*', in Christopher N. Henshilwood and Francesco D'Errico (eds), *Homo symbolicus: The Dawn of Language, Imagination and Spirituality*, Amsterdam: John Benjamins, pp. 205–24.

Barrow, J. D., 2011, *The Book of Universes*, London: Bodley Head and Vintage.

Bartlett, F. C., 1950, *Religion as Experience, Belief and Action*, Oxford: Oxford University Press.

Bateson, Patrick and Peter Gluckman, 2011, *Plasticity, Robustness, Development and Evolution*, Cambridge: Cambridge University Press.

Bauckham, Richard, 2006, *Jesus and the Eyewitnesses: The Gospels as Eyewitness Testimony*, Grand Rapids, MI: Eerdmans.

Behe, Michael J., 1996, *Darwin's Black Box: The Biochemical Challenge to Evolution*, Boston: Free Press.

Behe, Michael J., 1997, 'Letter to *The Boston Review*', http://www.arn.org/docs/behe/mb_brrespbr.htm, accessed 29 January 2006.

Behe, Michael J., 2007, 'Irreducible Complexity', in William Dembski and Michael Ruse (eds), *Debating Design: From Darwin to DNA*, Cambridge: Cambridge University Press.

Bekoff, Marc and Jessica Pierce, 2009, *Wild Justice: The Moral Lives of Animals*, Chicago: University of Chicago Press.

Berger, Peter L., 1967, *The Sacred Canopy*, Garden City, NY: Doubleday.

Berger, Peter L., 1969, *A Rumor of Angels: Modern Society and the Rediscovery of the Supernatural*, Garden City, NY, Doubleday.

Berry, R. J. and Malcolm Jeeves, 2008, 'The Nature of Human Nature', *Science and Christian Belief* 20.1, pp. 3–48.

Birch, Thomas, 1999, *The Works of the Honourable Robert Boyle*, reprinted from the 1772 edition, with a new introduction by Peter Alexander, Bristol: Thoemmes Press.

Blumenberg, Hans, 1983, *Die Lesbarkeit der Welt*, Frankfurt: Suhrkamp.

Bowler, Peter J., 2001, *Reconciling Science and Religion: The Debate in Early Twentieth-Century Britain*, Chicago: University of Chicago Press.

Boyer, Pascal, 2001, *Religion Explained: The Human Instincts that Fashion Gods, Spirits and Ancestors*, London: Vintage.

Boyle, Robert, 1690–1, *The Christian Virtuoso*, London: Edward Jones.

Boyle, Robert, 1772, *Works*, T. Birch (ed.), 6 vols, London: J & F Rivington.

Broglie, Louis de, 1943, *Licht und Materie: Ergebnisse der neuen Physik. Mit einem Vorwort von Werner Heisenberg*, Hamburg: H. Goverts.

Brooke, John Hedley, 1991, *Science and Religion: Some Historical Perspectives*, Cambridge: Cambridge University Press.

Brooke, John Hedley, 2003, 'Darwin and Victorian Christianity', in Jonathan Hodge and Gregory Radick (eds), *The Cambridge Companion to Darwin*, Cambridge: Cambridge University Press, pp. 192–213.

Brooke, John Hedley, 2009a, '"Laws impressed on Matter by the Creator"? The *Origin* and the Question of Religion', in Robert J. Richards and Michael Ruse (eds), *The Cambridge Companion to the* Origin of Species, Cambridge: Cambridge University Press, pp. 256–74.

Brooke, John Hedley, 2009b, 'Should the Word *Nature* be Eliminated?', in James D. Proctor (ed.), *Envisioning Nature, Science, and Religion*, West Conshohocken, PA: Templeton Press, pp. 312–36.

Brooke, John Hedley, 2010, 'The Legacy of Robert Boyle: Then and Now', http://www.gresham.ac.uk/lectures-and-events/the-boyle-lecture-the-leg-acy-of-robert-boyle-then-and-now, accessed 14 September 2011.

Brooke, John Hedley and Geoffrey Cantor, 1998, *Reconstructing Nature: The Engagement of Science and Religion*, Edinburgh: T & T Clark.

Brown, Warren S., 2006, 'The Brain, Religion and Baseball: Comments on the Potential for a Neurology of Religion and Religious Experience', in Patrick McNamara and Praeger (eds), *Where God and Science Meet: How Brain and Evolutionary Studies Alter Our Understanding of Religion*, Vol. 2: *The Neurology of Religious Experience*, Santa Barbara, CA: Praeger, pp. 229–44.

Bryant, Levi, Graham Harman and Nick Srnicek (eds), 2011, *The Speculative Turn. Continental Materialism and Realism*, Melbourne: Re.Press.

Bultmann, Rudolf, 1960, *Glauben und Verstehen*, vol. 3, Tübingen: J. C. B. Mohr.

Byrne, Michael and G. R. Bush (eds), 2007, *St Mary-le-Bow: A History*, Yorkshire: Wharncliffe Books.

Cantor, Geoffrey, 1999, 'Boyling Over: A Commentary', *British Journal for the History of Science* 32, pp. 315–24.

Carpenter, Edward, 1948, *Thomas Tenison, Archbishop of Canterbury*, London: SPCK.

Cartwright, Nancy, 1999, *The Dappled World: A Study in the Boundaries of Science*, Cambridge: Cambridge University Press.

Cartwright, Nancy and Eric Martin, 2013, 'Queen Physics: How Much of the Globe is Painted Red?', in Fraser Watts and Christopher C. Knight (eds), *God and the Scientist: Exploring the Work of John Polkinghorne*, London: Ashgate, pp. 67–76.

Chesterton, G. K., 1913, *Tremendous Trifles*, London: Methuen.

Clayton, N. and N. Emery, 2004, 'The Mentality of Crows: Convergent Evolution in Corvids and Apes', *Science* 306, pp. 1903–7.

Clayton, Philip, 2004, *Mind and Emergence: From Quantum to Consciousness*, Oxford: Oxford University Press.

Clayton, Philip, 2012, *Religion and Science: The Basics*, London and New York: Routledge.

Clayton, Philip and Paul Davies (eds), 2006, *The Re-emergence of Emergence: The Emergentist Hypothesis from Science to Religion*, Oxford: Oxford University Press.

Clayton, Philip and Steven Knapp, 2011, *The Predicament of Belief: Science, Philosophy, Faith*, Oxford: Oxford University Press.

Clayton, Philip and Zachary Simpson (eds), 2006, *The Oxford Handbook of Religion and Science*, Oxford: Oxford University Press.

Coakley, S. F. (ed.), 2013 (in press), *Spiritual Healing: Science, Meaning, and Discernment*, Grand Rapids, MI: Eerdmans.

Cobb, Jr., John B. and David Griffin, 1976, *Process Theology: An Introductory Exposition*, Philadelphia: Westminster Press.

Conway Morris, Simon, 2003, *Life's Solution: Inevitable Humans in a Lonely Universe*, Cambridge: Cambridge University Press.

Corcoran, K., 2005, 'The Constitution of Persons', in J. B. Green and S. L. Palmer (eds), *In Search of the Soul: Four Views of the Mind–Body Problem*, Downers Grove, IL: InterVarsity Press.

Cramer, Fritz, 1993, *Der Zeitbaum: Grundlegung einer allgemeinen Zeittheorie*, Frankfurt: Insel.

Cramer, Fritz, 1998, *Symphonie des Lebendigen: Versuch einer allgemeinen Resonanztheorie*, Frankfurt: Insel.

Crisp, Oliver, 2007, *Divinity and Humanity*, Cambridge: Cambridge University Press.

Cunningham, Conor, 2010, *Darwin's Pious Idea: Why the Ultra-Darwinists and Creationists Both Get it Wrong*, Grand Rapids, MI: Eerdmans.

Darwin, Charles, 1859, *On the Origin of Species by Means of Natural Selection, or the Preservation of Favoured Races in the Struggle for Life*, 1st edn., London: John Murray.

Davis, Edward B., 1994, '"Parcere nominibus": Boyle, Hooke and the Rhetorical Interpretation of Descartes', in Michael Hunter (ed.), *Robert Boyle Reconsidered*, Cambridge: Cambridge University Press, pp. 157–75.

Davies, Paul, 1992, *The Mind of God: The Scientific Basis for a Rational World*, New York: Simon & Schuster.

Dawe, Donald, 1963, *The Form of a Servant*, Philadelphia: Westminster Press.

Dawkins, Richard, 1986, *The Blind Watchmaker*, London: Penguin.

Dawkins, Richard, 1976, *The Selfish Gene*, New York: Oxford University Press.

Dawkins, Richard, 1995, *River out of Eden: A Darwinian View of Life*, London: Weidenfeld & Nicolson.

Dawkins, Richard, 1996, *Climbing Mount Improbable*, New York: W. W. Norton & Co.

Dawkins, Richard, 2005, *The Ancestor's Tale: A Pilgrimage to the Dawn of Life*, London: Phoenix.

Deane-Drummond, C., 2009, *Christ and Evolution: Wonder and Wisdom*, Minneapolis/London: Fortress/SCM.

Dembski, William and Michael Ruse (eds), 2004, *Debating Design: From Darwin to DNA*, New York: Cambridge University Press.

Dennett, D. C., 1995, *Darwin's Dangerous Idea: Evolution and the Meanings of Life*, Harmondsworth: Penguin.

Dixon, Thomas, Geoffrey Cantor and Stephen Pumphrey (eds), 2010, *Science and Religion: New Historical Perspectives*, Cambridge: Cambridge University Press.

Dostoyevsky, Fyodor, 1969, *The Idiot*, trans. Henry and Olga Carlisle, New York: Signet Classic.

Durham, William, 1991, *Coevolution: Genes, Culture, and Human Diversity*, Stanford: Stanford University Press.

Ecklund, Elaine Howard, 2010, *Science vs. Religion: What Scientists Really Think*, Oxford: Oxford University Press.

Evans, C. S., 2006, *Exploring Kenotic Christology: The Self-Emptying of God*, Oxford: Oxford University Press.

Evans-Pritchard, E. E., 1965, *Theories of Primitive Religion*, Oxford: Clarendon Press.

Evelyn, John, 2000, *The Diary of John Evelyn*, edited by E. S. de Beer, Volume 5, 1690–1706, Oxford: Clarendon Press.

Flieger, V., 2002, *Splintered Light: Logos and Language in Tolkien's World*, Kent, OH: Kent State University Press.

Fodor, Jerry and Massimo Piatelli-Palmarini, 2010, *What Darwin Got Wrong*, London: Profile Books.

Franks, Nigel, 2008, 'Convergent Evolution, Serendipity, and Intelligence for the Simple-Minded', in Simon Conway Morris (ed.), *The Deep Structure of Biology: Is Convergence Sufficiently Ubiquitous to Give a Directional Signal?*, West Conshohocken, PA: Templeton Press, pp. 111–27.

Gaukroger, Stephen, 2006, *The Emergence of a Scientific Culture: Science and the Shaping of Modernity, 1210–1685*, Oxford: Oxford University Press.

Gilkey, Langdon, 1985, *Creationism on Trial: Evolution and God at Little Rock*, Charlottesville: University of Virginia Press.

Gillispie, Charles Coulston, 1996, *Genesis and Geology: A Study in the Relations of Scientific Thought, Natural Theology, and Social Opinion in Great Britain, 1790–1850*, Cambridge, MA: Harvard University Press.

Goetz, S., 2005, 'Substance Dualism', in J. B. Green and S. L. Palmer (eds), *In Search of the Soul: Four Views of the Mind–Body Problem*, Downers Grove, IL: InterVarsity Press.

Goodman, D. C. (ed.), 1973, *Science and Religious Belief 1600–1900: A Selection of Primary Sources*, Bristol: John Wright in association with the Open University Press.

Gould, Stephen Jay, 2001, *Rock of Ages: Science and Religion in the Fullness of Life*, London: Cape.

Gould, Stephen Jay, 2002, *The Structure of Evolutionary Theory*, Belknap/Cambridge, MA: Harvard University Press.

Gray, P. M. et al., 2002, 'The Music of Nature and the Nature of Music', *Science* 291, pp. 52–4.

Gray, Terry, 1996, 'Re: Fw: Mere Creation conference' A debate with Bob DeHaan, http://www.asa3.org/archive/asa/199611/0144.html, accessed 29 January 2006.

Gregory, Frederick, 2003. 'Intersections of Physical Science and Western Religion in the Nineteenth and Twentieth Centuries', in Mary Jo Nye (ed.), *The Cambridge History of Science*, Vol. 5, Cambridge: Cambridge University Press, pp. 36–53.

Hall, Marie Boas, 1958, *Robert Boyle and Seventeenth-Century Chemistry*, Cambridge: Cambridge University Press.

Hall, Marie Boas (ed.), 1965, *Robert Boyle on Natural Philosophy: An Essay with Selections from His Writings*, Bloomington, IN: Indiana University Press.

Hallman, Joseph M., 1991, *The Descent of God: Divine Suffering in History and Theology*, Minneapolis: Fortress Press.

Harrison, Peter, 1998, *The Bible, Protestantism and the Rise of Natural Science*, Cambridge: Cambridge University Press.

Harrison, Peter, 2007, *The Fall of Man and the Foundations of Science*, Cambridge: Cambridge University Press.

Harrison, Peter, 2010, *The Cambridge Companion to Science and Religion*, Cambridge: Cambridge University Press.

Hartshorne, Charles, 1941, *Man's Vision of God*, Chicago and New York: Willett, Clark & Co.

Hasker, W., 2005, 'On Behalf of Emergent Dualism', in J. B. Green and S. L. Palmer (eds), *In Search of the Soul: Four Views of the Mind–Body Problem*, Downers Grove, IL: InterVarsity Press, pp. 75–100.

Haught, John F., 1993, *The Promise of Nature*, Mahwah, NJ: Paulist Press.

Haught, John F., 1996, 'Ecology and Eschatology', in D. Christiansen and W. Grazen (eds), *And God Says That It Was Good: Catholic Theology and the Environment*, Washington, DC: US Catholic Conference.

Haught, John F., 2000, *God After Darwin: A Theology of Evolution*, Boulder, CO: Westview Press.

Haught, John F., 2010, *Making Sense of Evolution: Darwin, God and the Drama of Life*, Louisville, KY: Westminster John Knox Press.

Hawking, Stephen and Leonard Mlodinow, 2010, *The Grand Design*, New York: Bantam.

Heidegger, Martin, 1962, *Being and Time*, trans. J. Macquarrie and E. Robinson, London: Routledge.

Hick, John, 1978, *Evil and the God of Love*, revised edn, New York: Harper & Row.

Holder, Rodney, 2004, *God, the Multiverse, and Everything: Modern Cosmology and the Argument from Design*, Aldershot: Ashgate.

Hooykaas, Reijer, 1997, *Robert Boyle: A Study in Science and Christian Belief, With a Foreword by John Hedley Brooke and Michael Hunter*, Lanham: University Press of America.

Howe, Günter, 1953, *Mensch und Physik*, Berlin: Kreuz Verlag.

Hunter, Michael, 1990, 'Alchemy, Magic and Moralism in the Thought of Robert Boyle', *British Journal for the History of Science* 23, pp. 387–410.

Hunter, Michael (ed.), 1994a, *Robert Boyle Reconsidered*, Cambridge: Cambridge University Press.

Hunter, Michael (ed.), 1994b, *Robert Boyle by Himself and his Friends*, London: Pickering.

Hunter, Michael, 1999, 'Robert Boyle (1627–91): A suitable Case for Treatment?', *British Journal for the History of Science* 32, pp. 261–75.

Hunter, Michael, 2009, *Boyle: Between God and Science*, New Haven and London: Yale University Press.

Hunter, Michael and Edward B. Davis (eds), 1999–2000, *The Works of Robert Boyle*, 14 vols, London: Pickering and Chatto.

Huuysteen, W. van, ND, *Human Uniqueness and Symbolisation: The Global Spiral*, http:/www.metanexus.net/magazine/tabid/68/id/10167/Default.aspx.

Jacob, Margaret C., 1976, *The Newtonians and the English Revolution 1689–1720*, New York: Cornell University Press.

Jaki, S. L., 1986, *Chesterton: A Seer of Science*, Urbana: University of Illinois Press.

James, W., 1902, *The Varieties of Religious Experience*, London: Longmans, Green.

Jammer, Max, 1954, *Concepts of Space: The History of Theories of Space in Physics*, with a Foreword by Albert Einstein, Cambridge, MA: Harvard University Press.

Jeeves, Malcolm, 1997, *Human Nature at the Millennium*, Grand Rapids, MI: Baker.

Jeeves, Malcolm and Brown, Warren, 2009, *Neuroscience, Psychology, and Religion: Illusions, Delusions, and Realities about Human Nature*, West Conshohocken, PA: Templeton Press.

Jenkins, Tim, 2009, 'Closer to Dan Brown than Gregor Mendel: On Dawkins' *The God Delusion*', *Scottish Journal of Theology* 62.3, pp. 268–81.

Kaufmann, Stuart, 1995, *At Home in the Universe: The Search for Laws of Self-Organisation and Complexity*, New York: Oxford University Press.

Kelly, Andrew and Melanie Kelly (eds), 2009, *Darwin: For the Love of Science*, Bristol: Bristol Cultural Development Partnership.

Kenny, Christopher, 1996, 'Theology and Natural Philosophy in Late Seventeenth Century and Early Eighteenth-Century Britain', PhD Diss., University of Leeds.

Kiefer, Julie, 2010, 'Primer and Interviews: Molecular Mechanisms of Morphological Evolution', *Developmental Dynamics* 239, pp. 3497–505.

Kierkegaard, Søren, 1944, *The Concept of Dread*, trans. W. Lowrie, Princeton, NJ: Princeton University Press.

Koselleck, Reinhard, 1979, *Vergangene Zukunft: Zur Semantik geschichtlicher Zeiten*, Frankfurt: Suhrkamp.

Laughlin, Robert, 2005, *A Different Universe: Reinventing Physics from the Bottom Down*, New York: Basic Books.

Lehn, Jean-Marie, 2002, 'Toward Complex Matter: Supramolecular Chemistry and Self-Organization', *Proceedings of the National Academy of Sciences* 99.8, pp. 4763–8.

Lovejoy, Arthur O., 1965, *The Great Chain of Being: A Study of the History of an Idea*, New York: Harper & Row.

MacIntosh, J. J. and Peter Anstey, 2006, 'Robert Boyle', in Edward N. Zalta, ed., *Stanford Encyclopedia of Philosophy*, Spring 2006 edition, URL http://plato.stanford.edu/archives/spi2006/entries/boyle/

MacIntosh, J. J., 2005, *Boyle on Atheism*, Toronto: University of Toronto Press.

Mackay, D. M., 1991, *Behind the Eye*, Oxford: Blackwell.

Macquarrie, John, 1978, *The Humility of God*, Philadelphia: Westminster Press.

Maddison, R. E. W., 1952, 'Studies in the Life of Robert Boyle, F. R. S., Part III', *Notes and Records of the Royal Society of London* 10, pp. 15–27.

Manson, N. A., 2000, 'Anthropocentrism and the Design Argument', *Religious Studies* 36, pp. 163–76.

Manuel, Frank E., 1968, *A Portrait of Isaac Newton*, Cambridge, MA: Belknap Press.

Marino, L., 1996, 'What can Dolphins tell us about Primate Evolution?', *Evolutionary Anthropology* 5, pp. 81–5.

Marino, L. et al., 2004, 'Neuroanatomy of the Killer Whale (*Orcinas orca*) from Magnetic Resonance Imaging', *Anatomical Record* 281A, pp. 1247–55.

McDowell, John, 1996, *Mind and World*, revised edn, Cambridge, MA: Harvard University Press.

McGrath, Alister, 2001, *A Scientific Theology*. Vol. 1: *Nature*, Edinburgh: T & T Clark.

McGrath, Alister, 2008, *The Open Secret: A New Vision for Natural Theology*, Oxford: Blackwell.

McGrath, Alister, 2009, *A Fine-Tuned Universe*, Louisville, KY: Westminster John Knox Press.

McGrath, Alister, 2010, *Why God Won't Go Away: Is the New Atheism Running on Empty?*, Nashville: Thomas Nelson.

MacIntosh, J. J. and Anstey, P., 2002 and 2010, 'Robert Boyle', entry in *Stanford Encyclopedia of Philosophy*, http://plato.stanford.edu/entries/boyle.

Meillassoux, Quentin, 2008, *After Finitude: An Essay on the Necessity of Contingency*, London: Continuum.

Middleton, J. R., 2005, *The Liberating Image: The imago Dei in Genesis 1*, Grand Rapids, MI: Brazos Press.

Miller, Patrick, 2004, 'What is a Human Being?: The Anthropology of Scripture', in Joel B. Green (ed.), *What about the Soul?*, Nashville: Abingdon Press, pp. 63–73.

Moltmann, Jürgen, 1968, 'Der Kategorie Novum in der christlichen Theologie' (1965), in *Perspektiven der Theologie*, Munich: C. Kaiser, pp. 174–88.

Moltmann, Jürgen, 1974, *The Crucified God*, trans. R. A. Wilson and John Bowden, New York: Harper & Row.

Moltmann, Jürgen, 1975, *The Experiment Hope*, ed. and trans. M. Douglas Meeks, Philadelphia: Fortress Press.

Moltmann, Jürgen, 1979, 'Creation as an Open System', in *The Future of Creation*, trans. Margaret Kohl, London: SCM Press, pp. 115–30.

Moltmann, Jürgen, 1985, *God in Creation: An Ecological Doctrine of Creation*. The Gifford Lectures, 1984–85, trans. Margaret Kohl, London and San Francisco: SCM Press and Harper & Row.

Moltmann, Jürgen, 2003, *Science and Wisdom*, trans. Margaret Kohl, London: SCM Press.

Moltmann, Jürgen, 2010, 'Natural Science and the Hermeneutics of Nature', in *Sun of Righteousness, Arise! God's Future for Humanity and the Earth*, Minneapolis and London: Fortress and SCM Press, pp. 189–208.

Monod, Jacques, 1971, *Chance and Necessity: An Essay on the Natural Philosophy of Modern Biology*, trans. Austryn Wainhouse, New York: Knopf.

Murchie, Guy, 1978, *The Seven Mysteries of Life: An Exploration in Science and Philosophy*, Boston: Houghton Mifflin.

Murphy, Nancey, 2005, 'Non Reductive Physicalism', in J. B. Green and S. L. Palmer (eds), *In Search of the Soul: Four Views of the Mind–Body Problem*, Downers Grove, IL: InterVarsity Press.

Murphy, Nancey and Warren S. Brown, 2007, *Did My Neurons Make Me Do It? Philosophical and Neurobiological Perspectives on Moral Responsibility and Free Will*, Oxford: Oxford University Press.

Myers, D., 2007, *Psychology*, 7th edn, New York: Worth.

Nagel, T., 2007, 'Science and the Mind–Body Problem', in *What is Our Real Knowledge About the Human Being? Scripta Varia 109*. Vatican City: Pontifical Academia Scientiarum, pp. 96–100.

Naito, H. and N. Matsui, 1988, 'Temporal Lobe Epilepsy with Ictal Ecstatic State and Interictal Behaviour of Hypergraphia', *Journal of Nervous and Mental Disease* 176.2, pp. 123–4.

Newberg, A., E. d'Aquili and V. Rause, 2001, *Why God Won't Go Away: Brain Science and the Biology of Belief*, New York: Ballantine Books.

Newberg, A., A. Alavi, M. Baime, M. Pourdehnad, J. Santanna and E. d'Aquili, 2001, 'The Measurement of Regional Cerebral Blood Flow During the Complex Cognitive Task of Meditation: A Preliminary SPECT Study', *Psychiatry Research* 2, pp. 113–22.

Nichols, David E. and Benjamin R. Chemel, 2006, 'The Neuropharmacology of Religious Experiences: Hallucinogens and the Experience of the Divine', in Patrick McNamara (ed.) *Where God and Science Meet*, Vol. 3: *The Psychology of Religious Experience*, Westport, CT: Praeger, pp. 1–34.

Nietzsche, Friedrich, 1973, 'Über Wahrheit und Lüge im aussermoralis-chen Sinne', in Giorgio Colli and Mazzino Montinari (eds), *Nietzsche Werke*, Berlin: Walter de Gruyter.

Nowak, Martin A., 2006a, *Evolutionary Dynamics: Exploring the Equations of Life*, Cambridge, MA: Harvard University Press.

Nowak, Martin A., 2006b, 'Five Rules for the Evolution of Cooperation', *Science* 314.8, pp. 1560–3.

Osler, Margaret J., 2001, 'Whose Ends? Teleology in Early Modern Natural Philosophy', in John Hedley Brooke, Margaret Osler and Jitse M. van der Meer (eds), *Science in Theistic Contexts: Cognitive Dimensions*, Chicago: University of Chicago Press, pp. 151–68.

Pannenberg, Wolfhart, 1977, *Faith and Reality*, trans. John Maxwell, Philadelphia: Westminster Press.

Pannenberg, Wolfhart, 1988–1994, *Systematic Theology*, 3 vols, Grand Rapids, MI: Eerdmans.

Peacocke, A. R., 2007, *All That Is: A Naturalistic faith for the Twenty-First Century*, ed. Philip Clayton, Minneapolis: Fortress Press.

Persinger, M. A., 1983, 'Religious and Mystical Experiences as Artifacts of Temporal Lobe Function: A General Hypothesis', *Perceptual and Motor Skills* 557, pp. 1225–62.

Persinger, M. A. and K. Makarec, 1987, 'Temporal Lobe Epileptic Signs and Correlative Behaviours Displayed by Normal Populations', *Journal of General Psychology* 1114, pp. 179–95.

Persinger, M. A. and K. Makarec, 1993, 'Complex Partial Epileptic Signs as a Continuum from Normals to Epileptics: Normative Data and Clinical Populations', *Journal of Clinical Psychology* 49, pp. 33–45.

Peters, Ted, 1992, *God – The World's Future: Systematic Theology for a Postmodern Era*, Minneapolis: Fortress Press.

Pettitt, Paul, 2011, 'The Living as Symbols; the Dead as Symbols: Problematising the Scale and Pace of Hominin Symbolic Evolution', in Christopher N. Henshilwood and Francesco D'Errico (eds), *Homo symbolicus: The Dawn of Language, Imagination and Spirituality*, Amsterdam: John Benjamins, pp. 141–61.

Picht, Georg, 1980, *Hier und Jetzt: Philosophieren nach Auschwitz*, vol. 1, Stuttgart: Klett-Cotta.

Polkinghorne, John, 1987, 'Creation and the Structure of the Physical World', *Theology Today* 44, pp. 53–68.

Polkinghorne, John, 1996, *Beyond Science*, Cambridge: Cambridge University Press.

Polkinghorne, John, 1998, *Belief in God in an Age of Science*, New Haven, CT: Yale University Press.

Polkinghorne, John (ed.), 2001, *The Work of Love: Creation as Kenosis*, Grand Rapids, MI: Eerdmans.

Polkinghorne, John, 2005a, *Exploring Reality: The Intertwining of Science and Religion*, London: SPCK.

Polkinghorne, John, 2005b, *Science and Providence: God's Interaction with the World*, West Conshohocken, PA: Templeton Press.

Polkinghorne, John (ed.), 2010, *The Trinity and an Entangled World: Relationality in Physical Science and Theology*, Grand Rapids, MI: Eerdmans.

Prigogine, I. and I. Stenger, 1997, *End of Certainty: Time, Chaos and the New Laws of Nature*, New York: Free Press.

Principe, Lawrence, 1998, *The Aspiring Adept: Robert Boyle and his Alchemical Quest*, Princeton: Princeton University Press.

Quash, Ben, 2005, *Theology and the Drama of History*, Cambridge: Cambridge University Press.

Rahner, Karl, 1969, *Theological Investigations*, Vol. 6, trans. Karl and Boniface Kruger, Baltimore: Helicon.

Ramachandran, V. S. et al., 1997, 'The Neural Basis of Religious Experiences', *Society for Neuroscience Conference Abstracts*, p. 16.

Rattansi, P. M., 1972, 'The Social Interpretation of Science in the Seventeenth Century', in Peter Mathias (ed.), *Science and Society 1600–1900*, Cambridge: Cambridge University Press, pp. 1–32.

Ratzinger, Joseph, 2007, *Jesus of Nazareth*, London: Bloomsbury.

Re Manning, Russell, 2007, 'Mere Summing Up? Some Considerations on the History of the Concept of Emergence and its Significance for Science and Religion', *Science and Christian Belief* 19.1, pp. 37–58.

Re Manning, Russell (ed.), 2013, *The Oxford Handbook of Natural Theology*, with John Hedley Brooke and Fraser Watts (consultant eds), Oxford: Oxford University Press.

Rees, Martin J., 2000, *Just Six Numbers: The Deep Forces that Shape the Universe*, New York: Basic Books.

Reiter, Johannes, 2006, 'Bild und Sprache der Gentechnik: Zur Hermeneutik naturwissenschaftlicher Rede und Argumentation', in K. Hilpert and D. Mieth (eds), *Kriterien biomedizinischer Ethik: Theologische Beiträge zum gesellschaftlichen Diskurs*, Freiburg: Herder, pp. 337–53.

Rendell, L. and H. Whitehead, 2001, 'Culture in Whales and Dolphins', *Behavioral and Brain Sciences* 24.2, pp. 309–73.

Richards, Robert J., 2009, 'Darwin's Theory of Natural Selection and its Moral Purpose', in Robert J. Richards and Michael Ruse (eds), *The Cambridge Companion to the Origin of Species*, Cambridge: Cambridge University Press, pp. 256–74.

Rubenstein, Mary-Jane, 2012, 'Cosmic Singularities: On the Nothing and the Sovereign', *Journal of the American Academy of Religion* 80.2, pp. 485–517.

Rumke, H. C., 1952, *The Psychology of Unbelief*, London: Rockliff.

Ruse, Michael, 2000, *Can a Darwinian Be a Christian?: The Relationship between Science and Religion*, New York: Cambridge University Press.

Ruse, Michael, 2003, *Darwin and Design: Does Evolution Have a Purpose?* Cambridge, MA: Harvard University Press.

Salzman, Mark, 2000, *Lying Awake*, New York: Knopf.

Sargent, Rose-Mary, 1995, *The Diffident Naturalist: Robert Boyle and the Philosophy of Experiment*, Chicago: University of Chicago Press.

Saver, J. L. and J. Rubin, 1997, 'The Neural Substrates of Religious Experience', *Journal of Neuropsychiatry* 9, pp. 498–510.

Scheler, Max, 2009, *The Human Place in the Cosmos* (1927), trans. M. Frings, Evanston, IL: Northwestern University Press.

Schloss, J., 2002, 'From Evolution to Eschatology', in T. Peter, R. J. Russell and M. Welker (eds), *Resurrection: Theological and Scientific Assessments*, Grand Rapids, MI: Eerdmans.

Shapin, Steven, 1994, *A Social History of Truth: Civility and Science in Seventeenth-Century England*, Chicago: University of Chicago Press.

Shapin, Steven, 1996, *The Scientific Revolution*, Cambridge, MA: Harvard University Press.

Shapin, Steven and Simon Schaffer, 1985, *Leviathan and the Air-Pump: Hobbes, Boyle and the Experimental Life*, Princeton: Princeton University Press.

Shattuck, R., 1997, *Forbidden Knowledge: From Prometheus to Pornography*, London: Harcourt Brace.

Sheldrake, Rupert, 1988, *The Presence of the Past*, London: Collins.

Sherrington, Charles, 1951, *Man on His Nature*, Cambridge: Cambridge University Press.

Skinner, B. F., 1972, *Beyond Freedom and Dignity*, New York: Bantam.

Southgate, Christopher, 2008, *The Groaning of Creation: God, Evolution, and the Problem of Evil*, Louisville, KY: Westminster John Knox Press.

Sperry, R. W., 1966, *Bulletin of the Atomic Scientists* 22.7, pp. 2–6.

Sperry, R. W., 1988, 'Psychology's Mentalist Paradigm and the Religion / Science Tension', *American Psychologist* 43.8, p. 609.

Stewart, M. A. (ed.), 1979, *Selected Philosophical Papers of Robert Boyle*, Manchester: Manchester University Press.

Strawson, Peter, 1974, *Freedom and Resentment, and Other Essays*, London: Methuen.

Sterelny, Kim, 2008, 'Social Intelligence, Human Intelligence and Niche Construction', in Nathan Emery, Nicola Clayton and Chris Firth (eds), *Social Intelligence: From Brain to Culture*, Oxford: Oxford University Press, pp. 375–92.

Stern, David L. and Virginie Orgogozo, 2009, 'Is Genetic Evolution Predictable', *Science* 323, pp. 746–51.

Stern, David, 2010, *Evolution, Development and the Predictable Genome*, Greenwood Village: Roberts & Co.

Tanzella-Nitti, Guiseppe, 2004, 'The Two Books Prior to the Scientific Revolution', *Annales Theologici* 18, pp. 51–83.

Teilhard de Chardin, Pierre, 1964, *The Future of Man*, trans. Norman Denny, New York: Harper Colophon.

Teilhard de Chardin, Pierre, 1969, *Christianity and Evolution*, trans. René Hague, New York: Harcourt Brace.

Teilhard de Chardin, Pierre, 1970, *Activation of Energy*, trans. René Hague, New York: Harcourt Brace Jovanovich.

Teilhard de Chardin, Pierre, 1999, *The Human Phenomenon*, trans. Sarah Appleton-Weber, Brighton and Portland, OR: Sussex Academic Press.

Thomsen W. and H. Holländer (eds), 1984, *Augenblick und Zeitpunkt*, Darmstadt: Wissenschaftliche Buchgesellschaft.

Thouless, R. H., 1971, *An Introduction to the Psychology of Religion*, Cambridge: Cambridge University Press.

Till, H. van, 2000, 'Partnership: Science and Christian Theology as Partners in Theorizing', in R. F. Carlson (ed.), *Science and Christianity: Four Views*, Downers Grove, IL: InterVarsity Press, pp. 188–94.

Tooby, Aaron John and Leda Cosmides, 2009, 'Formidability and the Logic of Human Anger', *Proceedings of the National Academy of Sciences*, 106.35, pp. 15073–8.

Tooby John and Leda Cosmides, 2010, 'The Evolutionary Psychology of the Emotions and their Relationship to Internal Regulatory Variables', in M. Lewis, J. M. Haviland-Jones and L. Feldman Barrett (eds), *Handbook of Emotions*, New York: Guilford, pp. 114–37.

Torrance, Thomas T., 1981, *Divine and Contingent Order*, Oxford: Clarendon Press.

Turtledove, H., 1988, *A Different Flesh*, New York: Congdon & Weed.

Visala, Aku, 2011, *Naturalism, Theism, and the Cognitive Science of Religion: Religion Explained?*, Burlington, VT: Ashgate.

Vining, Joe, 2004, *The Song Sparrow and the Child: Claims of Science and Humanity*, South Bend, IN: University of Notre Dame Press.

Waal, Frans de, 2009, *The Age of Empathy: Nature's Lessons for a Kinder Society*, London: Souvenir Press.

Wagoner, B., A. Gillespie and G. Duveen, 2007, 'Bartlett in the Digital Age', *The Psychologist* 20.11, pp. 680–1.

Ward, Keith, 2008, *The Big Questions in Science and Religion*, West Conshohocken, PA: Templeton Press.

Watkins, Eric (ed.), 2013, *God's Order, Man's Order, and the Order of Nature*, Oxford: Oxford University Press.

Watts, F. N., 2007, *Jesus and Psychology*, London: Darton, Longman & Todd.

Watts, F. N. and M. Williams, 1988, *The Psychology of Religious Knowing*, London: Chapman.

Weizsäcker, Carl-Friedrich von, 1953, *Die Geschichte der Natur*, Göttingen: Vandenhoeck & Ruprecht.

White, Lynn, 1967, 'The Historical Roots of our Ecologic Crisis', *Science* 155, pp. 1203–7.

Whitehead, Alfred North, 1967, *Adventures of Ideas*, New York: Free Press.

Whitehead, Alfred North, 1968, *Modes of Thought*, New York: Free Press.

Whitehead, Alfred North, 1978, *Process and Reality*, corrected edition, ed. David Ray Griffin and Donald W. Sherburne, New York: Free Press.

Whiten, Andrew and Carel P. van Schaik, 2008, 'The Evolution of Animal 'Cultures' and Social Intelligence', in Nathan Emery, Nicola Clayton and Chris Firth (eds), *Social Intelligence: From Brain to Culture*, Oxford: Oxford University Press, pp. 189–216.

Williams, George C., 1995, 'Mother Nature is a Wicked Old Witch!', in Matthew H. Nitecki and Doris V. Nitecki (eds), *Evolutionary Ethics*, Albany, NY: State University of New York Press, pp. 217–31.

Wilson, David Sloan, 2011, 'The Human Major Transition in Relation to Symbolic Behaviour, Including Language, Imagination and Spirituality', in Christopher N. Henshilwood and Francesco D'Errico (eds), *Homo Symbolicus: The Dawn of Language, Imagination and Spirituality*, Amsterdam: John Benjamins, pp. 133–9.

Wilson, Edward O., 1998, *Consilience: The Unity of Knowledge*, New York: Knopf.

Wilson, Edward O., 2012, *The Social Conquest of Earth*, New York: Norton.

Wojcik, Jan, 1997, *Robert Boyle and the Limits of Reason*, Cambridge: Cambridge University Press.

Wright, C. J. H., 2004, *Old Testament Ethics for the People of God*, Leicester: InterVarsity Press.

Zakai, Avihu, 2010, *Jonathan Edwards's Philosophy of Nature: The Reenchantment of the World in the Age of Scientific Reasoning*, London: T & T Clark.

Zilhao, J., 2011, 'The Emergence of Language, Art and Symbolic Thinking: A Neandertal Test of Competing Hypotheses', in Christopher N. Henshilwood and Francesco D'Errico (eds), *Homo Symbolicus: The Dawn of Language, Imagination and Spirituality*, Amsterdam: John Benjamins, pp. 111–31.

Zurek, Wojciech, 1991, 'Decoherence and the Transition from Quantum to Classical', *Physics Today* 44, pp. 36–44.

Zurek, Wojciech, 2002, 'Decoherence and the Transition from Quantum to Classical – Revisited', *Los Alamos Science* 27, p. 14.

Index